Eating Pomegranates

A MEMOIR OF MOTHERS, DAUGHTERS,
AND THE *BRCA* GENE

Sarah Gabriel

Scribner

New York London Toronto Sydney

🔥

Scribner
A Division of Simon & Schuster, Inc.
1230 Avenue of the Americas
New York, NY 10020

Names and identifying characteristics have been changed.

Copyright © 2009 by Sarah Gabriel
Originally published in Great Britain in 2009 by Jonathan Cape,
a division of Random House

First Scribner hardcover edition March 2010

SCRIBNER and design are registered trademarks of
The Gale Group, Inc., used under license by Simon & Schuster,
Inc., the publisher of this work.

For information about special discounts for bulk purchases,
please contact Simon & Schuster Special Sales at 1-866-506-1949 or
business@simonandschuster.com.

The Simon & Schuster Speakers Bureau can bring authors to your
live event. For more information or to book an event contact
the Simon & Schuster Speakers Bureau at 1-866-248-3049 or
visit our website at www.simonspeakers.com.

Manufactured in the United States of America

1   3   5   7   9   10   8   6   4   2

Library of Congress Control Number: 2009049524

ISBN 978-1-4391-4819-8
ISBN 978-1-4391-5813-5 (ebook)

To my beloved parents

Contents

Eating Pomegranates

Prologue

I ALWAYS THOUGHT I would write novels about relationships. Subtle psychological studies of the contemporary family, its disintegrations and reformations; the long shadow play of gender; generations across time. Exquisite things in the realist-symbolist tradition, where the fictional creatures took off from the page and held you in a separate rapture, about which there was nothing of shame or disclosure.

But reality supervened. It crashed onto the page. The third-person narratives got stuck. I couldn't get my creatures up in the morning, let alone dressed and out of the house. They sat as if in a roomful of outgrown toys, slumped in the corner, when the children have long gone on to other things. They reproached me, with their twisted limbs, their ratty fur, glass eyes hung out on wire.

Instead, something else got up and running. It wasn't nice. I didn't like it. But I have to admit it had a certain vitality. The hideous familiarity of certain close relatives, or one of Dostoevsky's drunks. Affable and manipulative, emptying out its pockets. What's mine is yours, my dear. Including my degradation, of course. Any comparison of offerings is vulgar; you know it yourself. It chuckled at me softly as I fled, and returned at night, when I was jumpy.

I took a mallet to its hands, as they crept under the shutters. I went for its knees; it just kept on coming. I am the way and the life, it said. Or your life, at any rate. I've got your card. It's marked.

Eventually, it wore me down. The broken beginnings. The

slumped dolls. Misery at any length is deadening. The banality of suffering. So I turned and faced it: let's be having you, then. Bring it on, whatever you may be.

And here I was startled. Yes, its face was ravaged by disease. A cheek, or an eye socket, had fallen away like a piece of cliff. But it was still a face. Recognizably human. It had expression, a set of feelings, a certain intensity of presence. In the family of specters, you could call it *jolie laide*.

OK, I said. Peace. We hunkered down together like an old married couple. Jealous of our habits. Considerately hostile. And I set about studying it, this "I" I had managed to generate from my sickness. For the first person was its preferred form, culpable and suasive. Sylvia Plath's "ich," stuck on the wire and doomed to endless repetition. Ich, ich, ich, ich.

I didn't choose it. Certainly, I didn't choose it. I would have chosen almost anything else. But then, what life chooses its subject? Where it's born, to whom, and what becomes of it? Isn't it an aspect of maturity to know this? And yet to serve. Isn't this the challenge?

THE STORY STARTS on March 14, 2006. Or at least, that was the day when my disease was given a name. When the proper authorities— doctors, radiographers, pathologists—gathered to bestow a title on it, christening it a creditable member of the family of diseases meriting genuine abhorrence and horrible treatment.

Or perhaps you could say it began on the day my grandparents conceived my mother, a midsummer day, 1937. My grandfather was a clerk at the Bank of England, with prospects. My grandmother was a picture-postcard model. There are little yellowed postcards of her wearing a bathing cap and a dark swimsuit reaching down to her thighs, which are plump and tender. Her smile, too, nothing like the models' of today. She came from a family of Russian Jewish émigrés. Her father managed to set up a small garage in south London; he even kept a greyhound. She and my grandfather loved each other, or so the story went. On her death, stacks of billets-doux were found in the attic, dating not just from the days of their courtship but blossoming again at each separation thereafter for business or family affairs. Once a year, my grandparents left their home in Surrey and went to the Dorchester hotel in London for a night to celebrate their wedding anniversary. So I am sure that the lovemaking that conceived my mother was passionate and promising. But this was no constraint. Disease is no respecter of persons; it makes no distinctions. Disease is the true democrat.

Alternatively, instead of focusing on the particular life, you could say this story began tens, even hundreds of thousands, of years ago, when the family DNA was happily multiplying through our Paleolithic ancestors. Like a bluff mayor presiding over a tombola stall, it threw out blue eyes here to attract a mate, a sharpened canine there the better to tear flesh, the opposing thumb without which *Homo habilis* would not have been possible, the endlessly enlarged cerebellum.

And then somewhere along the line, it threw out a googly—that's its job after all (it's only via such random events that the race advances), the trillions upon trillions of mutations without which the great experiment of life would come to a halt—a rogue mutation with a vicious amount of sidespin, enabling it to career through the generations. M18T is its name. It doesn't sound like much. It isn't much. Just the tiniest chemical alteration of one of the bases on a nucleotide on a gene known as *BRCA1*.

But way down there, in the DNA foundry of life, it counts for something. The *BRCA1* gene is responsible for cleaning up faulty DNA, particularly in cells destined for breast and ovarian tissue. It is the keeper of the gates of genetic purity. If for any reason it's not working properly, the dodgy DNA goes on to make copies of itself. And then copies of those copies. And before you know it, you've got a clump of several million cells grappling, surrounding blood vessels to ensure proper nourishment, and then packing their bags and making travel plans, setting off to other more interesting sites in the human body.

So somewhere back then, among my caveman ancestors, the women start dying young. Holed up in a cave in the south of France, 10,000 BC, one woman develops abdominal swelling. For a time she scarcely notices it. It's just an ache, an urge to urinate more often. Then the swelling becomes marked, the pain specific. Gradually the disease spreads to the base of her spine, and to her pelvis. The women of the tribe gather round. They bring her brews of juniper and acorn. Her children brush the earth around her bed and look at her with frightened eyes. Others disappear, unable to watch. They will turn up again at the rim of the settlement, like famished ghosts, when the job is done.

The old women light candles of moose fat, which throw shadows on the ceiling. The dying woman yearns toward them, a question in her eyes. The women bat the smoke and look away, studying the flickering patterns on the walls. They do not mean to be unkind. If the dying woman gathers strength and reaches forward, at cost of breath, to snatch at their hands, they swat her off like a fly. No woman easily takes on the burden of another's children.

Afterward, hers are scavenger children. The tribe instinctively shuns them, neglected and famished as they are. They threaten scarce resources of food and affection. Nonetheless, they are allowed to thrive in a certain haphazard sort of way. Shooed away from the inner sanctuary of cave and family, given the last cuts of meat, sleeping rough: you could not say they have a cheerful existence, a blessed life. But if they beat off death from starvation, random violence, infection, or war, they have time to reproduce. Their offspring will be without a grandmother. It is possible that they, in turn, will lose their own mother young, but failing other disasters, these children may make it to adolescence, even young adulthood, before calamity strikes.

In any case, each life only ever had a fifty-fifty chance of inheriting the rogue mutation. One chromosome from Mum. One from Dad. One dud, one sound. In the grand scheme of things, such odds are magnificent.

So genetic diversity is maintained—the mutation not deadly enough to have caused its own extinction—and M18T comes all the way down from my ur-mother. But for the purposes of this story, we'll skip on down the generations until we reach this one, stick a pin in the genealogical map, and get on with it. Because all creatures have got to get up and out of the house in the morning, after all. Even if it is only for a diagnosis of disease.

Chapter One

On the Eve

I T'S MARCH 13, 2006. I am propped up on the sofa with a pink leaflet about how to perform breast self-examination open on my chest and a glass of Chardonnay by my side. R (husband) is at the other end of the sofa, watching Manchester City play Tottenham Hotspur on the TV.

Strictly speaking, R does not like Chardonnay. He says it is a "nasty" drink, laden with chemicals that thicken his head in the morning. But he keeps me company loyally. Has done for many years.

His mother's drinking has always been a problem for R. So he drinks to limit me to my half of the bottle, in case I go the same way. As a result, at times he has had a half-a-bottle-of-Chardonnay-a-day habit. When he goes to visit his mother, it's worse. Whiskey. Maybe if he keeps pace with her, is true to her in the place she has to go, she won't have to go there. Maybe she will turn about and focus the mother's mirroring gaze on him. My darling child, how could I desert you? And for what, after all? A mess of toxins at the bottom of a bottle.

It never works. He never stops. He is the wandering knight to her Belle Dame Sans Merci. So a psyche is born.

"It says here you draw the hand in concentric circles outward to the perimeter of the breast and then bring it back again in radial lines."

I am reading aloud to distract myself. Everything from the nasty salmon-pink color of the leaflet, a standard-issue Pantone number favored by government departments and the National Health Service (NHS), to the brutal anatomical diagrams, to the remote possibility of finding something, combines to make this task distasteful.

"What do you think it means by . . . ?" I am confused by a description of a dimpling of the skin that can occur when a lump is pulling at it from within. Examining the smooth, clean skin of my breasts, I see nothing. But maybe I just don't know how to look?

"Mmmn?" says R, without focusing. He is concentrating hard to follow the commentary on the game, which is turned to low volume. This is our compromise. Chardonnay for football. Low volume for public breast examination. The continual trade of marital relations.

"What do you think it means . . . ?" If he had a page in front of him, in a patch of sunlight, and I were a cat, I would leap lightly across and curl myself up on it to get his attention.

But the Spurs striker has just done a header that clipped the goalpost. There is the collective gasp, a sotto voce roar, of male disappointment. A crash of testosterone up and down the country, which R, throwing himself back on the sofa in our narrow living room, echoes loyally. "Idiot!"

I turn back to the diagram with a sigh. Confronting me, in fuzzy black-and-white print, is a semicircle standing on its tip. It looks like a protractor, or a rubber drain plunger perhaps. Inside it, a tangled mass of black lines converge angrily on a knob at the end. These are the ducts. In any one of these ducts, I am told, designed to carry milk from the fatty tissue to the nipple in response to a baby's sucking motion, a lump might form. Struggling to map this bleak geometry onto the living body, I finger my breast desultorily, unsure how to distinguish its naturally grainy texture from anything more sinister.

Writing this, I am aware that this woman has something childish about her. Dishonest, even. She should be upstairs, in front of a mirror, without a glass of wine, doing the job properly.

Embarrassing. The instinct is to move on. So instead we'll do the opposite and move in closer. Lean over on creaking knees and take a little look. What is going on there? There is a picture of me at thirteen. The bedroom of a manse in Scotland, a little chilly, windows open onto a view of hills. I have a few drops of bright blood between my legs. I found them earlier, in the toilet, freshly staining the skin. I am frightened. I have managed to tell my mother. This was not easy. She had five children and was almost always hard-pressed.

My mother appears. She is carrying a contraption made of white pads and cotton ropes. I have no idea where she got it, whether it is one of her own or whether she had it in waiting for this moment. It looks like a kind of harness for the bottom half of the body. The packet it has emerged from is called "Dr White's." I remember the dirty pink and turquoise colors of the wrapping, aimed to capture femininity and hygiene and somehow soiling both. "You have your period now. You need to wear this," says my mother. Then she turns to go. "But how?" I manage to get out, horrified, the contraption dangling from my hand. Her voice accelerates, seems to become more chilly. "The girdle goes round the waist, the pad down below. It's perfectly simple. You'll work it out." And she is gone. There is supper to cook, the washing to put out, the dogs to walk, the little ones to take care of.

The next image is of a scuffed green prefab building, 1970. Primary Seven, the last year before secondary school. We are gathered to hear a lecture by head teacher Mrs. Cormack on The Facts of Life. Diagrams are pinned to the blackboard showing a man's penis, the insinuating twin-bean shape of the ovaries connected by the pendulous U of the fallopian tubes. I have seen these shapes for years inscribed on toilet walls and bus shelters. To see them posted up on a blackboard in this way seems obscene. A calculated affront.

Mrs. Cormack explains that to make a baby, the man's penis is inserted in the woman's vagina. This releases something called sperm. The sperm fertilizes the egg, which is implanted in the lining of the womb and fed via the umbilical cord with nutrient-rich blood from the mother. "If you have any questions about this process, please feel free to ask. You may do so confidentially." She invites us to write our questions anonymously on pieces of paper and put them in a basket. Can you have a baby without the man's penis going inside the woman's vagina? I write solemnly, folding my little note many times. At the front, she unfolds it and frowns. "This class was set up for serious matters," she says, tossing it aside. "If anyone is going to turn it into a joke, I'll put a stop to it immediately."

Later, the consequences of this self-hatred, the internalized phobia of the feminine. A yo-yo pattern of binge eating and dieting. No, Mother, I will not become you however hard you try to fill me with the food that will turn me into you. I will stopper up my mouth. Your cooking, which you so poignantly love (God knows why; how can it rescue you?), is a poison that I am determined to vomit up. I shall defy you, refuse to grow belly, thighs, breasts. If you force the issue, I shall refuse to grow at all. I will not be destroyed by pregnancy after pregnancy until I am tired and broken and old beyond my years. I will not surrender myself to the tyranny of the male will. To be granted only half a place at the hearth. To be forced to offer cups of tea, meals, compliance, concession, admiration, desperation, anything to buy off the outpourings of male frustration and discontent.

And I shall not die. Suddenly and catastrophically at age forty-two. Leaving five children and a husband behind.

So perhaps it's not surprising that I am unable to examine my breasts properly. Childish? Yes, certainly. Until my dead mother walks back into the bedroom, kneels before me, and talks me tenderly through how to put on that contraption, with her eyes resting calmly on mine, her voice kind and measured, how am I to grow up? Half-made woman? Yes, certainly. I may be forty-four. I may have children now myself. But I am still waiting. Didn't Orpheus look back for his Eurydice though it was mortal folly? Didn't Persephone eat the pomegranate pips though it condemned her in perpetuity to six months of every year in the underworld? For how long did Hades have to press them on her before she ate? And what did those sweet seeds taste like? Did they carry the bitterness of his kingdom? Or did they taste of the great green upper world, and the tumult of her mother's longing for her daughter? Isn't mitosis— self-division—at the very heart of things?

"R, I think I might have found something."

"Mmmn?"

"Really, R, I think I might have."

"Wait a minute," he says, attention focused on the screen, where someone is gearing up to take a penalty.

My first reaction is simple curiosity. As I examine my left breast, as instructed, with half a mind charting the strategy of the match and the emotional barometer of R's masculinity, my finger rolls over a lump. At first it feels like nothing, or rather, like something so insignificant the mind scarcely registers it. You are crossing a level terrain. All around you the smooth and even surface stretches out. But you step off a tiny shelf. It is so shallow, there is no disruption whatsoever to your feet, which carry you evenly onward. It's just that somewhere in the base of the spine, there is a flicker of anxiety, the uneasiness of weight being redistributed.

I put down my glass and finger the lump with fascination. It is about a centimeter in diameter and neatly spherical, with a shallow raised ridge. It feels like finding the shilling in the Christmas pudding.

"Look, I'm sure . . ."

"Mmmn? I can't feel anything."

R leans toward me on the sofa, touching my breast absentmindedly, while he gazes back at the screen. "No, really, I can't feel anything."

The Marriage of the Arnolfini, Jan Van Eyck, 1434. The Flemish merchant Giovanni di Nicolao Arnolfini stands with his wife in their intricately depicted bedchamber. Their surroundings are rich: ornate brass chandelier, fur-trimmed costumes, splendid red bed with its woolen bolsters and drapes. But affluence is not what strikes us about them. They are as stark and bare as saints. The natural light from the window touches them, he with his tapering hand upraised, she with her hand laid in his, palm up, as if giving herself without constraint or condition to their union. It is easy to see why scholars thought the painting might be a form of legal witness to a marriage. Their gazes are solemn, their gestures grave. Meantime, the little dog at their feet, terrierlike, with its bright eyes and tatty fur, suggests affectionate, domestic moments (some have seen it as an icon of lust, or fidelity), while the wooden patterns on the floor to their left tell of the street beyond, muddy and turbulent, full of trade and competition.

But in this room, now, there is stillness. What is meant by the merchant's upraised hand? What is meant by the woman's inclined head, face plump with shadow, the tenderly gathered folds of green velvet at her belly? And what is meant by the spectator, reflected in miniature in the convex mirror behind them? Is he a witness to the ceremony, as some have inferred?

This is northern light, the painter seems to tell us. Not so much fleeting as scarcely emergent. Much of the room is already in shadow. And these two, blessed by it at the height of their union when everything is full of promise—from the pendulous red bolsters suspended from the bed, to her swollen belly; from his mysterious gesture of command, to her subtle half-screened smile—are already in the act of vanishing.

Now, in an inversion of the painting, I take R's hands, which I have always loved, which are not tapering like the merchant's but have a masculine blunting at the tips and are dusted with hair at the knuckles, and place them carefully at the site of the lump.

"Oh, yes." And in his voice I hear the mirror of my own curiosity. Not fear. Just a detached kind of wonder.

"Maybe I should tell them tomorrow?"

"You think?" he asks uncertainly.

Tomorrow we are due to report to the Cancer Genetics Clinic of the Royal Marsden hospital in London, where I will have a routine annual check for breast cancer. I have inherited M18T, a mutation on the *BRCA1* gene, a gene known to be involved in the body's suppression of tumors. We don't yet know for certain whether M18T is harmful, or "deleterious." Only a hundred or so of the many mutations that can crop up on the long and complex *BRCA1* gene adversely affect its function. But if M18T is one of them, then I have a very high risk of developing breast or ovarian cancer at a relatively young age. At present, the head of the Cancer Genetics Clinic at the Marsden has described M18T as, technically, "of uncertain clinical significance." But it's not looking good. There's my own mother, who died of ovarian cancer at age forty-two; her mother, who also died of ovarian cancer; and a cousin in my generation who developed breast cancer at the same age also of forty-two.

You might have thought that all this would make me particularly careful in my breast examinations. But no. It doesn't seem to work like that. If I think of my mother and her premature death, I become a little breathless. At forty-four, I already have the sense of living on borrowed time. But I had a mammogram eight months ago that pronounced me clear of cancer. And in general, the new knowledge that medicine has offered does not always tend to make me more careful. What it actually makes me, in respect of my own risk of contracting breast cancer, is running scared. And that is something different.

"I think I should probably tell them tomorrow, shouldn't I?" I repeat.

"No," says R, more decisively. "I really don't think they're for bothering with *that*. If you're worried about it, you should take it to the GP."

Suddenly, I'm angry. More than angry. So furious that I can hardly get my words out.

"Well, what are they *for* exactly? This so-called cancer genetics clinic. At the Royal Marsden *Cancer* Hospital. Which is supposed to help me not to get *cancer*. Which otherwise I am pretty certain to get. When my mother died of ovarian cancer at forty-two. When a cousin had breast cancer at the same age. When I have been told I have an eighty-five percent chance of getting breast cancer myself, if you remember. What exactly are they *for*, R, if not for *bothering*?"

Poor R blinks in the sudden blaze, while the screen erupts with a roar in the background.

"Well, tell them, then," he says mildly. "If you think it's that important."

"Thank you. Thank you *so* much. For taking my life *so* seriously."

And I have completed the circle. It is he who does not care about my life, who prevaricates, who dandles this possibility of disaster before us and tosses it away like a trinket from the pram. I roll up my sleeves for a fight. I am energized, in good shape, my enemy before me. With hindsight, I see the pair of us with tenderness, like Miranda and Ferdinand in *The Tempest,* bent over a chessboard at the edge of the sea. We are playing at dread. Soon the storm will pick us up, whirl us about until we have lost sight of each other in the dark and our fingers cannot meet, tearing our proud puerility to shreds.

Chapter Two

What's in a Hospital?

*Now, gentlemen, I want to found a hospital for the treatment
of cancer, and for the study of the disease, for at the present
time we know absolutely nothing about it.*

—William Marsden, 1851

I T WAS A thirty-one-year-old William Marsden, newly admitted
to the Royal College of Surgeons after serving his apprentice-
ship with surgeon John Dale, and walking home one evening in
1827, who encountered a young woman slumped in the doorway of
St. Andrew's Church, Holborn, and stopped.

It is not known why he stopped. St. Andrew's was the church
in which Marsden and his wife, Elizabeth-Ann, had been married
seven years previously. It was also the church where his three children had been christened. Epidemics had claimed the lives of the
first two before their first birthdays. But the third, Libby, was alive
and strong and had been baptized there only a few weeks previously. It may be that his thoughts returned to these happier occasions as he contemplated the high railings and gaping porch, the
steep and rubbish-strewn steps that gave on to High Holborn Hill.

At any rate, the girl was young, seventeen or eighteen years old,
and perhaps judging by the soiled blue cape twisted beneath her, a
prostitute.

Marsden would have asked her where she lived. She would have signaled that she had no address. He would have asked her whether she had family. She would have shaken her head in that speechless way of people whose lives have been too chaotic even to begin to account for their disattachment from family. He would have cast about, looking for some friend or well-wisher to whom he could entrust her—there must be someone who acknowledged some minimal human tie with her, some distant but inevitable responsibility—and wondered whether he might just get up and go.

It had been a long day, and Elizabeth-Ann would be waiting for him. Anxiously so, since the death of their first two children had made her more clinging, as if only her husband's physical presence might stand between them and a third calamity.

There was no one. The crowd pressed this way and that, oblivious of the individual life drawing to a close in its midst. A woman selling eggs on the steps was packing up for the day; when Marsden asked her a question, she muttered loudly about the cold and her rheumatism. A hackney driver flogged on his horse over Marsden's wave. And a butcher whom Marsden could have sworn was watching him from his doorway, surrounded by sides of beef on hooks, disappeared inside his shop when Marsden made a move toward him.

Marsden sighed. His surgeon's eye had taken in the girl's state: her shortness of breath, the telltale rash on face and neck. It was syphilis, and the disease was advanced. Covering her with his coat and lifting her, he was shocked, despite himself, by her negligible weight. She seemed scarcely heavier than baby Libby, and in a disturbing echo, her head inclined helplessly on his shoulder, the rough texture of her hair grazing his chin.

Not much has been written about William Marsden, founder of two of London's principal hospitals: the Royal Free Hospital in Holborn and the Royal Marsden in Chelsea. In 1960, his great-granddaugher Frieda Sandwith published a biography of him, *The Surgeon Compassionate,* in which she describes William's father as a yeoman farmer, a "hard, unimaginative man," with whom Marsden was obliged to do battle before being released from his job as an apothecary in Yorkshire to pursue his vocation as a surgeon. But Neil McIntyre, former emeritus professor of medicine at the Royal Free Hospital and University College London Department of Medicine and author of a paper on Marsden's Yorkshire family, casts doubt on Sandwith's claims. He cites baptismal records in Sheffield for David Marsden's children in which the father is variously reported as a victualler, bookkeeper, and shopkeeper. Never as a yeoman farmer. The same uncertainty of facts surrounds William's mother, Elizabeth.

We do know that Marsden was born in Sheffield in 1796, the eldest of eight children. We know that he had proved himself sufficiently before the age of twenty to be offered a partnership in his employer's apothecary business. This he turned down, not something that the sons of tradesmen generally did, and especially not the eldest of eight children. He left for London in 1816 and became an apprentice to surgeon John Dale, who worked in Holborn Hill and had an extensive practice among the poor. He also learned anatomy at the Anatomical School of Joshua Brookes. Brookes had converted the basement of his house in Blenheim Street in London's West End into dissecting rooms, where he taught the leading surgeons of the day. In the rooms upstairs, he kept a collection of bones for comparative anatomy. Brookes was reviled by society as a resurrectionist. Since the law forbade the acquisition of corpses for dissection, he bought them illicitly from gangs of grave robbers. So Marsden was already familiar with having to forge alliances that took him outside society's comfort zone.

For whatever reason, Marsden found it unacceptable to leave the girl there. Taking her to the foot of the church steps, he waited as cab after cab passed. Eventually, by dint of physically detaining a driver and offering to pay him a multiple of the usual fare, he secured one. "St. Bartholomew's Hospital!" he said, propping the girl against the backseat. "Fast!"

This hospital was his alma mater, if he could be said to have one. It was here that he had reported to the overflowing egg-shaped lecture theater to hear the famous surgeon John Abernethy, no longer in his physical prime, but with ripe wit and invaluable experience. It was here that he had shared in the uproarious laughter of his colleagues when the dissecting man, for a lecture on surgical bandaging, appeared swathed to his eyeballs and had to be guided to the podium. Here that he had done his first gallstone operation, under Abernethy's supervision, and had taken refuge in the medieval chapel when his profession left him exhausted in mind and body. In the early years in London, St. Bartholomew's had been a second home, or the nearest thing he had had to one since leaving Yorkshire.

But at the hospital, he encountered a problem. Despite the fact that he offered to pay for the girl's sheets and cutlery, also for her burial, costs that were traditionally met by the patient, the warden refused to admit her. "No letter, sir. We can't be taking her without a letter." At that time, governors paid an annual subscription for the upkeep of a hospital and in return exercised patronage over who was admitted. No patient could be admitted without a governor's letter.

"I don't have time to get a letter," said Marsden. "Look at her, man, for God's sake. She's dying!"

This statement had no other effect than to make the warden more obdurate. A shutter came down over his eyes, and he took a wintry pleasure in his next set of utterances.

"No admission without a letter, sir. Guv'nor's orders. Them's the founding rules."

It had begun to rain, a thin, needling rain that chilled to the bone. Marsden looked back at the cab, which he had asked to wait. They were no longer on a main thoroughfare, and passing traffic had thinned. Such cabs as there were would be quickly claimed on account of the weather. He was anxious that the driver, glimpsing trouble, would just deposit the girl on the street and make off. Giving the warden a level stare, he turned on his heel and left.

The next stop was St. Thomas' Hospital, south of the river. Here the result was the same, though the tone different. The warden at St.

Thomas' would have helped if he could have. It was a crying shame to leave a girl in such a state, shocking in fact, and on such a night. But rules were rules. To admit her would be to risk his job. And it was more than his job was worth to admit her. The same thing was repeated at Guy's. By the time Marsden returned to the north side of the river, with the girl keeled over beside him, half-conscious, he was not the same man he had been when he set out.

History is vague as to what he did with her at this point. The entry on Marsden in the *Oxford Dictionary of National Biography* offers no account. Neither does the Marsden Web site nor the archives of the Royal Free Hospital. Sandwith claims that he found a widow nearby who was willing to yield up her attic in return for a sovereign. But in the absence of documentary evidence, I prefer to believe that he took the girl home with him to his wife, and that they nursed her there until her death one week later.

We can imagine Elizabeth-Ann, fresh from feeding the baby, reacting with shock when her husband first appeared in the hallway of the house in Thavies Inn with his wretched bundle. His appearance, after a long day's work and his nocturnal tour, would have been wild, his mood dark. Of middle-class family, and just twenty-three years old, Elizabeth-Ann was entitled to her fear. You did not welcome prostitutes into a comfortable middle-class home. And particularly not those so obviously dying of syphilis.

But Elizabeth-Ann had her own history, her own tale of ambitions and losses, which had already determined pronounced choices. If Sandwith is to be believed, she lost her mother when she was twelve. When her father remarried, she found home life with her stepmother intolerable and was sent to live with a rich aunt, Mrs. Hamilton, in Chelsea. Like Marsden, Elizabeth-Ann was seeking a world elsewhere. It is claimed that the pair first met on the coach to London.

They kept up their friendship by attending Sunday services together at St. Luke's Church in Chelsea. Marsden was at first welcomed into Mrs. Hamilton's drawing room on account of his intelligence, energy, and charm, qualities he must have had in abundance. But when the older woman found out his connection with Joshua Brookes and the anatomists—grave robbing, at however distant a remove, was not acceptable—he was banned. Undaunted, Elizabeth-Ann won her resurrectionist surgeon with notes passed across the pews at St. Luke's and assignations for secret walks in Hyde Park.

Marsden always expressed gratitude to his first wife for her dedication to his work. When he came to found his free hospital for the poor, she was vital to her husband's fund-raising efforts, without which the hospital wouldn't have survived. As one newspaper put it, she "contributed in no small degree to the success of the Hospital in its earlier days by the geniality of her disposition and the social gatherings held at her house." It seems reasonable to suppose that she was not simply a passive bystander to her husband's life, but a force in her own right.

So I like to think that after her initial shock, she instructed the housemaid to make a place for the girl in the best front bedroom. When she saw the grudging ill will with which the housemaid set about her unreckoned-on set of duties, and especially for such a creature as *that*—slamming down the coal bucket, raking the grate furiously, smacking up the pillows, in a way that would have caused a person in rude health to shudder, let alone that slip of a girl so close to death—she quietly took them over herself.

For Marsden, the die was cast. The following year, 1828, he gathered a committee of twenty-seven businessmen of the City of London (he had won the backing of City Alderman James Harmer, who supported him until his own death in 1853), and raised enough funds to set up his dispensary: the London General Institution for the Gratuitous Care of Malignant Diseases. It offered free advice and drugs from a four-story house in Greville Street, Hatton Garden, one of London's poorest areas. The consulting rooms were upstairs, the apothecary below. No letters of admission were required. No governor patrons in powerful places. There were no conditions for entry beyond sickness and need. Though at first the hospital was mistrusted—when had anyone ever given the poor something for nothing?—by 1844, the Free Hospital, as it became known, was seeing some thirty thousand patients per annum.

Eighteen years later, when Elizabeth-Ann herself became ill with cancer (we do not know what type; it was recorded with no more precision than as "internal"), loss again spurred Marsden into action. He founded what was to be the world's first cancer hospital, opening a house at 1 Cannon Row, Westminster, for the care of patients with the disease. By this time, his network of supporters ranged from City businessmen to Sir Robert Peel, prime minister and founder of the Peelers, the first police force, and even King George IV. From the outset, the Free Cancer Hospital was intended to offer not just treatment but also research into the disease. Records were to be kept of all tumor types and treatments, along with outcomes. At first the hospital consisted solely of a dispensary, offering palliative drugs for the relief of symptoms. But the need for receiving "patients indoors" was soon recognized. The hospital moved site several times during the 1850s, in pursuit of larger premises. Finally, funds were raised to build a dedicated building on Fulham Road, Chelsea, where the hospital moved in 1862.

Which is how the Royal Marsden hospital (it was awarded its royal charter by King George V in 1910 and rechristened in honor of its founder in 1954) comes to occupy its anomalous position in one of the most exclusive urban environments in the world: in the heart of Chelsea, with the stuccoed eighteenth-century terraces of Sydney Street and Onslow Square stretching off around it.

Not much is still visible of its core Victorian building, surrounded as it is by stacks of Edwardian brick capped off by turrets, the inner courtyards crammed with twentieth-century additions. But you capture a sense of it in the main hallway, with its wide flights of stairs spiraling off to the principal wards, their wrought-iron railings interleaved with gold flowers and letters announcing: LABOR VINCIT OMNIA. The Victorian vision of progress: effort, cumulative enlightenment, eventually conquering poverty and disease.

In the course of our visits to the hospital, R and I are to pay several hundred pounds in parking fees and fines to the Royal Borough of Kensington and Chelsea. It's easy money for the borough, like mugging old ladies. Who's going to leave a relative in distress, or lose their place in the queue when waiting for important results, to go and feed the meter?

I never see it as money wasted. It's more like payment for a piece of theater, or for entry to an exclusive club. To belong, if only in fantasy, to these streets is a pleasure so keen you cannot resent the cost. To stare into the windows of the interior-design shops, with their hand-painted fabrics and sleek furniture, to wander into the boutiques, with their exquisite, understated tailoring, is to be transported to a different world.

The rich live better. The lives inside these rows of handsome stuccoed houses are different. In such wealth, there is no sickness, disorder, or degradation. Girls do not attempt suicide when their mothers are dying of ovarian cancer. There are no careers of depression and failed pregnancies.

Instead, they get married at the proper age to husbands who earn an appropriate amount of money. Their dresses are made of organdy and silk, and they throw their bouquets to girls with brilliant smiles, perfected through years of expensive orthodontia. With the capable and positive personalities inculcated by top girls' schools such as Roedean and St. Paul's, they go forth to wealth and happiness, producing three healthy children by the time they are thirty and supporting their husbands loyally as the men become the heads of multinational companies or partners in leading City law firms.

I know all this because the clipped box trees in their pots tell me so. The little wrought-iron balconies above the doorways with their slender Ionic columns; the rows of fragrant narcissi in the window boxes; the heavily ruched blinds in shades of oyster and taupe.

Staring into these windows, I want my life all over again. I want to have been born into one of these houses, into a nursery equipped with the finest wooden toys and hand-crafted furniture.

I want to have gone to one of those exclusive schools, which would have molded my personality into a capable, positive bent and made of it something serviceable to the world. I want to have married one of the fine red-blooded males the culture produces, who knows how to invest in stocks and shares and to feather his nest with affluence. I want the loyal and affectionate, if reticent, parents of such an establishment, taking their daughter out to tea in Claridge's when she is a student, buying her a winter coat each year, turning up faithfully to the weddings and christenings that mark the successful female life.

Such a fine young woman would never do something as benighted as lose her mother. She would not suffer a rupture with her father when he rapidly remarries, and be a thing without ownership or origin. A broken fragment, slivered and dislimned from her material sap.

And she would not have inherited a mutation of some wretched gene that would very likely kill her unless she amputated large chunks of herself, that threatened to leave her children in the same parlous condition she was left in herself. More scavenger children to encumber the earth. S'blood. Feed the meter, R. Let's go look in the shopwindows. We've all got to believe in something.

The Cancer Genetics Clinic is on the fourth floor of the hospital, at the end of a corridor that runs perpendicularly from the Breast Diagnostic Unit. Its little volley of rooms grows from the stem of the corridor like the leaves of a vetch, symmetrically facing, each equipped with the same standard-issue desk, a bed, a few plastic chairs, and a small mobile unit containing packets of rubber gloves, needles, and sample jars.

I have been in each one of these rooms over the past eighteen months, attempting to outwit death stalking in the form of an inherited predisposition to cellular malfunction. In one, toward the end of 2004, a friendly New Zealand nurse took the blood that was to reveal twelve weeks later that I had inherited a mutation on the *BRCA1* gene. She was quick to point out that we did not know whether this mutation was harmful. Phoning for the result, I overestimated my own strength. She wanted me to make a hospital appointment to hear the result of the test, according to the normal procedure. I pulled rank, said it was my blood, that I had to know. This was all on the assumption that it would be negative. Despite my family history, I had never truly considered any other possibility. So she told me. "I am very sorry, Mrs. G. You have tested positive for a mutation on the *BRCA1* gene. We are not sure of its significance because so few families have been shown to have it. But it is a mutation." The big bell is tolling. Draw the curtains midafternoon, take to your bed. It happens that R and the children are out; the house is so still you can hear mortar trickling within the walls.

Later that day, I take Michaela, then four, for a bike ride after school. It is mid-February, and exceptionally for Oxford in these last years, it is snowing. I understand this weather, it's what I grew up with. Throughout my childhood, in different manses in Scotland, we were snowed in, permitted to watch the world fall away until the furious snowplow came, headlamps blazing up the narrow lanes. I run beside my daughter while the snow whirls out of the darkness at us in brazen cosmoses of confusion. Michaela is exhilarated by her own speed, the sudden snow, her mother running beside her; I by something inchoate, antecedent to speech. Run. Run for your life. Something is coming for you. Death, is it? It that the name it goes by? Not ready? Run then.

In a room with a laminated desk wedged into a corner, and a window with no view, someone shows me a graph describing when the cancers are likely to attack. The dark line chugs along the x axis for a good long stretch (this is called youth; you are immortal, nothing can ever get you), then abruptly, when you are forty, the line sets off at the clappers: a spirited forty-five-degree assault that spends itself only in your seventies, when the line begins to chug along the horizontal again. How many stragglers are left by this time, unfelled by either ovarian or breast cancer? Better not ask. There is only so much you can take in at any one time.

Dr. Deborah Lovelace, head of the clinic, sets out the options clearly. She is tall and slim, with a cool, precise manner and a background in ovarian cancer. Her job is the management of risk. There are presently no reliable diagnostic tests for ovarian cancer, she tells me. The two tests available—the CA-125 blood test, which detects a marker in the blood, raised levels of which are associated with ovarian cancer; and transvaginal ultrasound, which uses sonography to build up a picture of the ovaries, including any suspicious lumps—are not reliable: they detect only a minority of cancers. I should be aware that ovarian cancer, generally caught too late, kills four in five women who get it. Removal of the ovaries—oophorectomy—is the only solution. It is duly agreed upon for August 2005. Followed by crash menopause. A spot of HRT to ease the symptoms? This may not be so good for the breast cancer risk. Estrogen has a well-documented relationship with breast cancer: higher lifetime exposure to it is thought to raise the risk of breast cancer. But if you are going out of your mind . . . Well, as a matter of fact, I am. Hot flashes, lapses of memory, disorientation at the sound of my children's voices. It's no fun being old before your time. Well then, take the minimum dose. No real data. The gene was only discovered in 1994, after all. HRT shouldn't do too much harm.

In another of these rooms, with its close, exhausted air, we attempt to trace a family tree. It would seem at first glance as if the gene descended from my maternal grandmother, who died of ovarian cancer at the age of seventy. But not so fast. My maternal grandfather's sister also died of ovarian cancer, and at age thirty-nine. We know this for sure: my uncle, the only remaining member of my mother's immediate family, has called up the death certificate. This is more likely to be the "smoking gun," as mutations on the *BRCA1* and *BRCA2* genes are responsible for early-onset cancers. A greataunt dead at thirty-nine of ovarian cancer. A mother dead at fortytwo. Yes, the mutation probably came down via my grandfather to my mother. My maternal grandmother's death from ovarian cancer at seventy is most likely to be coincidence. Just bad luck.

There is one way of being absolutely *sure* that the mutation descended from my mother. Oh yes? Tumor blocks, says Deborah Lovelace with careful neutrality. When someone has cancer, the hospital will often retain samples of the tumor stored in paraffin for future research. In which hospital was my mother treated? Aberdeen Royal Infirmary. In what year did she die? 1980. It might be possible, she says, her head inclined in reflection. If there are tumor blocks, it is sometimes possible to extract DNA from them, if the DNA is not too damaged, and check the cells for the mutation. Big pause. I have met Deborah Lovelace often enough to be able to detect in her careful clinical demeanor the flame of exhilaration, of discovery. Her even complexion is suffused with faint color. Her hands rest calmly on the papers on the desk in front of her, but they are the hands of a scientist who wants to be doing something. In their very stillness, and the muscular tension required to underpin it, there is a quality of acute attention. In the world of mutations, M18T is a new kid on the block. And although Lovelace has described it as "of uncertain clinical significance," she has also confessed to a conviction that it is highly suspicious. The area of the *BRCA1* gene where it occurs is known to be important for the correct functioning of the gene to suppress tumors. There's also my family history of early-onset breast and ovarian cancers. At present, she tells us, there is only one other family on the international breast cancer database BIC (Breast Cancer Information Core) with the same mutation. This family has "segregated" for cancer: those with the mutation have developed cancer, while those without it have not. But we would need more evidence before being able finally to conclude that M18T was deleterious.

This is cutting-edge science. Stout Cortez, "silent upon a peak in Darien," on first catching sight of the Pacific; a sky watcher with a new planet swimming into his ken. If the new group on the database—my relatives and I—goes on to segregate for cancer, Lovelace and her team may have scalped a new deleterious mutation. My mother's status in respect of M18T, given that she died of ovarian cancer, would be valuable additional data.

The light from outside becomes very white. It moves along the wall in a luminous blot. How could I possibly explain? So much of my adult life has been spent in longing to gather a few more remnants of my mother: stories, images, objects. When he married my stepmother, my father sold the house in which my mother died and many of their possessions. Too little remained of our joint family life. My sisters and I kept a cupboard of her clothes, which we fought over, wearing them until grief and time had unraveled the seams. And there is no grave. My mother, as if previsioning the medical mystery that her death posed, but not her children's horror, left her body to science.

And now this woman tells me that there may—in Aberdeen Royal Infirmary, perhaps, that place of horror where at eighteen I saw my lovely mother grow thin, thin, thin, her blue eyes deep as lapis lazuli, the wedding ring slip to the knuckle—be a tumor block containing some of her tissue.

The blot of light on the wall throbs and dilates. Scarves of light run from it like solar flares from a distant star: cataclysmic eruptions of silent grief. It is all so long ago. It is all so far away. It is decayed light that travels to us here; the event itself was done with years ago. And if there is a tumor block, what shall I do? Shall I fling off my clothes and cast myself upon it, sob and sob and chew the ground it inhabits, like a rabid dog? My mother. This woman says she may be able to reconstruct her DNA from a tumor block left a quarter of a century ago in Aberdeen Royal Infirmary. Let elephants fly. Let dead men walk. Let lovely Persephone return forever to her mother, Demeter, who stopped the grain, making the flowers and the grasses grow wherever she treads.

On the afternoon of March 14, Deborah Lovelace is busy in another meeting, so we are assigned to consultant Justin Dartwright. In his early thirties, with an elongated, intelligent face and blue eyes, he greets us with mild friendliness and invites us to sit down. He props his foot on his knee, twitching it up and down, and plays with his pen throughout, in a way that reminds me of my brother, whose long adolescent limbs would beat out just such a restless counterpoint to whatever conversation he was engaged in.

It has been a long day for Justin Dartwright. Outside, the sun is shining. The young are in the street. He must have a girlfriend somewhere. Perhaps a wife. At any rate, the claims of sickness are pressing today, and some inner resistance, the natural prerogative of youth and health, asserts itself in that twitching foot, that flipped pen, which at one point flies up and out of his hand, and lands on the floor below. He bends to retrieve it with a kind of shamefaced boyishness, a charming gaucherie, as if he were in the front row of the Latin class years back and a paper airplane had landed on his desk, causing the master to fall silent and the class to crumple in snickers.

We rehearse the predicament at a smart trot, now well versed in its intricacies. The threat from ovarian cancer has been defused via removal of the ovaries. True, there is a residual risk of peritoneal cancer, as the surgeon can never remove 100 percent of the tissue. But the risk is very small. What is small? Just 2 to 3 percent. And what is the survival rate for peritoneal cancer? Not so good. He shakes his head, looks at his hands. Well, what exactly? Can he put a figure to it? Oh, 95 percent mortality or thereabouts, he murmurs mildly. There is a pause. *Peritoneal* is not a word I know. In my geography of the human body, the peritoneum is somewhere off toward the anus and possibly involved in passing urine. Months later, checking a dictionary, I find that the peritoneum (I have confused it with perineum) is the membrane lining the cavity of the abdomen, covering the abdominal organs. If cancer develops in this thin, stretched membrane (it derives from Greek *peritonos,* or stretched around), there is little the doctors can do about it.

"And what is the life expectancy of a woman with a mutation on the *BRCA1* gene?" The question has been lurking in the recesses of my mind, but had not formulated itself clearly enough to be included in any of the typewritten lists that R and I prepare for meetings with the doctors. I feel R's startled gaze on me as I wander off message. "Life expectancy?" says Dartwright mildly, inspecting his pen. "Hard to say. The gene was discovered only ten years ago, we don't have a lot of data to go on." Some sort of clinical intuition? "Well, without developing a malignant tumor, it can be good," he says. "Yes, it can be good." And with a tumor? He gives a graceful shrug. "In that case, not so good. No, not so good."

There is a pause while we absorb this. I don't exactly shiver, but a dark wing clips the room. Like seeing sunshine in negative. When we resume our discussion, there is a little extra brio and acceleration lent it by fear.

So, moving on to the breast cancer risk? Well, hopefully, he explains, we have had an impact on that via oophorectomy. Oophorectomy removes much of the estrogen from a woman's body, and cutting estrogen appears to have a protective effect. In fact, if you remove the ovaries of a woman with a *BRCA1* mutation early enough, you can almost halve the risk of her developing breast cancer, as studies at the Mayo Clinic have demonstrated. We know that women who menstruate later, and have more pregnancies, have a lower incidence of breast cancer, possibly due to reduced lifetime exposure to estrogen. It's true that at forty-four I haven't gotten in there quite as early as I might have. But still, I can hope for some benefit.

Of course, there is always preventive surgery. He speaks more mildly as his subject approaches greater horror. "Bilateral mastectomy appears to cut the risk of a woman with a mutation developing breast cancer by up to ninety percent. That's a very significant reduction. A proportion of women do opt for this strategy." I shudder. "But of course," he continues, "bilateral mastectomy would not be recommended in the present situation. At this point, it is not known for certain that M18T is deleterious. The surgery itself carries risks. And there is research to suggest that bilateral mastectomy is associated with significant postoperative psychosocial morbidity." Please? "Well, women feel mutilated in some core part of their femininity." He fiddles with his pen, looking pained. It must be hard for a man in his thirties to talk about this to a woman ten years older than he, with her husband sitting beside her. "There is a higher incidence of depression, sexual dysfunction, and so on. So really, it could not be justified unless one were absolutely certain that M18T was deleterious."

We are all agreed. We don't need to go there. And as we acknowledge this, there is a lightening in the atmosphere. A feeling of levity,
of bustle, as of an examination successfully completed. We switch
the tape recorder off, start gathering our papers. There are smiles
all round. M18T can safely be put to bed for another year. We can
all escape this hot, close room with its exhausted air. Outside, I can
make my appointment for next year.

There is just one sour note, which later comes back to haunt
me. "Is it mammograms you are using to screen against the breast-
cancer risk?" asks Justin Dartwright, his pen raised over a form.
I nod. He pauses. I have a sense of pressure, as of someone shy
of expressing a concern. I wait. "Well, that should probably be
fine," he says, scribbling across the form. I do know, of course,
that MRI scans are more reliable for detecting tumors in women
with *BRCA* mutations? One reason for this is that *BRCA* tumors
strike younger women whose breast tissue is more dense, so that
tumors often don't appear clearly under X-ray. I had heard something about this, yes. Deborah Lovelace did mention it. She said
that NICE (the National Institute for Health and Clinical Excel-
lence) is currently considering whether to authorize MRI scanning for women with deleterious mutations. But how much more
reliable is it exactly?

"Well, for women with a mutation, the evidence suggests that
MRI scanning combined with mammograms can be over eighty
percent reliable," says Justin Dartwright. "That is, it detects cancers in eighty percent of cases, while mammograms alone detect
only twenty-three percent of tumors."

I am stunned. No one had informed me of this. How could I
have sat in so many rooms with so many different medical professionals and not ever heard such a significant fact? I think of the
mammogram I had eight months ago that showed me clear of
cancer. As a certificate of health, it was not worth the paper it was
written on. "But why would I have a test that is only twenty-three
percent reliable?" I say. Justin Dartwright doesn't answer. Instead,
he looks at the floor. "Maybe I should be getting myself an MRI

scan privately?" I say sharply. (I have no private medical insurance, and my treatment is under the NHS, but I have bought myself scans privately whenever it seemed necessary.) Again that hesitation. "Well, it might be an idea," he murmurs.

But even this news, which has shocked me profoundly, is not enough to interfere with my élan, the sense of wrapping up a good tutorial, and the drive to be gone. We shake hands warmly. Dartwright hopes that we do not get stuck in traffic on our way back to Oxford. We wish him a pleasant evening. And at that point, if Deborah Lovelace herself hadn't appeared, popping her head around the door and apologizing for being caught up in another consultation, I would have left without saying a word about the lump I had discovered the previous evening, as if the foregoing discussion were purely academic and had no possible application whatsoever to my own biological existence.

"I hope Justin has helped you," she says. "He heads a team doing important research into this very mutation. The field of breast-cancer genetics is really moving very fast." We chat about M18T, picking up from a few months ago. Does she have any news? "Well, as a matter of fact, there is something to report," she says. A cluster of families with the M18T mutation has been tracked down in Nijmegen, Holland. And they segregate for cancer. It is very early-stage data. Not possible to draw definite conclusions. But do we have any Dutch relatives? Not that I know of. Scottish lineage on my father's side, a Russian Jewish grandmother. My maternal grandfather was sandy haired, reddish blond, definitely Saxon. That's about as close as it gets. We laugh. The conversation is friendly, urbane. An image of the wretched family in Nijmegen, busily segregating for cancer, flashes up briefly. *Poor things,* I think, and move on. There is a feeling of camaraderie between colleagues, as if we have all worked together to defuse the threat of M18T and are now entitled to a little lighthearted exchange before going our separate ways. Soon we are shaking hands, promising to meet up again in a year's time, at which point I find myself saying, on the point of passing through the door, holding my briefcase full of papers and tape recorder, "Oh, by the way, it's probably nothing, but I think I may have found something . . ."

Not so much *Treppenwörter,* or afterthoughts on the staircase, as *Türknopfwörter,* words thrown out while gripping the door handle in the act of exit. Doctors must be familiar with the phenomenon. Lovelace does not break step. She is affable, assured: "We'll just have a quick look. Better safe than sorry." And within seconds, I am on the examining bed, naked to the waist and entering the spell that occurs when one lies prone in a medical setting, as if, in the act of lying down, you have become a different person, obligingly offering up pathology to whatever label the doctor has prepared for you.

Deborah Lovelace's hands are long and thin, like those of the merchant Arnolfini, and a little chill, for which she apologizes. She strokes my breast with soft, keen movements, bringing her hands inward along the radial line, and I am aware of something practiced and knowing, a precision that takes years of experience to achieve. I remember her clinical training in ovarian cancer and am both frightened and fascinated. What if she had examined my mother? When would that have had to happen in order to make a difference? 1980? No, by then it would have been too late. The cancer was advanced. 1978? No, it couldn't have happened then. The gene was only discovered in 1994. No one could have known of my mother's increased risk. Her own mother died a year after she did. No one would even have talked to her of her paternal aunt's death at age thirty-nine from ovarian cancer. Cancer itself was unmentionable, let alone gynecological cancers. If spoken of at all, it would have been in vague terms: Aunt Jane died young. Very sad. Some kind of internal problem. Just as we in another generation had spoken of my mother's death. "Cancer of the womb," I had repeated airily for years, if anyone asked, which mostly they didn't. It was all I knew. After his remarriage, my father scarcely mentioned my mother, and never the cause of her death. No doctor talked to us, nor did any family member or family friend. In the absence of any other information, cancer of the womb was the best I could do. It served an unconscious poetic need, too, encapsulating the basic point: death by fertility. Five children, mortality. The gates of life open to bring forth its end. It was only the developments in this generation—my cousin's early breast cancer, her referral to the Marsden, Deborah Lovelace's precise questioning—that forced my uncle to check the death certificates of his female relatives, bringing to light the actual cause of this aunt's death. For my mother, there was no hope. She was simply a woman in the full flood of life, with five children aged eleven to nineteen and a demanding husband. Who would pay the slightest attention if she got a bit of back pain, some abdominal swelling? She least of all. There were always children to attend to, washing to put out, dogs to walk, meals to cook.

"Is that it? There?" Deborah Lovelace's pale face appears above me. "There does seem to be something," she says quietly. "Excuse me." She disappears for a moment and returns again within minutes. "Dr. Jane Steward, our radiologist, is next door. She was about to go home, but I have asked her to stay and see you before she leaves." And again I have that numb, pleased feeling, a kind of detached wonder, as if I have done something clever, pulled the rabbit out of the hat, in turning up the lump the textbooks had said I should.

Jane Steward is a middle-aged woman, a few years older than I, with a roughly chopped salt-and-pepper bob and a warm smile. Deborah Lovelace has caught her on the point of leaving: her computer is switched off, her desk clear; her briefcase stands hopefully by the door with a mackintosh draped over it. "Top half bare if you wouldn't mind," she says. "And hop up on the bed."

Soon I'm facing her on the bed, naked to the waist, heels dangling, feeling like a child waiting for a spoonful of medicine. She asks me to hold my arms above my head, stretch them out to my sides, then hold them by my hips, while she examines, at a distance, the silhouettes formed by these movements. Then she steps forward to conduct a physical examination of my left breast—meticulous and gentle, an unconscious critical coda of my own coarse domestic parody the preceding evening—and immediately locates the lump. "Here?" she asks, describing the parameters with index and middle fingers.

I nod, feeling foolish. How could I have made such heavy weather of finding something that the doctors discover in an instant?

"Lie down on the bed now," says Jane Steward, picking up a tube and squirting out gel, which she proceeds to warm between the palms of her hands. "This will be a bit chilly, I'm afraid."

I am familiar with the ritual from repeated ultrasounds during my two pregnancies. After several miscarriages, I was under the care of the high-risk-pregnancy clinic at Oxford's John Radcliffe Hospital, and scanned on a regular basis. Those scans are among my most powerful memories of pregnancy. The darkened room. The cold gel on my stomach. The grave hush as we waited.

Now Jane Steward angles the screen toward me, just as the radiographer at John Radcliffe used to do. There is a quietness between us that echoes that sweet gravity of old, when the terror of finding nothing—an empty sac, an aching hollow where life should be—was replaced by a lurch of joy as the fetus swam into vision, tender and promising as the first bean of spring, nestled in its numinous grainy pod with its tiny cross-stitch heart at the center, miraculously opening and shutting at twice the rate of a born human being.

Except that this time the gel is applied to my breast instead of my stomach. Instead of charting its familiar fertile abdominal terrain, the probe is making its way across a murky stretch of breast tissue. And in place of that tender bean, its heart going like the clappers, we are presented with something very different.

Large and lobular as a child's drawing, deadly as the asp at Cleopatra's breast, it is very clear: a dark pearl. It is lodged in the striated humus of breast tissue like something well bedded and awaiting watering. And in place of the radiographer's quiet smile expressive of happiness on our behalf, triggering a cascade of ejaculations and banalities on our part—the idiocy of joy—Dr. Jane Steward, in a terrifying departure from medical etiquette, is leaning over me, her choppy hair falling across her face, and applying gentle pressure to my hand: "I'm so sorry. I'm so very sorry."

Chapter Three

Shock Is Another Country

S HOCK IS ANOTHER COUNTRY. Things happen differently there. The train is caught forever leaving the station, like a surrealist emblem, in full velocity, yet stationary. Chronology falls through a lift shaft without pulleys. You can't remember your children's names. House keys play gleeful games of peekaboo, hiding for hours or days at a stretch before they turn up by the bread bin, on top of the loo, in the front door itself. You can't give someone directions to your own street. Instead, a kind of locomotive scarecrow goes round all day, poked at and prodded by other people's questions, until it bursts into torrents of tin-man tears. You wake up at night with a heart pounding like Big Ben and sopping pajamas.

"You've got me mixed up with someone else!" says one woman, marching round the back of the doctor's desk and wresting her medical file from his hands. For weeks she believes this. She has a sick mother-in-law in a house in Berkshire. Her husband works long hours in London. One of her children has mild autism and needs extra support to manage at home and at school. There is no space in her schedule for illness. Someone else passes out before the doctor has finished uttering the diagnosis. She's already been through treatment for cancer in the opposing breast. The thought that she might have to go through it again is more than she can bear. The doctor is left blinking at an empty space in front of her. Beam me up, Scotty. I am taking the forty trillion or so cells that make up me to another planet, where conditions are more favorable to the propagation and continuation of human life. I'll leave modern medicine and its chamber of surgical and chemical horrors to someone else if it's all the same to you. So long. Been nice knowing you. Send my regards to the children. A third woman starts shouting: "Now listen here. I've got three children. Solo. Not out of choice, you understand. But because my shit of a husband left me when I was pregnant with the third. I work part-time in a shitty office where my boss bullies me; I can't afford to pay the cable bill; and most of my wages go to a childminder who gets a lot of flu. Myself, I've never had a day's illness in my life. I don't do ill. Do you get me?"

As for me, despite my genetic inheritance, despite knowing that it is really a case of when, not if, the disease lays its mark on me— what else does an 85 percent lifetime risk mean?—I find myself with my head down between my knees, holding it tight, while the floor comes up to meet me.

And I get busy with my thoughts, which run like this: if we had stayed in that next-door room and finished shaking hands with Deborah Lovelace as we should have, as common courtesy and closure dictated; if I had just passed through that door without needing to do that puerile attention-seeking stunt about my lump, with my hand on the very doorknob, how cheesy can you get; and if Jane Steward had been allowed to go home as she intended to do—there was her briefcase with the raincoat over it like a child's tea set laid out for a picnic the grown-ups are always too busy to attend—and as she was entitled to do, for God's sake, after a long day's work in a cancer hospital, none of this would have happened.

She would be long gone by now, swaying heavily into the crush on the tube, halfway to some comfortable home in Wimbledon or Ealing, thoughts focused on the evening ahead, her children, a favorite television program perhaps, a glass of wine, her feet up.

And I wouldn't be sitting in a plastic bucket chair with my head pressed between my knees with that nice woman Jane Steward—I thought she was a nice woman, I didn't ask to hate her—advising me to go home and, given my *BRCA1* status, given that my breast tissue had developed cancer once and was liable to do so again, carefully consider having both breasts chopped off at once.

"You mustn't lose hope. The lump is small. It has been caught early. The chances are you will be through this in a year's time and out the other side. And reconstructions nowadays can be really very good. When a woman has her clothes on, you wouldn't be able to see any difference."

It is Deborah Lovelace, phoning the evening after diagnosis. She would have left the hospital at the time of the ultrasound, returned to find my news the following morning, and made this call at the close of her afternoon clinic. "Yes," I say flatly, without having any notion of what I am assenting to. I have never heard the word *reconstruction* before in this context. I had no idea you could rebuild a breast. With what? How? My mind flaps wildly around the idea like loose tarpaulins on a building site when a gale is blowing.

"You mustn't get taken up with the sad cases you see in hospital," she continues. "They don't reflect the statistics. The majority of women are up and through this and getting on with their lives after treatment. You don't see them in hospital because they're not there."

Sad cases. Seven months ago, in August 2005, reporting to the hospital to have my ovaries removed, I met an attractive woman with long chestnut hair and a pale face. She was part of a confused crowd of people in the rear lobby of the hospital waiting for things to which they seemed to feel entitled—doctors, beds, clinics, results—but which were not forthcoming. I was one of them, having been promised a bed that was not available. The woman with chestnut hair was in the same position. Her husband, too, was crowding the secretary's desk, talking of letters and appointments. But while I became vocally outraged, she sat on her chair unperturbed, looking quietly ahead, her overnight bag by her feet.

Later, I was pleased to find myself sharing a room with her. She told me she had three children in a house in Norfolk and that her husband had had to take yet more time off work to bring her here.

We settled our bags and got ready for bed. As we did so, I noticed that she moved slowly, going to and from the bathroom, folding her clothes and placing them on the chair, as if physical movement required conscious deliberation. Her breathing was labored, like that of a woman in the late stages of pregnancy.

In the corridor, I overheard her husband talking urgently to a nurse. "*Please*. You've got to give her something stronger . . . she's really in a lot of pain."

Later that night, when our husbands had gone, I asked her what surgery she was having. She told me that there was no surgery the doctors could give her. The breast cancer she had contracted several years ago had gone into her bones, and then her lungs. She was, however, going to have radiotherapy to try and slow the spread of the cancer. "And would that deal with it?" I asked, with my heart in my throat. She explained gently that once the cancer had gone into your bones and your lungs there was no cure. All the doctors could do was delay the further spread, hold it back a little.

"I'm hoping that they will be able to make me more comfortable. And that I will be able to go home again soon." She spoke quietly, without emphasis or drama, as if such news required a special tenderness toward the person hearing it.

Afterward, I had difficulty sleeping. My thoughts were full of the children in Norfolk, the patient husband taking time off work, that beautiful woman moving about slowly with the obscene tumors choking her from within.

AT THE SHEPHERD'S Bush roundabout, on the edge of West London, where the A40 from Oxford turns into Holland Road, before traveling onward into leafy Kensington, Thames Water Authority has built a sixteen-meter-high water tower. It is made of stainless steel and plastic, in the shape of an upended oil pipe. Its transparent vertical cylinder is separated into five segments; in each, hidden valves throw out jets of water that wash aimlessly round the plastic sections before cascading downward.

The tower was built as a creative solution to a planning problem. A surge pipe was needed to accommodate sudden spikes in pressure within the London ring main, the eighty-mile-long circuit of pipes embedded eighty meters below ground that carries the city's water supply from reservoirs in Harrow to the west and the River Lea to the east. But Kensington and Chelsea Borough refused planning permission for what it judged an unsightly pipe in such a public location.

The Authority got round the borough's objections by commissioning two design students from the Royal College of Art and an architect, who came up with the idea of enclosing the pipe to form a kind of public barometer, something midway between sculpture and architecture, which would contain the underlying pressure in the water supply. With photovoltaic panels in the top of the pipe powering an electronic barometer capable of detecting minute changes in climatic pressure, and a microprocessor to trigger sprays of water at different levels within the tower, it is an extremely clever piece of late-twentieth-century design.

Making the journey to London on a near-daily basis in the wake of diagnosis, and often stationary at the roundabout, R and I find ourselves contemplating the tower's weird iconography. Its florid swirls of dyed blue water, its upended segments of pipe. Around it is chaos. The roundabout is being enlarged to accommodate increased traffic from north and west; its central reservation is full of diggers, breeze blocks, cement mixers, and a Nissen hut the size of a small supermarket.

"Opinions vary on what the changing water levels in the tower mean," says the Open Guide to London Web site. "Some think that it's a barometer, and the higher the water, the higher the pressure; others think that it's a pressure-balancing tower and the height is chosen to match the water table somewhere like Harrow."

For me, it becomes an icon of this time. The emblem of a dystopian universe, it marches in and out of my dreams. What is it doing there in the midst of this chaos? Whose idea was it anyway? What hopeless project for the decoration of the devastated?

* * *

"THE SITUATION CAN be managed," says a radiographer quietly, poring over the ultrasound screen as his right hand guides the probe across my naked breast and his left angles the screen for better vision. It is March 16. We are here for a core biopsy, in which tissue is withdrawn from the tumor and taken to the laboratory for analysis, offering 100 percent confirmation of diagnosis. Ultrasound is used to locate the center of the tumor.

He is in his late thirties, with a white shirt open at the neck and a shaved head revealing a beautifully shaped cranium. He is quiet and extremely focused, which is a mercy. But the young nurse beside him insists on asking questions about our children, the journey to the hospital, and what the weather is up to. Eventually, under the crushing impact of our silence, she falls silent herself, like a child caught running in a Victorian drawing room.

As the radiographer guides the probe across my breast, I am startled to see the tumor flash up again on the screen. I half expected it to have disappeared. Hospitals, doctors, ultrasound machines, biopsies, tumors: they are so many papier mâché effigies of horror. One blink and they will disappear.

But the radiographer seems to be taking the fiction seriously. Angling the needle carefully—we watch on-screen as the grainy probe nears its target—he releases a button. There is a loud crack as it withdraws. I jump like a shot hare; the nurse giggles fatuously.

"I'm sorry," he murmurs. "I should have warned you." He injects the contents of the needle into a plastic bottle; labels it; and continues his work. I allow myself to drift into a state midway between sleeping and waking, surrendering to the darkness, the warmth of the room, the grave calm of the radiographer's concentration. I have not slept for forty-eight hours. This brief passage on the bed, under medical supervision, represents an interstice in time in which I am momentarily released from the horror of my thoughts and can allow myself to drift into a state of pure passivity, a cradle of childlike suspension.

I am brought back by a sudden urgency as the radiographer angles the probe sharply this way and that to achieve a better vision of something on the screen. I turn my head to follow his gaze.

At which point I see not just one pearl-shaped lump, but another, and another. They are smaller than the first, but distinct. And beyond them, further dark grains, as if the flesh all around were going the same way. The radiographer starts to span the diameter of the tumors with a bleeping white broken line before entering the measurements on screen: 12 mm, 8 mm, 6 mm.

"How many of them are there?" I begin to sob in horror. "How many? This is hopeless, isn't it?"

"The situation can be managed," he murmurs quietly, leaving me to contemplate the meaning of the word *managed* in this context while he continues work with his electronic calipers. We are not talking cure here. We are not talking getting well, getting through, and going on to lead a normal life. We are not talking about forgetting the "sad cases" because they do not concern us. We are talking about a situation so irremediable, so terminally spun out of control, that its only hope is to be "managed."

"My children are five and three," I sob, at which point the nurse moves forward to take my hand in a manner clearly instructed by a textbook but nonetheless welcome. "My children are five and three."

Swish, swish, goes the water at the third segment of pipe. *Swoosh, swoosh.* And then it dies, a weak deliquescent wash, against the horizon of West London rooftops. I feel my life fading out with it. Home, security, the meanings of family, a bankable future. At a stroke, these sureties have vanished. How could this have happened?

We have all worked so hard. What has life been for the last two years except the struggle against this mutation? What did all those hospital visits mean? The endless sessions in cancer genetics. Long hours poring over research papers on the Internet. Trawling round specialists: oophorectomy or not oophorectomy. Surely there must be some alternative to amputation, we had argued. It seems so drastic, primitive even. There are all the negative consequences on health: heightened risks of osteoporosis and heart failure, not to mention lower-level effects such as reduced sexual and cognitive function. But no. It's not just Deborah Lovelace who insists on the unreliability of current screening tests. It's every paper we call up on the subject. It's also Professor Habermeyer, head of gynecological oncology at University College, London, and director of national research programs. Certainly, he says, we can expect reliable diagnostic tests in the future, enabling us to screen for ovarian cancer. There are a number of hopeful candidates in the pipeline; our children should be the beneficiaries. But there is nothing that will be up and running in time for me. I have entered the period of risk. We only have to look at my mother's age at her death. And here he does what doctors are not supposed to do when advising on these matters, but which for me is the single most valuable thing they have to offer: he expresses a personal opinion, based on many years' experience on the clinical coalface. His working life has been spent in the care of women with ovarian cancer, he says quietly, and he believes it would be better if I never went there.

So there was no choice. My ovaries had to go. In August 2005, there is the final tumbrel ride on the trolley to the operating theater. I have the urge to jump off (for what would I do, sad woman, with any remaining fertility I have but try for another baby?), and I have to summon up my children's faces to stay put. Some ethical choices are not free: they are made for us by what has gone before.

Meantime, there are mammograms to manage my risk of contracting breast cancer. Deborah Lovelace herself, a nice New Zealand nurse in Mammography, and a consultant breast surgeon all at different points pronounce me clear. "Nothing sinister there, Mrs. G," says the nurse, squeezing my breasts tight between two glass plates. "Nothing untoward at all. You can go ahead and make an appointment for this time next year."

And all the while it was there inside me, the deadly flower, at the heart of things. Just a millimeter in diameter perhaps. Too small to be detected. But several million cells' worth already. Sending out feelers into the surrounding tissue. Grappling a blood supply to itself. A process known as angiogenesis. From Greek *angeion,* vessel, genesis, creation. And it's off the blocks. Nothing can stop it now. Guzzling up quarts of blood to accelerate replication. The cells to be numbered in the billions now, reproducing at a rate far exceeding that of any surrounding tissue.

"MUMMY, MUMMY, I've made a bed for Rabbit!" Michaela flies along the corridor to meet us, holding up a shoe box with Rabbit in it. Rabbit is her "best-beloved," in R's mother's phrase, the soft toy to which she has bonded since birth. With long ears and a soft, yielding body, Rabbit has accompanied her everywhere: to a child-minder at five months, on every family holiday in France or Scotland, on the big adventure to live in Dublin for two years, and then back again to Oxford. His once-lovely pale fur is now grey and matted. Banned from the washing machine, he is slightly whiffy to the objective nose, although to me he still smells of babies' heads, white wool crocheted blankets, and mother-of-pearl nails so tiny they cannot be cut by any scissors, but have to be nibbled trim by their father.

She has covered Rabbit with a sheet and a piece of woolen blanket. Around him in the shoe box she has placed pinecones, flowers, buttons, some cups and saucers from a miniature tea set. It is a version of a Neolithic burial mound, Wayland's Smithy perhaps, or an ancient Egyptian tomb.

"Do you like it, Mummy? It's a bed for Rabbit."

But I can't speak. For some reason the whole thing seems unbearably poignant to me. If I open my mouth, I will start howling.

At this moment Katja, known to us as Kitty, streams toward me with a stack of little cards. "Mummy, Mummy, I've made cards for you!" They proliferate with symbols of flowers, butterflies, kites, her own jubilant icons, in emerald and rose, yellow, indigo and violet, as if she were running a home printing works at the kitchen table. They have been finished off with a wobbling eccentric script that is an integral part of the design: "Mum, I love you, Kitty," followed by rows of kisses, each more lavish than the last.

I gather their gifts into my arms while they look at me expectantly. Normally, I would be full of praise. But now I have no words. The silence is ghastly. A look of fear crosses Michaela's face. She glances at R and seems to shrink back a little. Kitty, standing on the bottom step of the stairs, giggles. It is the kind of giggle that sometimes escapes people when an announcement of calamity is made: someone has had a terrible accident, or is about to get a divorce. Then she presses her face firmly into my leg. "Mama," she says. "I love you."

"Come on," says R. "Mummy is tired. It's been a long day. Let's all go through to the kitchen and make supper."

"IT IS MULTIFOCAL CANCER. In such cases lumpectomy, or simple removal of the lump, is not possible. The surrounding tissue is too unstable. We have no choice but to do a full mastectomy. Pathology has shown that your tumors are Grade III, and estrogen negative, as is common in *BRCA* cancers. The estrogen-negative status means that hormonal treatments such as Tamoxifen or Arimidex won't be relevant. It is likely that you will be given chemotherapy. Now, have you thought about reconstruction yet?"

It is Nicky Perrone, consultant breast surgeon, a few days later. Short, slight, with a quick, precise manner and intelligent brown eyes, he has forgotten that he has met me before.

It was around this time a year ago. I underwent a physical breast examination on this same bed, at the end of which he pronounced me clear of cancer. I remember the delicate concentric circles he drew on my breasts, up into the armpit to check the lymph glands, back down again toward the nipple. Afterward, as I put on my clothes, released into hopefulness by his verdict, I asked questions about diet, how I might attempt to combat my genetic predisposition through nutrition. Should I avoid dairy products, as some experts advocated? I mentioned a book I was reading by Professor Jane Plant, linking higher rates of breast cancer in affluent countries with their dependence on animal fats and carcinogenic chemicals. Should I eat more fish? Take supplements?

"In the great scheme of things, anything you can do with diet is a tiny saucer compared with the great bucket of your inherited risk," he pronounced in his swift, decisive manner. "You are clear of cancer. Go away. Live your life. Better not to think about it."

AT THE WHITE CITY OVERPASS, I look down into the little streets, which spread out like a child's model. The lintels of the houses have been painted white. There are little market barrows with striped awnings, rows of toy cars parked tidily. The odd tree has erupted into blossom, looking like a Japanese character suspended against the brick scroll of the houses.

When I was twenty-one, my friends from university left in a bright group to live in London, in a flat in Shepherd's Bush. They had been offered jobs in advertising and management consultancy, the civil service, or journalism. I would hear stories about them from time to time, and catch glimpses of their busy and energetic lives. There was Xanthe, catching a cab from a function at work, being sick afterward because she had drunk too much, but not before she had secured a major new account for her advertising firm. There was Luke, whose mathematical brilliance and wit brought him to the attention of senior people within the Treasury, so that he was appointed private secretary to the Chancellor of the Exchequer at an exceptionally young age. There was Anna, sending back reports from war zones across the world, mountaineering in the Himalayas in her spare time. And Liz, who was happily married with three children and a house in the country before any of us realized that either was a possibility.

Meanwhile, I stayed in Oxford. Wrote a little heap of lyric poems, drank too much, was clinically depressed. There was something wrong with me. That was for sure. But none of us knew how to fix it. Life went by: days, months, years of it. Gradually, I began to grow other possibilities, almost in spite of myself. There was therapy, and a career of sorts as a journalist. I married. Eventually, I even had children. The balance of life shifted: I discovered the charms of simple happiness. It is this that diagnosis has smashed.

"I don't want to go home," I say to R, thinking of the children's faces. "I can't bear to go home."

WHEN MY MOTHER DIED, I was afraid to sleep. I knew that if I put my head on the pillow and gave in, at some point I would have to go through the business of waking again. Whatever nightmare my unconscious mind was spinning, it could not compete with the uncontested horror of that reality.

In the weeks following diagnosis, I lose the power of sleep again. "Don't worry, S. I'll be there with you," says R. "You don't have to do it if you don't want to. Heck, we can give up sleeping for a while."

So we wake at two, or four, or five o'clock. We get up, we make cocoa, we watch the dawn. We hold each other, with that cautious, tender touch of those in shock who seek nothing except the presence of another's hand in theirs, quite still, the proof of skin against skin.

"WE NEED TO find out whether the cancer has traveled to your lymph glands. You will need to have a sentinel node biopsy. It's minor surgery—a night or two in hospital at most."

Nicky Perrone again. A small cubicle off the Outpatients section. He is leaning against a bed, in a white coat, his arms crossed, flanked by a nurse to one side, a stack of brown files to the other.

In the past, he explains, surgeons would automatically remove the lymph nodes after a diagnosis of breast cancer. But this often led to lymphedema, a chronic condition in which the arm becomes swollen because the glands have been removed, leaving the lymph nowhere to escape to. Doctors looked for a different way of doing things. They developed the sentinel node biopsy. Blue dye, together with a radioactive isotope, is injected into the breast at the site of the tumor. This enters the lymph system, passing from the breast toward the first node—the sentinel node. The surgeon can then locate this, remove it, and examine it for signs of cancer. If nothing is found, no further glands are removed. If cancer is found, the woman will undergo full axillary clearance, or the removal of her underarm lymph glands.

Perrone presses some forms into my hands. "Take these to the Old Brompton Hospital on the day before your surgery. Radiography. Fourth floor. If you have any more questions, please ask the breast-care nurse."

He indicates the young woman at his side, who bears a plastic printed name tag on her chest saying JOY DUGGAN, and who beams at me obligingly. I lean forward, ignoring her and addressing myself directly to him. "And what if it *has*?" I can't help myself asking. "Traveled into my lymph system, I mean. What are my chances *then*?"

He makes a gesture of dismissal and straightens up. "Too early to say. Not enough information. We need the results from the sentinel node, and the pathology report from the mastectomy. Then we'll be in a better position to make an estimate. Now, have you had time to think about reconstruction?"

CANCER FOR ME takes place in nineteenth-century buildings: in old stacks of brick, seamed with soot from an era of railway and coal, buildings that have borne their load, done their bit, been rattled by trains and bombs and trucks. Buildings that have stood firm beneath the passage of feet and have made their accommodations over the course of the twentieth century to the demands of modern medicine. It takes place in errant back passages, gloomy stairwells, in lifts that rattle up two floors and give out, to be exchanged for flights of concrete steps found at the opposite end of the building. Along rumbling plywood rampways, tacked down to level out differences of height for wheelchairs and trolleys. In makeshift prefab units, dropped into gloomy courtyards to house new administrative operations, or an outsize piece of scanning equipment.

Particularly, it takes place in miles and miles of corridor painted chocolate brown or cream; not rich and buttery, a wholesome farmhouse cream, but thin and wheyish, the shade of a persistent yeast infection or some other eruption of exhausted white blood corpuscles.

It is the essential warp and weft of these buildings that captures the prevaricating, backtracking nature of the disease, a disease that cannot be caught hold of directly and faced down, but which defies predictions; a disease that lies in wait for years or decades before answering a mysterious internal clock and leaping into life again. Deceitful, opportunistic, dilatory, dark, and deadly. In the end, the decay and shabbiness of the buildings is essential to the experience of hope, without which one could not endure treatment: the feeling that if one were only to transform the architecture, let the light in, the disease itself might be capable of solution. I can't imagine what it would be like to be treated in modern, lucid spaces. More chillingly terrible, perhaps. We would have reached the end of human ingenuity—the very best shot we could give it—and *still* it would be there.

IN THE FIRST DAYS after diagnosis, we visit rooms of every shape and size throughout the hospital. There are darkened rooms for ultrasound scanning. There is a brilliantly lit room where I go for a CT scan, to be placed inside a large plastic cylinder and bombarded with X-rays. The computer builds these into a three-dimensional image to confirm whether the cancer has spread to my lungs. All I know is that I am left alone in a machine, naked, while everyone else leaves the room. There is a visit to the Preoperative Assessment Unit for an electrocardiogram. Anesthesia and chemotherapy both place extra pressure on the heart. Little blue rubber disks attached to wires are scattered across my body like confetti by a technician too uninterested to look at me or speak. Behind a grey curtain, a young Irish nurse directs me to blow into a tube to test lung capacity.

There are endless blood tests. I become familiar with every cubicle of the phlebotomists, their shabby grey curtains, the raised padded chairs. I become familiar with the phlebotomists themselves, the way one likes to decorate her booth with cloying pictures of kittens, the natural austerity of another. In the basement, we make our way past large yellow bins marked RADIO-ACTIVE WASTE to the X-ray department. I stand undressed to the waist while a woman pulls heavy metal screens about my chest, before withdrawing to a glass cubicle. There she and a young male technician joke about David Beckham's new pay packet and his dismal performances for Real Madrid. At the end, R and I take my scans with excessive deference, like a pair of elderly refugees. The young ones hardly look at us. We are learning. It is the beginning of a long journey into the kingdom of the sick, as Susan Sontag called it. For suffering isolates. Make no mistake. It is only relatively recently in human history that anyone sought to explain disease as anything other than divine retribution for a crime committed.

"ARMS OUT, BACK STRAIGHT, feet firmly on the floor, and look straight at me. Thank you. Perfect."

We are in the basement of the Marsden again, a room marked PHOTOGRAPHY, and a middle-aged woman called Yelka with a kind face and grey roots showing through her dyed auburn hair is pulling up heavy iron studio lights on extendable hinges. They look like something from a 1930s film set. I am sitting on a stool before a grey backdrop, wearing nothing but a pair of knickers. She snaps on the lights and trains them on my upper torso.

"Both breasts?" she inquires in an eastern European accent.

I nod.

She makes a sympathetic clicking noise. "How come?"

"A mutation. *BRCA1*."

She nods. "Reconstruction?"

"I don't know."

Before removing body parts, the hospital likes to take photographs in case a reconstructive surgeon needs to consult them later. No one needs to justify the process as far as I am concerned. It answers to a powerful documentary urge I feel myself. We have already spent an afternoon with a professional photographer near Oxford who shot several reels of film to prove to the children later, if need be, that their mother was attractive; that their parents made a handsome couple; that there were happy times when we lived together as a family.

"The surgeons can do a lot now," says Yelka, looking down her heavy black tripod. "In the past, women had nothing." She shrugs. "In my country, still they have nothing."

Something about the improbability of the situation, the strangeness of such photography before butchery, and the laconic kindness of this woman as she gives me instructions, releases loquacity in me.

"I can't make a decision. Every night I read the leaflets and can't make sense of it all. When I try to concentrate, my mind goes blank. I suppose it's denial. I think about the children, what they'll make of it. I breast-fed them both, you see. I think about my husband. He says it won't make any difference to him. But how can he know what he'll feel?"

She indicates an Alpine scene to the right of me on the wall. "Turn that way, please. I need a profile," she murmurs. And then: "Perhaps you should trust him if he says it doesn't matter. Why should it, really? And if you have breast-fed your children, well . . ." She shrugs. "They have done their job."

The picture is all snowy peaks and wildflower meadows. Kitsch as it is, I think that perhaps it represents something in her childhood and feel a pang of affection for it. While the flash goes off, with its improbable retro glamour, she tells me that she left Serbia when she was nineteen to study in the West. Now she goes back twice a year. Her father used to own the orchards at the foot of these mountains—they have now passed to a cousin—and whenever she comes back to London, she brings a suitcase full of apples from them. They taste completely different from anything you can find in the shops here. "When I first came here, I walked the streets. Buying, buying. Looking for something that tasted like apples at home. Nothing. I felt I had lost a sense."

At the end, she passes me the form and takes my hands. "Good luck," she says. My eyes fill with tears. When you are this vulnerable, kindness is a dangerous force.

"WE NEED TO talk to the children," says R. "They're disturbed."

"Do you think I don't *know* they're disturbed? My own children. Do you think I don't *know* what they are?"

It is the second day running that Kitty has turned up from school wearing someone else's clothes. She has wet herself there, not something that has ever happened before, and the school has given her a spare set. "We had a little accident," says the teacher. "We were quite upset, Mummy. But we dusted ourselves down and got cleaned up. But we were rather quiet afterward. Not ourselves. A little withdrawn, I should say. Is anything happening at home, maybe? Anything unsettling her in the home background?"

For the past year, this teacher has had long, unexplained absences, turning up perhaps three days out of five, leaving her band of three-year-olds leaderless and rudderless. Parents have gone on more than one occasion to register their unhappiness with the headmistress, who says that her hands are tied because of employment law. I feel that Kitty has suffered from a lack of continuity in her first experience of school. Looking into the squashy, evasive face of this woman, now pressed close into my own with suffocating concern, I decide furiously that I will not be forced into intimacy with her.

"I will wash the trousers," I say icily. "You'll have them back first thing tomorrow, without fail."

The night before, Michaela appeared at bedtime with a book about dinosaurs, a large-format Dorling Kindersley book we had bought together one happy afternoon in the basement of Waterstone's. It has a picture of Tyrannosaurus rex on the front baring its teeth at smaller dinosaurs. "This is what I want."

"I'm sorry, Michaela. I can't."

"You *can*," she insists.

"I can't. I'm very sorry."

Her eyes narrow. The thick lashes meet to become a menacing sooty streak, and her skin, naked after her bath, begins to flush. As a baby, her skin was always a barometer of feeling. After breastfeeding, the finely grained opalescence would take on a deep rosy tinge. How I loved those golden mother-and-baby fugs, the pair of us enveloped in a milky haze, her curls clinging damply to the nape of her neck as we drifted off into sleep. The window was open to the green outside: snatches of birdsong, an ozone exhalation from the river. If we walked downriver, past the willows and the weir, to where the fields open out and the water is bordered with steeply wooded banks—quite common to see a heron on a post or the flash of a kingfisher—she would fall asleep in the papoose and the blood would recede from her skin altogether. Then she took on an unearthly pallor; it was like looking at an abbot carved in a Provençal church, a stone angel fallen to earth.

But now it's something else that flushes through her. In one irresistible beat, from the cushioned pads of her toes through short, strong limbs to the tiny rosebud nipples, her five-year-old body expresses rage. Vigorous, healthy, righteous rage.

"You *can*," she says, shoving the book into my face. "Of course you can. Why *not*?"

"You'll need to find something else, Michaela."

"Well, I'm not having *any* story, then!"

The door slams and she disappears into her own room. A little later, I hear R's voice, low and sonorous, rolling out sentences about the days, seventy million years ago, when giant lizards ruled the world. When Tyrannosaurus tore the head off Compsognathus; when meteors from the asteroid belt orbiting the sun some hundred million miles away, out there between Mars and Jupiter, rained down upon the earth, causing untold devastation, nights that lasted for months, winters that lasted for years, and the extinction of many thousands of species, including, perhaps, the dinosaurs themselves.

R AND I had our children late, in our late thirties and early forties. There were three miscarriages along the way. So there is scarcely a day when we have not been conscious of the blessing of them, derived joy from each gesture and smile, each game or burst of laughter, each act of physical or verbal dexterity. In short, we have doted on them, in the way of older parents who have looked into the face of childlessness.

But overnight, they have turned into baggage, something to be managed. There is a constant attempt to off-load them: friends, acquaintances, after-school club. We juggle addresses, street maps, pick-up times, as we lurch back from hospital appointments in choked traffic. R calls friends from the mobile phone on the motorway to say that we will be late. I know I should take this task from him, but can't. If anyone asks me how I am, I will break down. In front of other people's houses, I hunch down in the passenger seat so that no one can see me. R goes to the front door. Warm light spills out. Chatter in the hall. Why is it that other people's domesticity always looks so inviting, so unreachable? Then the children's faces appear, like crumpled flowers in the dusk. They are pale, streaked with dirt and neglect. They seem like strangers to me. So quickly the biological bond is broken. Afterward, there are horrible screaming bedtimes because nothing is the same and they don't know what's happening to them.

"We need to say something to them," R repeats one night in bed. "They're disturbed. They need some sort of explanation."

"Got any ideas?" I say nastily.

R props a pillow behind him. "You can tell them you are ill. That you have . . . cancer." I notice that he struggles a little over the word. "You can tell them that you will have to go into hospital. And that the doctors are going to make you better."

"And what if it's not true?"

I reach into a drawer, extract a pill from a silver blister pack and place it under my tongue. Lorazepam, I love you. This tiny blue pill (eventually we went to the doctor, who prescribed tranquilizers) will ensure me a few hours of oblivion. Not rest exactly, for I wake up in the small hours turbid and confused, as if I have been sitting for an exam while under the influence of alcohol, but the temporary extinction of consciousness.

"We don't need to think about that," he says. "They just need to know what's happening now."

"I'm not ready," I say sharply. "Don't push me. I'm not ready."

For in truth, what am I to say to them? That I am going to die, as my mother did before me. That I am going to grow thin, thin, thin. That my eyes are going to hollow out until they are so intensely blue they will follow them for the rest of their lives, waking and sleeping. That I will be sick in a bowl because of the agony I am in. That the sight of their golden faces is not possible for me anymore because I know I have to leave them. That they will have to watch death claim me, their beloved mother, and be helpless to do a thing about it.

If I talk to them now, I will traumatize them. So I say nothing. I avoid them ruthlessly. I can hardly bear to touch them. My kisses at night are perfunctory. I refuse to meet their gaze. Their high piping voices are a torment to me. And I have become incapable in relation to them, can do nothing for them: not brush their teeth, comb their hair, wipe their bottoms, make them a meal. I am buying time. Like a creature with amputated limbs, wrapped in an enormous bale of bandages until blood flow is stanched. All of a sudden, as a mother, the very best I can offer is to refrain from damage.

Chapter Four

Bride of Frankenstein

THERE ARE THREE principal methods for rebuilding a breast."
It is Nicky Perrone again, in delivery mode, arms akimbo,
more than a little impatient. The stack of brown files on the examining bed beside him is a foot high. His waiting room is full. The
electronic board on the wall outside is already announcing delays,
and the afternoon clinic has only just begun. "You've got implant-
only reconstruction. Implant-assisted latissimus dorsi. And a vari-
ety of autologous flaps. With bells and whistles."

As Perrone talks, you see him in class at age six or seven, always
the brightest, the teacher already struggling to keep up with his
need for stimulation. At university, he absorbs theory, data, surgical
methods at a rate that leaves his peers far behind. Now he handles
a workload that might comfortably be shared among three. Packed
clinics and theater lists; the management of systems and training; endless clinical meetings, conferences, international travel. In
another life, he might have been a top athlete or modernized a factory. He is compassionate, too. The sight of suffering tends to make
him silent. He watches it with quiet attention. I learn from a friend
later that while her daughter was dying of cancer, he took special
care of her. When she was hospitalized repeatedly with episodes
of acute pain, he would visit her each day on the ward, ruffling her
hair, or what was left of it, and pausing to chat with her awhile. He
also attended her memorial service. But whatever his gifts, adapt-

ing his delivery to a patient stupefied by shock is not foremost among them. Nor does the practice of medicine within the NHS at this level allow much space for it.

As he talks, I become more and more dazed—by the speed of delivery, the complexity of the information, and the sheer improbability of what he is describing. I can't shake off the feeling of having taken up residence in a science-fiction novel: Dr. Moreau's evil island, where wicked genius is busily grafting animals together in new and unnatural ways; *Bride of Frankenstein,* perhaps; the book of Genesis. Anything where mad scientists run amok, creating new life, with weird erotic overtones.

"The simplest method is implant-only." Perrone is off the blocks. "You place silicone or saline bags under the pectoral muscle and expand them over the course of a few months. As the implants are filled, the skin is stretched. Later, there is more surgery to replace the expander implants with permanent ones. The downside of this type of reconstruction is the same as with any foreign material introduced to the body. The body forms a scar of tissue around it. If this capsule of scar tissue contracts around the implant—capsular contracture—it can cause pain or aesthetic distortion. Depending on its severity, you might need secondary surgery: excision of the scar tissue, repositioning of the implant, or its replacement altogether. On the aesthetic level, the results of implant-only reconstruction can be"—he hesitates—"pretty good. You get a youthful shape: high, flat, but no ptosis."

"Ptosis?"

He makes a fluid gesture, in which the shape of a woman's breast is captured. The aching pendulousness. That precise curve where the pear begins to swell. Something about falling and flesh. Ptosis is surgeon's speak for sagging.

"And what is the risk of capsular contracture?" I have a list of typewritten questions in front of me, and a tape recorder running. A journalist by trade, the interviewing habit dies hard. It is impossible to shake off the conviction that knowledge—enough of it, early enough, and well-enough digested—will protect.

He shrugs. "Estimates differ. No center keeps statistics in the same way, so it's hard to compare. But most people would agree it's in the order of thirty percent within ten years."

"High," I murmur.

"Reconstruction is seldom a one-stop solution," he says briskly. "It's a commitment to repeated rounds of surgery, sometimes across a lifetime. You are a work in progress. With implant reconstruction, it's like parts in a car. You get some service, then they wear out and have to be replaced."

Work in progress . . . parts in a car . . . Lovely metaphors. So it's back to the surgeon for bodywork for the rest of your life, however long it is.

"And what about the nipples?" I force myself to be explicit. "What happens to them?"

"The nipple is part of the breast, period," he rattles off. "In your case, mastectomy is being performed for cancer-prophylactic as well as cancer-therapeutic reasons. In *BRCA* cases, reduction in breast tissue is correlated with a reduction in the risk of developing another cancer. We can never remove a hundred percent of breast tissue, because the breast does not start and finish at a single point. It constitutes a milk line, as in any mammal, up to the clavicle, down to the abdomen. But I would aim for maximum clearance: between ninety and ninety-seven percent. Of course, it's your choice whether to retain the nipple. But you could argue that there is a contradiction in removing maximum breast tissue for prophylactic reasons while retaining the nipple for other reasons."

Thank you, Nicky Perrone. That is clearly put. And it is the kind of clarity that saves lives. So no nipple. It's part of the breast. Period.

My thoughts are full of something cloudy. Something diaphanous and drifting, like the webby crystal sometimes found at the bottom of a bottle of fine wine. There is the sensation of a man's hands, the fingers blunt and fine, dusted with hair at the knuckles, held over my breasts. The heat thrown from these hands, at a distance of about half a foot, is enough to make the small gold beads of the nipples rise. An ardent flame scours my belly. Bushfire. Where does the erotic self reside, after all? Is it in the mind, as some say, in the image of oneself in the eyes of another? Is it in the skin, the circuitry of hormones, the potential to suckle an infant, or in none of these? Is it like the soul in medieval theology? Will it migrate at death, to take up residence in a better place? Or will my poor breasts haunt me with ghost memories, referred sensation, as some amputees report?

Preoccupied by these thoughts, I miss a chunk of what Perrone is saying and have to ask him to repeat it. He looks at the clock pointedly. He is doing this under duress; he would prefer to devolve communication to the breast-care nurse. But she can't answer questions about rates of capsular contracture, about the impact on physical mobility of different types of reconstruction, about the implications for *BRCA1* women of retaining the nipple. She gives an enormous smile and hazards a guess, which is not acceptable. So it's got to be Nicky Perrone.

"The second principal method of reconstruction is latissimus dorsi, after the latissimus dorsi muscle on the back," he continues, indicating a chart on the wall of a male skeleton partially clad in muscles. He points to the muscle that fans out just below the shoulder blade. "You take this muscle, tunnel it under the armpit to the front, then, placing an implant underneath for volume, you resect it to the chest wall. The aesthetic results can be excellent, softer and more natural in appearance than implant-only reconstruction, especially with skin-sparing mastectomy."

"Skin sparing?"

"Mastectomy is performed while the skin is left intact. Generally, a periolar incision is adequate."

He draws a diagram. The surgeon makes a circular incision round the nipple, scoops out the breast tissue, tunnels the latissimus dorsi muscle from the back round to the front, places it over an implant inside the hollow of skin, and stitches it up again. What remains externally is a small circular scar. Neat. Perfect even. Part of me appreciates it detachedly; it's like the seams I used to make inserting a sleeve into a sleeve hole when making doll's clothes as a child.

"Afterward, you can have a nipple tattooed, or apply a nipple prosthesis, in which case it's sometimes possible to cover the scar altogether," he adds.

"And what is the downside?" I have read enough in the leaflets to know that in the world of breast reconstruction, there is no gain without pain.

"You add to your scar collection, of course," says Perrone, quickly sketching a diagram of a woman's back with two long horizontal incisions below the shoulder blades. "And this is major surgery. Four turns on the table. You would have limited mobility for several weeks. You have the risk of capsular contracture later, as with implant-only reconstruction. And there is sometimes some donor-site morbidity: a slight reduction in overarm strength. In the normal run of things, you wouldn't notice it. But if you played tennis at county level, say, or were a strong swimmer, you might."

I have always been proud of my crawl. A fine scissoring motion that clips the surface of the water with scarcely a splash, giving me force in excess of my body weight. In a French swimming pool once, age thirteen, a boy fell in love with me purely on account of it. So is it good-bye beautiful crawl?

Perrone sets off again at the clappers. "Finally, you've got tummy flaps. Basically, you take abdominal tissue and transfer it up to the chest. If the woman hasn't got enough tummy fat, you might use the thigh or the buttocks. In the case of TRAM reconstruction, the surgeon makes a hip-to-hip incision below the navel, takes the transverse rectus abdominus muscle, hence the name, and tunnels it up under the skin to the mastectomy site, while keeping it attached to its original blood supply. The trouble with TRAM is that you end up with a weakened abdominal muscle and a higher risk of hernia. DIEP is an improved version, since you cut away fat and skin but very little muscle. Here you remove the flap completely, taking the principal blood vessel with it, the deep interior epigastric perforator—hence the name. You resect it to the chest wall, reattaching the blood vessels to those in the chest. Later, there's more surgery to tidy it all up. At this point, it's enough for the surgeon just to get the flap up there. Aesthetically, autologous flaps can offer extremely good results. The breasts are made of your own tissue. They can be soft and natural. They put on or lose weight with you, and age with you, too. There's no risk of capsular contracture later, because there's no implant. And if it works, you're done. There should be no need for further surgery."

At this point, I'm feeling light-headed. We had lunch at the Marsden café—some kind of pasta bake, dense with cheese and sodden vegetables—and it's beginning to sit rather heavily in my stomach. "And what is the downside of this type of reconstruction?" I ask. By now this question is uttered dutifully, more out of loyalty to the printed list in front of me than a genuine desire to find out.

But Nicky Perrone is not to know this. All he knows is that he has to get to the end of this monster tutorial that is threatening to derail his clinic, and start chomping through that pile of files. So there is a burst of acceleration as we near the end. "This is major surgery: ten hours for two breasts. With all the risks that go with it: infection, hematoma, a thrombotic event, and so on . . . And of course, with this type of surgery, there is always a risk of failure . . ."

"Failure?"

"The big thing with flaps is to get the blood supply going. The blood vessels from the flap must be individually attached to the vessels in the chest. This is very intricate work. The surgeon has to be skilled in microsurgery. If it fails for any reason, you're in trouble. Only last week, we were in theater until three a.m. with a case of bilateral DIEP reconstruction where the vessels in the flap were poor." He shrugs. "But it isn't common. You're young. Slim." He checks the file. "No history of diabetes. Nonsmoker—smoking reduces blood supply to the vessels. You would probably be all right . . ."

"What is the overall risk of flap failure?"

"National statistics: ten percent. In your case, less. I couldn't put a figure to it."

"And if the flap fails? What then?"

"It must be removed."

"And the reconstruction?"

"You revert to Plan B."

In the art of medical understatement, this is a small gem, I gather from later reading a little of what flap failure might involve. The woman is kept very warm after surgery, wrapped in tinfoil blankets, to open the vessels and encourage blood flow, a little like a bloodletting of old. At the first sign of the flesh on her chest mottling—indicating inadequate blood supply—she is whisked back to theater, where everyone does their utmost to save the flap. But if this fails, and the tissue doesn't have enough blood supply to function, it suffers necrosis—surgeon's speak for rotting. Lovely. You've been diagnosed with cancer. Both your breasts have been cut off. A large section of your abdomen has been sliced out. You won't be able to bend over or hold your children for months. You've had ten hours of surgery with all the attendant risks. And now, to cap it off, you're lying in bed with a piece of your own living flesh stitched to your chest and rotting.

"I'm not sure whether I could go through with that, given such a high risk of failure," I say unsteadily.

Perrone pushes his glasses back up his nose. "It's not for the fainthearted. Certainly."

"What would you recommend in my case?" I ask now.

He shoots his swivel chair toward me, grabs hold of the rim of fat around my abdomen, and squeezes it hard between his two hands. "Plenty of abdominal laxity here. But not enough abdominal adiposity to create two full-size breasts. DIEP is ruled out in your case, I think, unless you want to drop a bra size. And you're not that big in the first place. For you, I would recommend bilateral implant-assisted latissimus dorsi reconstruction. Provided the lymph nodes are clear."

* * *

"WHY ARE YOU looking at me, Mummy?" asks Kitty, sitting in the bath with Michaela.

"I'm not."

"You *are*." She giggles. "You were looking at my breastes."

The cluster of consonants is too difficult for her. So she lengthens the word to two syllables, pronouncing it a little like the Robert Burns poem: Wee sleekit cow'rin tim'rous beastie. O, what a panic's in thy breastie . . .

She's right. I had lost myself staring at their nipples: a slipped stitch in the otherwise perfect flesh. Hard to imagine that at age ten or twelve, they will start to swell. Become fully fledged breasts, capable of attracting men, being stimulated, suckling a child.

And for them? Will this be their fate? What of each egg that went into making them, with its complement of twenty-three chromosomes, each a random mix of genetic material from my parents. Did it get the bit of the *BRCA1* gene from Mum? Or the bit from Dad? No one thought to lower the barrier and interrogate it: little egg, you look so propitious, so full of fortune, such a magical recombination of everything humanly possible, but do you in fact carry a speck of imperfection, an infinitesimally small chemical alteration, the mutation called M18T? In which case, however miraculous a recombination you are, however much nothing your like has ever been seen before in nature, nor ever will again, you may be doomed to disaster, to amputations, or to an early and painful death.

Later, when I am chasing them to bed, they stuff damp towels down their pajama tops and prance around the narrow landing outside the bathroom with their chests stuck out.

"Look, Michaela, look, I've got breastes!" says Kitty. Michaela bumps into her with her chest. They are helpless with laughter. "No, Kitty, no! I've got boobies and they're bigger! Look, mine are bigger!"

The future veers away from me. I am standing on a pier, staring down into sunlit water. The rusted coils of many hawsers curve away below me. On the surface, brightly painted fishing boats bob up and down. Where do these hawsers go? I can see no end to them. The iron coils stretch backward in time. They stretch forward. Determinacy. My love is not more strong. Can it be that for the people one loves most, one is this helpless?

THE DATE FOR sentinel node surgery arrives. We report to the Old Brompton, where I am injected with radioactive dye, which will travel into the lymph system, allowing the surgeon to locate and remove the sentinel node. My father and stepmother, Miriam, arrive from Scotland to look after the children. They have made five separate journeys by rail and ferry to get here, and by the time they arrive, Miriam is ill and has to go to bed. Kitty, too, is ill. She is running a temperature of 104°F. We haven't had time to take her to the doctor. When I go upstairs to say good-bye to her, she looks pale and unsavory, in the way of sick children. "We won't be long, Kitty," I say. "Just two nights."

But I'm not reaching her. She makes a mewling noise and turns her head away. I lay my hand on her forehead, which is burning. The gesture recalls my mother. I remember the sensation of her hand on my own forehead. The cool, flat palm. The fleeting warmth of her fingertips as she withdrew them. Then the flash of glass as the thermometer was shaken back and forth. She would examine the bead of mercury, checking to see whether it had climbed sufficiently, and invariably place the thermometer back again. My tongue over the glass tube felt like a swollen limb. But if the results were good, it was plumped pillows and trays of mashed bananas. It was iced water and stories by the bucketload. It was rare that my mother, preoccupied with her younger children, could spare such attention.

Will this gesture disappear from Kitty's life vastly earlier than it did from my own? Will she have no memory of it, except as a subliminal thing? Will she spend her life searching the immense vacancy left by a mother's tenderness, never able to recover or reach it, whatever strange men's beds she climbs into, whatever friends she struggles to bond with, whatever form of intimacy she fashions for herself with a husband, only to bump up against her absolute solitude at times of difficulty and stress?

The hospital, when we get there, is hot and porous. R feeds the meter and we sit in the Transitional Care Unit while a bed is prepared, leafing through sticky copies of *Hello!* and *Country Life*. There is a dense silence in the room, which has been sectioned from the interior of the building and has no windows.

Mostly, people are quiet. But at one point, an incident breaks out. A young woman on the other side of the room starts murmuring something about a friend of hers on Ellis Ward who died that day at 12:30 p.m. She has been waiting in TCU since 9:00 a.m. and wasn't allowed the chance to go and see her friend. This is not right, she says. Her neighbor agrees. A young doctor comes out to talk to her, listens to the details, and falls silent. The woman starts to become more vocally upset. "I've been waiting here while she was dying. It's not right. They should have let me go. I needed to see her. I wanted to say good-bye."

The doctor goes away and comes back with a nurse, a middle-aged Chinese woman wearing black tights and a black belt round her tiny waist. "It wasn't nice, the last few hours," she says. "She didn't want visitors. Isn't it better to remember her the way she was?"

"I needed to say good-bye to her," the original woman repeats, inconsolable, like a child who has lost the favorite pebble she took home from a day at the beach. "She was my friend!" Suddenly the nurse changes tack, sits down on a chair beside her, and puts an arm round her. "She was my friend, too," she says with the open, unfinished consonants of a native Mandarin speaker fluent in English. "Mine, too. But it wasn't nice at the end. She didn't want visitors. Honest. I wouldn't lie to you. Better to remember her the way she was."

From the moment we enter Ellis Ward, a feeling of comparative calm steals over me. It is an old-style Edwardian ward, with a high ceiling and rows of orderly beds on each side. At the end of the ward large windows give on to the Fulham Road. The ledges of these windows are full of flowers. Every morning an old lady comes to pick the dead blooms out of these bouquets, and to change the water, because the patients themselves are often unable to bear weight or move their arms.

I am shown a bed and life shrinks to its dimensions. There is a little bedside cabinet where I place my belongings and a curtain that can be pulled round for a cursory privacy. Photographs of the children go on the board behind me and a few books, which I will not read, but which supply a feeling of well-being, go on the trolley. I have a phone card and enough money to buy a newspaper; I pass my valuables to R to take home.

In this giving up of objects and relationships, I experience peace. I am able to think of the children but take no responsibility for them. Released from the pressure to look into their faces, and care for them, I can quell for a few moments the anguish of wondering what life will be like for them if I do not survive. Sharing time with R, but not domestic duties or a bed, I can at last cocoon my shattered mind with the privacy it needs.

The ward wakes at 6:00 a.m. with a rumble and jolt of trolleys. The nurses are doing their rounds. They arrive with blood-pressure cuffs, electronic thermometers, and plastic beakers full of pills. The women who have had surgery are helped, their dressings checked, the pillows plumped behind them. Some of the older ones are taken to the bathroom, the nurses following behind like bridesmaids with armfuls of tubes and drains and mobile IV stands. Sheets are changed; surgery lists checked.

I have been told I am first on the list, but am bumped due to the arrival of other urgent cases. Nicky Perrone appears with a retinue of juniors and a blue felt-tip. He draws a cross on my left breast to make sure there are no mistakes. I stare at the doors of the ward until midday, unable to concentrate. By 2:00 p.m., light-headed from lack of fluid and food, I have become tearful. The ward sister makes a phone call and shortly afterward a young woman appears with a silver box and a towel. "The sister tells me you've been waiting awhile," she says in a gentle voice. "Can I offer you a foot massage?"

Many years ago, R and I made a trip to Thailand. Like every good tourist, we reported to the temple of Wat Pho in the center of Bangkok to visit the Reclining Buddha. After trudging round the enormous figure, all forty-six gross golden meters of him, as no guidebook fails to tell you, we emerge tottering into the blinding light of midday Bangkok.

Weaving our way across the blazing paving stones of the esplanade, stupefied by the heat and humidity, we reach a low pavilion, fashioned out of wood whose jade green paint has faded to a soft pewter. The carved filigree of the arches, open to the outside, seems to offer shade. We dip our foreheads into the wood, as if in an attempt to butt our way into the cool within.

All of a sudden, we are surrounded by women with brilliant smiles and long colored skirts. "Massage? Massage? You want massage?" They congregate in the doorway of the pavilion, in a loose throng, like children or a host of butterflies. When I hesitate, they insist. R has gone ahead. They smile at me encouragingly and seem less concerned with losing an earning opportunity than with my missing out on an important experience. "You, too. Is lovely. Please!"

At first, I can see nothing in the darkened interior. Gradually I make out enormous fans on the ceiling, antique helicopter blades revolving in a slow, creaking motion. Low stone benches run down the sides of the walls and the center of the room. The shadows of the women move among them.

A woman with long black hair tied back in a ponytail shows me to a stone bench, which is covered with a ticking mat. "No clothes," she says, smiling. She is short and strong. Her jet-black hair is so sleek as to seem oiled. Her ponytail accentuates the sweet gravity of the forehead. At first, her face appears as unmarked as that of a girl. But then you realize she's older—maybe quite a bit older.

Undressed to the waist, I lie facedown on the mat, resting my forehead on my knuckles, while she squats over my back. She begins to rub oil into my shoulders with a firm motion that speaks of experience. The surface of my skin begins to quicken with warmth, like the air just before dawn, a fine fabric against which the sun is pressing.

But she is not content with surfaces. With a vigor and focus that tell of her dedication to her work, she presses on, kneading her way below the skin. Layers of tissue begin to breathe, as well as the musculature beneath. If I had had the knowledge then, her touch might have enabled me to discriminate the trapezius, the deltoid, or the latissimus dorsi.

Up above, the fans revolve on the ceiling, with just enough motion to cast a measure of tepid breeze on my back. I lose track of time and space. The women's voices, rising and falling, are sometimes close, sometimes far away. They divide the air like birdsong, staking out an invisible floating architecture of sound. Minutes pass, or perhaps an hour. When the woman attending to me dips her hands in a bucket of water to rinse them, the sound of the drops into the bucket reaches me from far away, a green shade falling down a green well. The sound is so plentiful, so reverberating, it seems to go on forever.

My mother and I are in a garden somewhere. I am small. Her legs move beside me in the grass, strong and tall and tanned. I think she may be wearing a blue dress, a shift of some sort, printed with pink flowers. We are looking in the flower bed. She has promised me that today I will pick my own peony to put in the silver bowl at the center of the table. She shows me where to look among the plants: geraniums, roses, scabious. The peonies grow in clumps, with stalks fanning out like medieval rib vaulting into glossy palmate leaves. Underneath the stems is a cathedral of shade. The space has layers: the air is cooler on top, silvery blue, like the underside of the leaves, while lower down it stores warmth from the earth. When I pick my peony, the snapped stem fills the pocket of shade with a wild, tart smell. Like an explosion of scented gas in a box. Warm tears cover my face. And just at that moment, the doors of the ward fly open and two burly hospital porters appear pushing a gurney, one with a green tattoo up his arm of a naked woman with outsize cartoon breasts: "Thought we'd forgotten you, eh? No such luck!"

LATER THAT NIGHT, a young woman with a clipboard and a pen comes to my bed and pulls round the grey curtain. "I've come to do a psychological assessment, Mrs. G." She beams at me with a very white smile. "I've been told you're a little distressed. I'm doing a special module for my degree, you see, on mothers coping with breast cancer. I haven't done anyone with the *BRCA* gene yet," she confides, sitting down cozily on the edge of my bed. "Now, tell me. Your mother died of cancer, is that right? What was the date of that, then?"

In another frame of mind, I might be able to make short work of this woman. But weakened by surgery and anesthesia, with R gone home for the night, lonely and frightened, I am low on defenses. "Nineteen eighty," I answer obediently. She draws a circle on her page, writes "mother" under it in a large, babyish hand, draws a crosshatch through the circle, and adds the date of my mother's death. "And your grandmother? On your mother's side?"

"She died of cancer, too."

Another circle appears, above the one for my mother. She draws a crosshatch through this one, too, along with the date of death. Then she connects them both with a black line.

"And you, Mrs. G? What is your date of birth?"

"Nineteen sixty-one."

A third circle appears. How long, I wonder, before this is all that's left of me? A circle with a crosshatch through it on some submission for a student's degree?

"And do you have children yourself?"

My eyes fill with tears. "Two."

Soon there are two circles on the page for Michaela and Kitty. Fortunately, she refrains from putting a crosshatch through these; otherwise, I might have found the strength to pick up the bed and do something to her with it.

She turns to me now with a special intensity. "And what would you say is upsetting you most, Mrs. G?" she says in an earnest, confidential tone of voice. "What is it that you find most distressing in your situation?"

At first I am left speechless by this. The impudence, the sheer crassness of it. The fact that some clinical psychologist, or whoever designed this psychic binary punch card, has risen to the unutterable broad-mindedness of an open-ended question. Words, words, words, as Hamlet said. The rubberneckers, as Ruth Picardie called them, commenting on the number of acquaintances who suddenly wanted to know her again when she was dying. Watch out for them. They will come to you with soft voices, whispered questions, the outward forms of kindness. But their eyes, when you catch them, are cold.

"That I've got to have both my breasts cut off? That I might not live to see my children grow up? That I lost my mother before I could really know who she was? That my children might be left motherless, like me? That that's not something I can bear?"

She sucks the end of her pen. "Mmmmn-hmm," she says slowly, looking at me with a cool gaze. "And you haven't mentioned chemotherapy? The fact that you will lose your hair? That it won't be the same if it grows back? What about that? Most women find that a little distressing."

"Does no one get the same hair back again?" I inquire, a catch in my voice.

"No." She shakes her head earnestly. She is just twenty-one or so. She can't resist the thrill of imparting privileged knowledge.

"How does it come back, then?" I know I shouldn't be asking this question. But I can't resist.

"It often comes back curly. Or grey. Or bushy. Never the same." She gives another beaming smile. "But most women are grateful. Just to have anything at all."

I throw my head back on the pillow. My hair. My signature shoulder-length, straight blond hair, the hair I have had since my teens, that has carried me through my twenties and thirties, been eked out by highlights in my early forties. My hair as I have known it is over. It will come back curly. Or grey. Or not at all. And for this I am supposed to be grateful.

Shutting my eyes, I summon up my mother. She died with breasts intact, with her hair on her head. She was thinner, for sure. The cancer had eaten her flesh. But she was lovely to the last. Beautiful in death, as she had been in life.

"I think I need to sleep now," I say, promising myself a double dose of Lorazepam to survive this woman's "psychological assessment." "I think I need to sleep."

"R, IF I CAN'T DO THIS, will you help me?" We are at the Shepherd's Bush roundabout again. The cylinder is quiet. Its vacant plastic refracts the light. Beyond it you can see a horizon of cranes across West London. Then suddenly, from nowhere, a spurt shoots up to the summit, before cascading jerkily down through the levels of the pipe. R looks ahead, his face white and closed. "Will you help me?"

When he was a baby, R cried too much. His mother, encased in plaster from a back injury, struggled to cope. She already had a three-year-old boy. Her husband was busy with his academic job, and the burden of child care was hers. Things came to a head toward Christmas. R was sent to the local children's hospital. Later, I realize it is the Park psychiatric children's hospital, not far from us now. The narrative is vague as to how long his stay lasted. But on one thing it's clear. "When he came back, he looked straight into my eyes and I looked straight into his and we knew we had a deal," says his mother. She talks with panache. Lauren Bacall in a sharp suit taking a drag on her cigarette. She is relating an episode in the chronicles of parental derring-do. The deal was: No Tears.

R's ability to shut down, which I have always related to this episode, is beyond any power I have ever had. In the thrust and parry of marital relations he can always checkmate me. Withdrawal is effortless, instantaneous, catastrophic, while at the same time he remains in the role of the nice guy, the extremely polite shell of a person. As a tactic, it never fails to reduce me to gibbering rage, which puts me instantly in the wrong.

"R?" I say, trying to suppress the menace in my voice. This matter is too serious to allow it to be derailed in the stalemate of marital conflict. "If I can't do this? Will you help me?"

R and I were married twenty years ago, in a ceremony in a registry office in Oxford's Westgate Shopping Centre. It was four years after my mother's death and I still slept with tablets under my pillow, needing to know I had an escape route. My father was present at the wedding, with my stepmother. So were R's parents. We made a dismal passage through the concrete shopping concourse for an understated ceremony, after which the two sets of families made awkward little sallies toward each other across the crowded room before giving up and talking among themselves. I drank too much in order to blot out my anxiety, and my father gathered up the unused bottles of champagne with a view to taking them back to the shop. My memories of that occasion do not rise clear of the general unhappiness of those years, and I retain no spiritual significance to the words "I will" as I signed up to love, honor, and obey for the rest of my life until death did us part.

But about that commitment on the Shepherd's Bush roundabout, in front of the red light, one morning toward the end of March, I have very different feelings. We are in our midforties. There are no hopeful relatives to look on and bless the occasion. We are the commanding generation now, beyond the parental gaze. "The theater of all my actions is fallen," as George Eliot says in *Middlemarch* of "an antique personage when his chief friend was dead." This vow is for ourselves alone. "I will," says R with great gentleness, cementing our union in a way that that ceremony twenty years ago never had. "I will."

Chapter Five

Doing a Geographical

WHEN I WAS YOUNG, perhaps six or seven years old, I used to spend hours playing grass houses in the garden beside our house. My father would mow the grass and I would gather the cuttings into sunlit heaps, then ravel them out into long lines demarcating houses.

My plans were nothing if not ambitious. The houses had dining rooms, playrooms, bedrooms, dressing rooms, bathrooms by the bucketful, ballrooms, studios, and stables. Miles and miles of corridor, marked out by parallel lines of grass, meandered across the soft turf, doubling back on itself until it burst open onto a fresh cornucopia of rooms.

Later, that same expansiveness, the delight in scaffolding a dream, a world at will, appeared in a love of languages and travel. During adolescence, when depression had dammed the impulse into bookish channels, one of my favorite pastimes was to sit with the Larousse French dictionary, following the etymology of words. The words opened up worlds, as the grass houses had. I would write down idiomatic turns of phrase, and practice them in imaginary conversations until I could say them with a flourish: *Il faut savoir séparer le bon grain de l'ivraie.* You need to know how to separate the wheat from the chaff. *Il n'y a pire imbecile qu'un vieil imbecile.* There's no fool like an old fool. *Il pourrait aussi bien s'appeler Harpagon.* His middle name is Scrooge.

As a journalist, the high point of my career—if that mixture of botched opportunity and postponement could be said to have formed a career—was writing travel features for the *Independent on Sunday*. Jeremy Atiyah, a friend who spoke seven languages, from ancient Greek to Arabic and Mandarin (who as a student had a habit of fixing on the barest, most uncontoured square inch of the *Times Atlas of the World* and saying, "There! There's where I must go!"), had become editor of the travel pages of the paper. He suggested I write some pieces for him. For a few years, before miscarriages and children put a stop to it, I experienced the joy of getting on and off planes, touching down in strange cities, deciphering speech, signs, geography, before returning to write about them—rambling, joyful pieces about food and fashion, architecture and history. No paid writing task had ever given me greater pleasure.

Little wonder, then, that confronted with the cul-de-sac of life-threatening illness, something of this old expansiveness rises up. Movement, the outward-bound impulse. We are travelers by nature. Didn't we always have to seek food for survival, animals upon which to prey, animals with which to mate, climates in which to nourish our young? The settling bit came later. Husbandry and tilth. Predictable constellations, a roof over our heads.

So on March 30, R and I find ourselves on a flight from Heathrow to Düsseldorf, for an appointment with Professor Werner Wiesbach, breast-cancer surgeon and director of the breast center in Gerresheim, a suburb of Düsseldorf. We have left the children with R's brother and his wife in the village of Childrey near the Lambourn Downs.

In the previous week, we heard that the disease is not present in my lymph nodes, adding about 10 percent to my survival odds and pressing the green light for immediate reconstruction. "Bilateral mastectomy, please, with immediate reconstruction—latissimus dorsi," I said to Nicky Perrone upon hearing the results of the biopsy, as if I were asking for an ounce of penny chews in a sweet shop. "As soon as possible."

Perrone had sprung from his position leaning on the edge of

the gurney with the energy of a man of action forced to sit on his hands for too long. "Okeydokey. Now, when can we book you in for?"

But the earliest surgery date he could offer me was six weeks hence. Six weeks during which the cancer might travel into the lymph system. He assured us there was little risk in waiting—breast cancer is a slow-growing disease. But my tumors were Grade III, the fastest-growing, most aggressive type. When we asked for evidence that there was no risk in the delay, there was none to hand. We sought appointments with breast-cancer surgeons in Oxford to hear their opinion of such a delay, but they were fully booked. So R contacted a former colleague at Oxford University, who talked to his wife, who talked to her neighbor, a professor of urology, whose wife happened to have a cousin who was married to a leading German breast-cancer surgeon.

When R talked to Wiesbach on the phone, the German professor was adamant: there was indeed little risk in the delay. But the planned surgery itself was a mistake. "Too much all at once. There is evidence to suggest that surgical trauma risks proliferating cancer cells through the body. Also, it confuses cancer treatment and cosmesis. I don't recommend it."

The little airport of Weeze-Niederrhein, west of Düsseldorf, is clean and futuristic. It has a view of low-lying hills from the glass atrium of the arrivals hall, planes standing in ranks, like flocks of patient birds. With its orderly and transparent arrangements, it reminds me of all the regional airports I touched down in during my travel-writing days.

Soon we are bowling through the sunlit German landscape in an air-conditioned Mercedes. The driver, screened off from us by a Perspex partition, listens to the news on the radio. With his leather jacket and Rolex watch, he exhibits just the quiet, obsessive concentration needed to drive safely at speed.

There is something comforting about this landscape—the uninhabited fairy-tale forests on either side of the motorway—and the powerful car that gives us a sensation of invincibility, as if, with the right vehicle, we could speed through our troubles as effortlessly as this.

By noon, we draw up at a block of buildings on the outskirts of the city marked KRANKENHAUS GERRESHEIM. There is a small tower, with a complex of lower-lying buildings at its foot, punctuated by ambulance bays and glass-covered walkways. BRUSTKREBSZENTRUM says a pink granite slab at the entrance to one of the walkways, in cinder-black letters. The glass doors spring open noiselessly at our approach, to reveal gleaming corridors with blue and white signs saying: SENOLOGIE, RADIOLOGIE, CHEMOTHERAPIE. By this time, the sunshine, the speed of the car, and the new vocabulary has induced a state of mild euphoria in me. Now, this is really something! Who could have dreamed that the lonely girl gobbling up the dictionary in a bedroom in Aberdeen all those years ago, looking up one word in three in a German novel, would be making her way through a breast-cancer hospital in Düsseldorf all these years later?

"Ah, the English couple!" says Professor Wiesbach, a short, slim figure about sixty years old, with the hint of an energetic hunch, and extremely blue eyes. "Welcome. Your flight was OK? Come this way."

He leads us to a well lit, comfortable waiting room decorated with portraits of women. They are women of all ages, with hair or without, smiling or not, in scarves, hats, earrings. Their faces are eager and full of life. Little plaques below record their names and dates. After studying them for a few moments, I realize that they are all dead and that most died relatively young. I assume that these are women whom Wiesbach treated who did not survive.

It makes a positive impression on me. The Marsden deals with cancer on an industrial scale: more than forty thousand patients per year and almost every type of cancer. Its survival rates equal those of anywhere else in the world, according to its doctors, despite the fact that the "hairy" cases from the rest of the country are funneled toward it. The royal blue carpet of the central lobby is vacuumed assiduously each day, the banisters and ironwork polished with care. And the grand staircase is decorated with a few smoky oil paintings of great men, physicians and benefactors, along with an anomalous portrait of Princess Diana in a ball dress and tiara. But of patients' images, there are none.

The Gerresheim center, being smaller, can be more familial. It can afford to record some of its members. I wander through the little gallery, enjoying the fact that the women in the portraits are given their names and dates. Since diagnosis at the Marsden, I think it's fair to say that no doctor has found it necessary to commit my name to memory. I am Hospital No. 704329, one of a stack of files to be pulled out, dealt with, dispatched. Nurses and doctors will read my name from the cover of a file. Each exchange is courteous and kind, with the appropriate gravity and focus due the situation. But there are simply too many of us for doctors to undertake the task of remembering our names. We leave no individual mark. The record of us is in carefully kept databases, archives of blood samples for future research, the pathology slides of our tumors.

"This lady . . ." says the professor of oncology, of me and twenty others a morning, in a kind of compressed coda of courtesy that skids right over the top of my head. "This lady . . ." I can hear him say at the in-camera medical meetings where the heads of divisions reach important decisions about our treatment. My promotion to lady at this stage of life—hitherto, I have been girl, daughter, woman, wife—makes me uneasy. It seems to be related to the gradual stripping away of anything that might make me one. What is a woman without ovaries, breasts, hair, or name? A lady, clearly. So the professor flaps his linguistic fig leaf over the nakedness that threatens to gape between us.

But I never learn to recognize myself in the formula. The "lady" who has come into existence is an effigy, a piece of sinister bourgeoisification. When she goes out, she runs on little wheels discreetly concealed beneath voluminous skirts. Behind her trails a dachshund, to which she feeds morsels of Sachertorte in opulently shaded drawing rooms. And when she has said good-bye in the morning to her husband, who receives his silver-tipped cane and briefcase from her with the barest inclination of the head, she takes the heavy heart that lies beneath her skirts to bearded professors on the other side of town.

I don't know whether it matters that the person responsible for saving your life doesn't know you by name. In medical terms, probably not. But in personal terms, it makes a difference. It seems to be a bad omen, the sign of a worrying lack of commitment to keeping you here.

So it is with pleased surprise that I watch Wiesbach pausing over my name as he takes a clinical history with a fountain pen, seated at a large desk on the fourth floor with an open view of sky and trees. He is the first doctor since diagnosis to have taken a consultation with me sitting down. "And your children, how old are they?" he inquires. As I supply the information, he pauses. Again, I am grateful. For me, it has the grace of acknowledgment. "Young," he comments. "Very young."

His office door is ajar, and a traffic of professionals—radiologists, pathologists, plastic surgeons—come and go with respectful ease, checking on various points, offering information as needed. I get a sense of a close-knit team, with permeable boundaries, a highly functional family run by a benevolent patriarch.

When Wiesbach has finished taking the history, he shuffles through the little heap of biopsy reports and X-ray materials that have been faxed from London.

"There is no MRI scan here?" he inquires.

"I never had one."

"Why not?"

This is a painful subject. My discovery, on the evening of diagnosis, that the mammograms I was depending on to screen against my breast-cancer risk were only 23 percent reliable for women like me had filled me with dismay. If, in July 2005, I had had an MRI scan, as well as a mammogram, where would I be? MRI scans detect tumors from 0.5 cm. It is quite possible that such a scan would have detected at least the larger of my tumors and that my odds of survival would have been very different. Instead, the mammogram showed me clear of cancer, and my tumors were given another eight months to establish themselves.

It is now best practice for women with deleterious mutations of the *BRCA* gene to be routinely screened with a combination of MRI scanning and mammogram, as had been the case in many clinics in the United States for some time. But in 2005, in the United Kingdom, NICE had not yet recommended the use of MRI for screening women with *BRCA* mutations. The Marsden would have been acting beyond NICE guidelines to have offered it to me. Nonetheless, I can't help feeling let down. Why had no one told me of the massive discrepancy in reliability between the two scans? It was not a matter of a few percentage points after all, but a whopping 60 percent. Had I known it, I would have been free to buy myself an MRI scan, as I had bought myself other tests in the past.

Later, I raise this point with Deborah Lovelace herself. "This was potentially lifesaving knowledge," I said. "I feel I had a right to it."

"You need to remember that at the time you were being offered screening with mammogram, we didn't know for sure that the M18T mutation was deleterious," she says. She had, however, expressed a strong clinical hunch that it was. "Also, MRIs throw up a lot of false positives, which lead to anxiety and unnecessary surgery. And in any case, we are currently pressing for NICE to offer MRI screening to women with known deleterious *BRCA* mutations. I am confident that it should be through by the end of the year. It should be a relief to you to know that you are probably in the last batch of *BRCA1* women in this country to be offered mammograms alone, as opposed to mammograms in conjunction with MRI scans."

I can't say that it is. Beware of doctors. Ultimately, however brilliant, however professionally committed, however kind, hardworking, and responsible (and most of them are), it is your life, not theirs. They sit behind the desk; you, in front of it. Part of their responsibility is to implement national guidelines of treatment, arrived at via an analysis of cost versus benefit. Yours is to yourself and to your children. How unbearable to think that my own children face the possibility of being left motherless when the private purchase of a scan might have prevented it.

"MRI can sometimes give the surgeon important information about the position of the tumors," says Wiesbach, filling in a form with his energetic script and passing it across. "It costs about four hundred and fifty euros. Here. Take this downstairs. Bring the results back in two hours and we'll discuss treatment options."

Downstairs, a man in jeans and a lumberjack shirt shows me to a cubicle, where he instructs me to leave my clothes and valuables in a plastic crate and don a hospital gown. Then he runs through a checklist with me. "You have no jewelry, watch, gold teeth, brace, shunt, stent, or any other metallic object on your body?" he asks in that flawless English that Germans seem to acquire effortlessly in their properly organized schools. I shake my head. "During the scan, it is important you don't move," he says. "The scanner uses magnetism to construct a three-dimensional image of the body. If you move, this can blur the image. Then the scan must be repeated. For the same reason, you must breathe lightly." He gives a demonstration of the required level of breathing, so that the soft flannel of his shirt undulates faintly at my eye level. "Not too deep—otherwise the position of the breasts can change and threaten the image. Do you understand?"

He leads me through a darkened room where banks of computer screens display digitalized images. There are swirling neon shapes—red, blue, yellow, green—in which you can just make out livers, lungs, and breasts. Behind them, spines and rib cages stand out in stark monochrome. Something about the gaudiness of color slapped over the exquisite precision of skeletal structure makes these images arresting and beautiful; they could be served up as a video installation in a chic gallery. Radiographers sit in the darkness studying them in silence.

By contrast, the MRI room is starkly white and empty, except for an enormous cylindrical machine made out of hard white plastic running down the center. It looks like a felled *Apollo 7*.

A tall girl with blond hair scraped back into a ponytail instructs me to lie facedown on the Plexiglas tray in front of the machine. She points to shallow indentations, in which I am to lay my breasts, and tells me to lift my arms above my head. She raises her arms in a balletic pose to show me what she wants. But this is difficult, as the sentinel node biopsy has left a painful swelling on my left side. "It's sore. *Es tut mir weh.*"

She looks at me sharply, as if to judge whether I am malingering, then pronounces with casual certainty: *"Ein Seroma."* Later, I find out that seroma is a common consequence of surgery to the breast, caused when blood plasma rushes to the site of the wound to protect against infection. No one had warned me of it. In my confused state, this subcutaneous lump seems an extension of my tumors and, as such, fills me with terror and shame.

The girl pushes my arms higher above my head, causing a stab of pain. After rechecking the positioning of the breasts in their plastic molds, she claps a set of headphones over my ears ("The machine is very loud"), presses a small rubber ball attached to a wire into my right hand ("If anything goes wrong, press this, OK?"), and disappears.

And I am alone. I know that R is waiting for me in the corridor outside, but I've passed through so many rooms to get here, I no longer have any idea where this might be. He seems unreachable, as if in another lifetime, so sealed off am I in this white room.

The man with the lumberjack shirt is long gone. And now the girl with the ponytail has disappeared, too. I am aware of a control booth in the corner of the room. Shadows move about behind the almost opaque glass. The radiographers, who must limit their exposure to radiation, monitor things from afar.

The walls of an MRI room are lined with copper to prevent distortion of the magnetic field by any external signal, giving the room the atmosphere of a giant vacuum. I feel as if humanity has withdrawn from me utterly, decreed for me an absolute untouchability, leaving me—and my disease—to the uncradling arms of the machine.

With an edge of panic, I remember the instructions and set

about breathing in to a count of three, out to a count of four, as if on a jog. I haven't been doing this very long when there is a buzzing in my right ear, discrete and sinister. Hidden rollers are released and the Plexiglas tray begins to move backward, propelling me slowly into the machine heels first. Soon I am completely encased in the hard plastic tube.

More silence. It seems to go on for a long time, though probably it's only a matter of a minute or two. Just as I am beginning to relax into the rhythm of my breathing again, there is an explosion of noise from somewhere above my head.

It sounds as if a teenager has slung himself down at an electronic drum kit after a furious row with his parents. There is a crashing of cymbals as he releases the first flower of his rage, closely followed by a pumping of pedals as he settles into articulating the more habitual monotony of his murderous feelings toward them. From time to time, this is relieved by a thrashing of drums, centrifugal, spinning off in fluent, dynamic pulses. Then he is back to the cymbals again. More demonic rage, as he expresses the torture of being held fast by the parents who will never change and cannot be escaped. The theme repeats itself, with variations, all the while gathering volume, louder and louder, until it seems it can't get any louder without breaking sound itself. Then, all of a sudden, it's finished. Gone. Like violins after a crescendo guillotined by a great conductor.

Silence again. In which I attempt to pick up the broken thread of my breathing. But it seems that the more I try to steady my breath, rationing my consumption of air, the more grasping and unstable the intake becomes, until I am in danger of taking dizzying gulps that will rock my torso and threaten the scan.

As I wrestle with this problem, there is another burst of noise, this time from somewhere off to my left, below me in the darkness. It is a strange booming sound, eerie and haunting. It reminds me of once having heard an Aborigine play a didgeridoo on the quayside by Sydney Opera House. We had just gotten off the ferry and were heading toward the cafés that line the harbor. And there he was.

Sitting cross-legged in a doorway, his long pipe resting on the pavement in front of him. Stuck all over with bits of feather and cowrie shells, blue paint smeared on his leathery face. He was lost in his music, eyes shut, as the crowds of tourists flowed past him. The long notes of the pipe seemed to tell of great tracts of space and time: teeming bushland, gum trees, carcasses picked clean in the arid soil. The sounds are harsh, ugly even, but they have a mystery, a throaty insistence that arrives, in the end, at beauty. They search out dark places in the soul, touching them as nothing more familiar or gentle could. This sound, too, rises up, becomes louder and louder, threatens to flood the cavity of my brain, before suddenly—like the other—it falls dead.

At this point, facedown, breasts stuffed into their Perspex vice, left arm cupped over my head and in some pain, I am overtaken by what I take to be a panic attack.

It's no longer the plastic tube of the MRI machine I am lying in, but a long ash box on the conveyor belt of a crematorium chapel. The box is stationary on a raised platform in front of the nave.

It is just the kind of building I have always hated. Starkly modern but "churchy," with rows of heavily lacquered pews, mock-Gothic windows, and an organ whose pipes are so shiny they look as if they have been spray-painted. There are vases of plastic flowers stationed on each window ledge. Even the most devoted would be hard pressed to drop a knee here: you'd have more spiritual leanings in the frozen-food section of Tesco. In front of me are my family and friends. Behind is a dark blue velvet curtain with a little stiff frill, through which the ash box will eventually pass.

They are singing "The Lord Is My Shepherd." R's idea: he knows that it was a hymn in which I remembered my mother. But their voices are wavering and uncertain. No one really has the heart for it.

I try to sit up to make the situation clear, but immediately hit my head on the lid of the box. So I lie back down and start banging with my fist on the fresh-planed wood above me. But from this angle, I can't get much purchase. And anyway, no sound emerges.

Like the MRI room, the box is encased in something of such molecular density that it prevents all noise from escaping.

Instead, I focus my efforts on individuals. There is my father in the front row. White haired, erect. Age has drawn a little of his height from him, perhaps, a little of his furious physical energy, but not much. He doesn't need to study the words. He knows the psalm by heart. The sorrow he feels for his daughter, his firstborn, is evident. His features are grimmer, his face more set. But he leans his shoulder into the wheel. Many years ago, after my mother's death, there was an acceptance of transience. There are things in life about which nothing can be done. They are terrible. It is better not to dwell on them; life has to go on.

Next to him in the front row is R. He is wearing the dark suit we had bought him twenty years ago in which to sit job interviews. Its fine tailoring is still apparent. But it is unpressed, nudging shabbiness. He looks frail and diminished. My long illness and death have exhausted him. At this moment, he is preoccupied by the music. He has chosen some of my favorites: Beethoven's *Cavatina;* Handel's *Ode for the Birthday of Queen Anne;* a Bach cello suite. But it hasn't come off. Piped through the chapel sound system, the recordings are scratchy and thin. Because he is musical, and because he loved me, this is bothering him.

Beside him is Michaela. Her huge brown eyes, flecked with gold, are focused on the hymnbook. Little Big Eyes, I used to call her when she was a baby. How many times have I stood beside her in church and followed her singing out the words of the hymns. Scrambling to locate the right page in the book, scrambling to get to the end of the long lines in time to join in the tune. Belting it out with joyful force when she gets there.

She always manages it. And she is managing it now. I can rely on her to do this. She is just five, but she will continue. She will accept every challenge, go forward in life. The only sign of the tremendous strain she is under is the intense pallor of her face. A troubled darkness to her gaze, which I can sense from here. The not-yet-begun-to-be-deciphered pain of traversing life without a mother.

At the sound of my banging she looks up, her gaze resting on the ash box for a moment. The openness and intelligence of her gaze stops my heart, as it did the first moment I saw her when she was lifted up to me after birth. Beloved. Then she turns back to the hymn book in front of her. It is taking all her concentration to follow the words.

Only Kitty, unable to follow the lines of the hymn, wanders in her attention. She looks round dazedly. As I bang on the box, her little owl eyes widen. Her mouth drops open. She leans into R's arm and twists on his hand. "What is it?" He bends toward her. She looks over at the box on the platform, wanting him to follow her gaze. But he is preoccupied. He lifts the hymnbook in front of her. "Kitty, sweetheart, you need to sing. Just hum the tune if you can't follow the words." Her face takes on a confused look—the same look she had when she stole Michaela's last chocolate egg from its hiding place under the bed and had it stripped of its brightly colored foil and devoured before anyone, including her, knew what she was up to. She knows it is her mother banging away in that box. She knows someone should be doing something about it. But to get her point across she would need to pit her own sense of reality against that of the grown-up world. She is just three, and the strength required to do that will take a lifetime to develop.

So it is done. I am released through the stiff little velvet frill of the curtains and propelled backward on invisible rollers. Ahead of me are the symmetrical jets of blue flames, as neatly spaced as railway sleepers.

"What's wrong? What's wrong?" The girl with the ponytail looks cross. Her supple skin, pressed close to mine, has taken on unexpected indentations. This is what she will look like when she's old, I think.

I must have squeezed the rubber ball without realizing it. And now she has pressed a switch that has brought me back out of the scanner, posthaste. She checks my shoulders, my back, the position of my breasts on the tray, and when she has ascertained that everything is in order, she becomes severe. "If this does not go correctly, you will have to do it again. *Verstehen?*" she says, peering emphatically into my face.

I get the gist. If I sabotage this one, I am going to have to do it again. She prods my left arm higher with a punitive little jab and presses the rubber ball back into my hand.

"*Verstehen?*"

"YOU HAVE SIX TUMORS," says Wiesbach, pinning up the dark sheets of film on the wall and indicating a corolla of sooty disks that spiral through the milky breast tissue. "Four are probably malignant. The others look like DCIS, ductal carcinoma in situ. These might eventually progress to malignancy. One is quite close to the chest wall. When tumors are close to the skin, or to the chest wall, radiotherapy is a possibility, even where the lymph nodes are clear," he continues. "This is an argument against immediate reconstruction, as radiotherapy tends to damage the skin and can destroy it. But more importantly, you are *BRCA1*. In your case, mastectomy needs to be particularly meticulous."

He pauses for a moment to allow us to absorb the reasoning. Then continues.

"Bilateral mastectomy with immediate latissimus dorsi reconstruction is big surgery. Ten hours, maybe twelve. Several turns on the table. There is an argument for separating the roles of cancer surgeon and plastic surgeon: they have conflicting objectives. The first is dealing with the cancer, the plastic surgeon with cosmesis. What happens when the plastic surgeon, for aesthetic reasons, wants to preserve something that should go?" He shrugs. "We are all human. Altogether, I believe this surgery is unwise. It is too much." He laughs. "Too heroic—even for me."

I am silent, shocked by the directness of the opinion.

"This is not what we were told."

"No."

"So what would you recommend?" R asks.

"Immediate left-side mastectomy. Deal with the cancer first.

Reconstruction can come later, together with prophylactic right-side mastectomy."

"But then I would wake up with no breast."

"Correct."

Another pause while we absorb this. Wiesbach continues: "Believe me, I understand the sorrow of losing a breast. No kind of reconstruction can take this away. But you have Grade Three invasive cancer . . ." He shrugs again, a shrug that I translate roughly as follows: Please wake up. You have invasive cancer. And two young children. At this stage, whether you lose a breast or two is neither here nor there. Cancer is not a beauty program. Please do reorder your priorities. "Our main job is to get you safely home to your children," he says. "And your grandchildren."

That does it for me. Since diagnosis, no one has been willing to venture an opinion on my likely survival. In the vacuum of information, I have myself dispatched long before my children grow up. In my wildest dreams, I have not dared to think I might live to become a grandmother. "OK," I murmur. "That sounds like a good plan. OK."

IN THE LITTLE TOWN of Goch, a few miles from Niederrhein airport, I look out the window of our hotel bedroom to a thin stand of trees beyond a flat pebbledash roof. I know, for the first time, that I will lose my breast. It is as if the confusion of reconstruction had obscured this fact. Like cramming a sweetie into a child's mouth when the child has cut a knee; sweetness splits open in the mouth while the pain centers in the brain continue screaming. Confusion. No. I acknowledge it now: this amputation will take place.

It is a private feeling, between me and myself. Curving off in time is the vivid body that R loved, that I loved, golden skinned, clean limbed. That ran, skipped, hopped, jumped, sped across fields, leapt up hills, swam, danced, laughed, curled, crept, slept, wept. What delight it has given me, in all its manifestations. In clothes, or out of them. Free as the wind or under men's hands. So I am to lose it. Or a part of it. And something else will be born.

R rummages with wallet and hotel keys, stuffing them into his inside jacket pocket. He looks tired, battered. "We need to eat," he says with a drained expression. I turn from the trees with scarcely a sigh. When your life is at stake, what time is there to regret lost youth?

In the restaurant, waiters in crumpled white shirts and gold-brocaded waistcoats that have seen better days bring us large plates of food. The menu seemed of a piece, page after grubby laminated page of *Bratkartoffeln* and Schnitzel in different combinations. We choose at random, and eat without enthusiasm, while I study the couples at the surrounding tables.

In the United Kingdom, one in twelve women will develop breast cancer in her lifetime. In the United States, the figure is one in eight. The majority develop it after the age of fifty. The couples around me are older, in their fifties and sixties. At a conservative guess, there must be two or three women sitting here who have gone through this. What has it meant to them? What has it meant to their husbands? And now I am to join them, this secret sect of one-breasted women.

After a meal of formulaic heaviness, we head back to the hotel. I phone my father and take a tranquilizer. But before sleep comes to me, the clickings and grindings of the MRI machine start up. Soon this mixes, in a drowsy auditory soup, with the buzzing of a crematorium conveyor belt, monotone and insistent. Above, the word BRUSTKREBSZENTRUM dances up and down in dazzling waist-high gold letters.

Chapter Six

Telling the Children

Back in the UK, spring is in full throttle. There is a lightness in the air that not even the weight of exhausted hydrocarbons round the airport can deaden. Daffodils on the motorway verges. A gauze of green in the trees. By the time we have cut off the M4 to head north over the Lambourn Downs toward Childrey, we have entered an idyll.

The great painter in the sky has decreed light. The Downs are washed in sunshine. We dip into redbrick villages, with their core of medieval churches, Tudor cottages, manor houses. Then up again onto remote uplands, where the high white rails of the gallops gleam in the sunshine: post after post, while the ground falls away softly, sheerly, from every angle.

When my parents were newly married, they lived in an early Victorian house in Kent called Parsonage Farm House. It was made of warm brick, double fronted, with white lintels and shutters. The front garden was bisected by a path that ran straight up to the door as guilelessly as a child's drawing. On the right, there was a weeping willow, circled by clumps of snowdrops in February. The shallow pediment on the door gave the house the charm of classical allusion, but without pomp. To the side was a larger garden, divided by rose beds and lilacs and surrounded by walls of ruddy brick along which grew espaliered apple trees.

This house is the set for some of my happiest memories. I spent long hours playing in the garden in summer. Exploring the blue-bell woods at the back of the house. Cycling the lanes. There was the odd trip to Margate for a day at the beach: buckets and spades; picnics; children spouting from every crevice of my mother's old Morris Minor, ice creams melting on the hot red leather; a visit to the dolphins if we were lucky. In winter, there was the church with its flint spire and processions of children under the lych-gate for freezing Nativity ceremonies with cardboard cribs and tinfoil crowns. This is my mother's world. A world of shuttered lanes and primroses, gentle rituals, social sureties.

I know pastoral is an urge that afflicts almost everyone in the spring. But this knowledge doesn't give me any more resistance to it. The urban life we are giving our children seems inadequate by comparison. What wrong turns, what signposts unheeded, have ended in exile from the garden, an angel behind me at the gate blocking reentry with a flaming sword?

In this disoriented state, we arrive at Summer Farm, the home of R's brother and his wife, on the edge of Childrey. It has gravel driveways, a view of hills from the west-facing windows, and ponies at the end of the garden. Inside, there is an atmosphere of warmth and settled good taste. Fine rugs, framed pictures, a few pieces of antique furniture.

Most of all, there is R's brother's wife herself, with her blond good looks, generous nature, and cheerfulness. "They've done *fantastically*. Been real little troupers," she says. "Eaten up their food, had their baths, had their stories, and gone off to sleep like a top. The cousins had a lovely time together. Didn't you?"

But I am incapable of responding in kind. In such health and good humor, I think darkly to myself, diseases do not take root. Mutations, genetic or otherwise, are quickly expelled. It is in my home, shabby and makeshift as it is, poor in space and spirit, that the conditions are right. Someone put a big sign up over our house: TRAGEDY THIS WAY, it said. COME VISIT. Oedipus at the crossroads. He didn't ask to sleep with his mother; to be forced to put out his own eyes (what punishment could possibly answer to the crime?); to wander forever from his native land. And my children, where have they gotten to? Ah, here they are, appearing shyly round the edge of a doorjamb, first Michaela, then Kitty, a little cowed already by our absence, by the large and lovely house, by the onerous business of being beholden. Will this be it? Failing a mother, will they be forced to be "real little troupers" for the rest of their lives?

As we drive back, the children weigh heavily on me. They are subdued, watchful, as if in the space of forty-eight hours we have become strangers to each other. Looking out the window at the green fields, Michaela's face has the drained look it gets when she has been trying too hard. Kitty, too, is wan; she kicks the back of the passenger seat, despite being told repeatedly to stop, and babbles to herself in the manic way she has when tired or disturbed.

"And did you have a *lovely time* with your cousins?" I trill at them. "Was it *fun*? Did you share a *room*? And did you go *riding*? You *lucky things*!"

There isn't much response to this. Michaela stares blankly out the window, sucking her thumb, while Kitty continues kicking the back of the seat. "Mummy, why were you in Germany?" asks Michaela eventually, turning from the window.

Green fields have given way to the suburban sprawl of Wantage, the prehistoric spine of the Ridgeway to the crisscrossing roads of South Oxfordshire; ranks of pylons; the glittering cubes of the new biotech buildings.

"We went to see a doctor, Michaela."

"Why?"

"Well, you know that I've got a lump in my breast. We wanted the doctor to have a look at it and tell us what it might be and what we should do about it."

"Cousin Chrissie had a lump in her breast."

"Yes."

"Cousin Chrissie's lump was cancer."

"Yes."

Michaela doesn't ask whether my lump is cancer. Instead she

falls silent. "Where's Rabbit?" she asks. We rummage about on the backseat, but can't find him. So we stop the car and extract him from a suitcase in the boot. She lifts him to her chin, putting her right thumb in her mouth, stroking his long floppy ears round her fingers. This is her default position, the one to which she reverts when she has been engaged in feats of derring-do with her friends (somersaults on the monkey bars, scootering, cycling, sprinting, ice-skating), when the burden of managing complex friendships outside the home has become too much, when she is disturbed by friction between R and me, or when she is taking the nightly journey into sleep.

"Rabbit is going home," she says.

"Good. And did he have a nice trip visiting his cousins? Did he have a good time with them?"

"It was OK," she says phlegmatically.

"Just OK?"

She won't be pressured. "It was OK." She turns back to stare out the window. Then adds: "Rabbit is going home."

THE LEAFLETS MAKE it sound so easy. "Children have an ability to deal with the truth that adults often underestimate," says one. "Not knowing things can make them feel anxious. Even very sad truths will be better than the uncertainty of not knowing what is happening. We cannot stop them feeling sad, but if we share our feelings and give them information about what is happening we can support them in their sadness." (*Talking to Children about Cancer,* published by Cancerbackup.)

"Children are very quick to pick up on secrets. If they feel left out, they may think they have done something to upset you or they may make up their own story about what is happening, which may well be far worse than the truth . . . The fear and uncertainty could have a damaging effect on their behaviour, their schoolwork, and their friendships." (*Talking with Your Children about Breast Cancer,* Breast Cancer Care.)

"Tell them what has happened, such as some details about the cancer," the first leaflet continues in a memorable move to the prescriptive. "Explain what will happen next, such as how it will be treated. *And leave them with feelings of hope that even though you are upset now, there will be better times ahead.*"

And there's the rub. The little matter of hope. Without which you have no business stuffing tragedy into the mind of a child.

I have a stack of speeches in my cupboard, and none of them answers to the job. Speech No. 1: Glass Half-Full. Sweethearts, you have your father, it begins. He will love you to the end of time. To the ends of the earth. He will wake you each morning, get you dressed, brush your teeth, wipe your faces, comb your hair, put clips in it correctly, scrub the food stains off your tunics, straighten your collars, darn your tights, teach you maths, check your spellings, explain your periods to you, vet your first boyfriends, feed you nutritious, well-balanced meals every day of your lives, help you choose your GCSE subjects, buy you winter coats when you are students, and be there for you later if your babies get ill or your marriages break down. And we know he's got longevity because both his parents are still here, despite decades of hammering their health with cigarettes and booze.

Speech No. 2: The Hard-Boiled Effort. So, kiddos, here's the rap. We all get sick. We all die. It's just a question of timing. Hell, you think you've got it hard. Just take a look at the rest of the human race. Life is "solitary, poor, nasty, brutish, and short," as Hobbes put it in *Leviathan*. And that's about right. You know, I spent years and years thinking about my parents dying, tossing and turning in a lonely bed through my teens. And then my mother up and did it. Just like that. Said not a word to me. By the time I came home, she had almost lost consciousness. You think you've got it hard. Hell, you haven't even begun.

Speech No. 3: The Poignant Metaphor: Life As a Journey. My loves, we don't know where we are going or whether we will ever get there. Some people come farther along the road with us than others. It's not that they don't love us and wouldn't go all the way with us if they could. But it isn't to be. They get tired, or ill, or just plain old. And it doesn't mean they're not still walking with us. In spirit. In our hearts we carry them always. The story I like to think of is Christ on the road to Emmaus. His friends are sad; they think he is gone forever. Then they see a figure up ahead of them on the road and fall into conversation with him. Without knowing why, they feel lighter. That's called the comfort of strangers. Then, in the evening, at table, they know him by the way he breaks bread.

As none of this seems the least sayable, I say nothing. Instead, I stuff them full of questions, like a French farmer fattening his geese for foie gras. The little rubber pipettes inserted into their throats to bypass the gagging reflex. "And how was it, did you have a fun time playing with your cousins? And who read you stories at night? Oh, how *lovely*. And did you ride the *ponies?* You *lucky girls!*" I hear my voice shrill. There is a stillness, in which they watch me stolidly. Children react to deception with silence. It makes them wary. Quite rightly, they put their minds to work on it. What is behind it? What dreadful secret is driving all this noise?

AT HOME, when R unlocks the front door, I have an urge to flee. Down the path, past the box hedge, along the street, through the park, and away. A bus to London, perhaps. Melting into the big city. Runaway. Runaway. A number on the Missing Persons Register. Adapted to living life in a cardboard box. All doctors have patients on their books who have refused treatment. You read about them in the leaflets. No one comes to arrest them. They are not taken into custody. They have a life afterward; it's just that it may not be long.

But there is too much stuff blocking the exit. Suitcases, holdalls, plastic bags full of Wellingtons, rain coats, crayons, reading books, coloring books, sleeping bags, soft toys, umbrellas, R's briefcase full of papers, and more plastic bags full of cancer leaflets from the hospital, now in both German and English. The dustbins, which haven't been emptied. The overgrown hedge. Most of all, the stolid little bodies of the children themselves, planted firmly in the path. Watching. And waiting.

So I am funneled onward. And with the burglar alarm shrilling like an electronic version of the raven on Macbeth's battlements, we burst in a slow-motion avalanche into the narrow hall. There is a smell of stale air. Chipped paint on the skirting boards. Cobwebs on the ceiling. The absence of pictures on the walls. What failure of will or personality has resulted in this threadbare home? Where are the photographs of relatives and happy moments? The proud family lines that buoy children up with a sense of legendary antecedence? It's all up in the loft. In Pickfords packing cases, where it went when we returned from Dublin. Everything here seems makeshift and cobbled together. Like my body, the house is small, grimy, and untrustworthy. No wonder I want to flee it.

"WHAT'S FOR SUPPER, Mummy?" Michaela comes to me while I am sorting through the heap of dirty laundry spread on the kitchen floor; shoveling away books and boxes of pencils; tossing muddy boots into the cupboard under the stairs; jabbing at the mold left by condensation behind the kitchen sink; and keeping half an eye on a pan of boiling rice.

"Rice and peas," I say defensively. Our default meal since diagnosis. No time to shop. No time to cook. It's the best we can do.

Michaela looks glum. "At Alice's house, we had shepherd's pie. In little dishes. We each had our own dish. It had melted cheese on top."

Since it is the longest speech she has volunteered to me in a while, I know I should pay attention. Instead, I push past her with a heap of dirty washing in my arms and a high, bright voice. "Really?"

Pause. "And we had pudding."

The intonation says it all. Carefully neutral. There's no need for emphasis; the word is dangerous enough all by itself. Pudding! And they file majestically past me, my mother's puddings, made with dedication each evening, rain or shine, across a childhood.

Because no meal was complete without one: apple pies made with fruit from the garden, so tart and fresh they had their own sweet sting, the pastry topped with delicately carved leaves and whipped cream; raspberry fool, the berries splitting into the cream; blackberry and apple crumbles, full of the husky sweetness of late summer. Then winter with its chocolate sponges, treacle tarts, and syrup pudding. This was a favorite, the syrup embedded under its mound of steaming dumpling, so that when the spoon cut into the sponge, it would break open like a honeycomb. Wood fires. Children's drawings on the walls. The dogs in their baskets, snuffling in their dreams.

I ram the dirty washing into the machine, slam the door, and skid the button round to the shortest cycle. "Well, we can't always manage that, Michaela. It's just not always possible."

"We *never* have pudding. *Ever.*"

"That's not fair."

"*When* do we?"

When Michaela was a toddler and was pulled away from something she loved—paints at a nursery, a trike, a chocolate biscuit—she would beat her feet up and down on the ground in a stationary blur, while being dragged along by an adult's hand. This standing her ground with me now reminds me of that passionate foot stamping. The signature of a will. Hope not yet to be extinguished.

"We *will*, Michaela," I say, still jabbing at the mold on the tiles behind the sink and hurting my hand in the process. "When things get a bit *calmer*. When everything calms *down* a bit."

Michaela may be five, but she knows an unposable question when she has one. She looks at me in silence as I start banging plates and glasses on the kitchen table. In the echo left by these rough gestures, the question hangs between us, no less clamorous for the fact that she doesn't dare ask it: "And when will that *be*, Mummy? When will that be?"

Supper is a miserable affair of scraped chairs, spoiled food, and voices cutting into one another. Kitty doesn't sit still for one minute at a time. She capers about her chair, forages in the fridge, puddles through the dirty washing. "Kitty! Sit down, would you!" we yell at her by turns. She resumes her seat and takes to rolling her head around on the back of it, grinning wildly with her eyes shut tight. "Eat!" we say. "Eat!" She picks up the spoon and jabs it toward her mouth with her lips shut, so that rice and peas scatter all around her.

"Achilti-achilti-achilti-*boo*!

"Dum-di dum-di dum-di *doo*!"

Standing up, R starts shoveling the food into her mouth with the scarce-suppressed violence of an abusive caretaker in an old folk's home. She accepts a few mouthfuls, her eyes still shut, before she opens them abruptly, inspects R's hand for a moment—with an air of lucid insouciance—and then bites it. Once initiated, the gesture unleashes its own momentum: she sinks her teeth farther and farther into the ball of his thumb.

"Jesus!" he yells, tipping back his chair and disappearing from the kitchen into the backyard holding his hand. "Jesus!"

Michaela and I stare at Kitty, who kicks the leg of her chair and looks about at the kitchen walls, the clock, the window, everywhere but at the drop of blood that has appeared on the scrubbed pine table in front of her.

"Oooh, golly! Has Kitty murdered Daddy? Will she go to prison?" asks Michaela.

"Kitty!" I say with shock. "What on earth . . ."

But Kitty isn't hanging around for any of this. She has hopped off her chair with the agility of a frightened lizard, streaked out of the room, and is up the stairs with a slam of her door before anyone can say another word.

In the backyard, R has wrapped his grubby handkerchief tight round the ball of his thumb, which he is holding like a wounded creature. "I was that close to hitting her!" he says. "That close."

I sigh.

Even in the dusk, you can see the slumped panels of the wooden fence. One panel has buckled outright, revealing the ugly building yard on the other side. The wisteria hedge growing against the fence seems to have decided to come down with it. Large bales of woody overgrown stems are suspended above the ground. Should it be pruned back? Or should we root it out altogether? On better days, I know that the garden might have potential. A decent-sized rectangle of green, with a few fine trees beyond it; surely something could come of it. But it needs work, time, money, a plan, none of which we are in a position to give it.

Upstairs, the door to Kitty's bedroom is shut. It gives me a lost feeling in the pit of my stomach, as if I were the child suddenly excluded from the love of my parents. And although she is just three years old, I have an urge to knock.

She is sitting on her bed under the window, by the radiator. With drooped head and slack shoulders, her whole body expresses misery.

"Kitty!" I murmur, kneeling down on stiff knees beside her. "Kitty, you can't just *bite* people. You really *hurt* Daddy."

From the moment she was born, Kitty was a blithe spirit. A little puckered bundle of joy and vitality. I had only to speak from a doorway and she would throw up her fingers and toes, grin from ear to ear, gurgle energetically. Holding her once, my stepmother told me that she could feel Kitty's heart racing faster when I spoke. The power of being Mummy. That incredible high. Why some women have baby after baby for as long as biology holds up. Three years of love and laughter she has given me. The scent of her head when she was breast-fed. Those tiny toes taking their first steps in a house in Dublin. The first words. Some spectacular tantrums at two. But never for long. Her sky-bound spirit always asserting itself as quickly again. Up and running. Up and dancing. Up and drawing. Up and laughing.

So who is this person on the bed? This person with sharp edges, with secrets. Complicated enough to exit a social gathering, to shut a door in my face. Her misery so palpable it almost smells. "Kitty? What is it, darling? What's happening? I don't understand."

Liar, liar, pants on fire. When grown-ups lie, their noses don't grow longer and longer in the middle of their faces. It's not that simple. But is there somewhere else they go, the lies that grown-ups practice, and the lies that they heap on top of those to prevent exposure? Do they come back on them in a vast, putrid mass that stops up breath and feeling?

"Kitty, I think I may have been unfair to you. I think I've left you on your own when I shouldn't have." I try out words without knowing exactly what I have to say, but it feels OK, as if any speech might be better than none. "The truth is I couldn't talk to you because I didn't know what to say. I needed time to think about things myself."

I place my hand on the side of her bed, the cool length of beech. It has a plain and sturdy construction, like a bed from *Goldilocks and the Three Bears,* the only concession to decoration a sweetly curved headboard. It is as simple and wholesome as childhood itself. On the other side of the room is one exactly the same for Michaela, except a foot longer. We bought them at IKEA the previous summer. Remembering that broiling afternoon of London traffic, Swedish pick 'n' pin logistics, and domestic dysfunction, I am filled with longing for it. It was BC: before cancer.

"Kitty, I'm really very tired. Do you think I could lie down?"

She moves grudgingly toward the radiator to give me more space. I climb up carefully. Gross as Gulliver in the land of the Lilliputians. The fate of mothers. I twist my head to make room for it on the pillow, and raise my knees to squeeze my feet in at the end. "That's better." After a while, she decides to lie down next to me. She lays her head on the pillow and raises her knees, too, in unconscious parody. They are diminutive and garlanded with bruises.

"Kitty, I should have talked to you. I thought I didn't need to because you were so young." The stupidity of this strikes me now. What difference does age make to the capacity to feel pain, or confusion, or fear? I sigh. "I was wrong." Then I run out of speech. What has changed after all? It's not as if I have a story prepared for her now. But it doesn't seem to matter; something has shifted, and she takes up the baton herself.

"I've got a friend called Canka, Mummy," she confides, her face pressed into my shoulder.

"Really?"

"Canka, banka, bonka, donca, onca, conka." She erupts in a peal of wordplay typical of her. Except that this time it reminds me more of the "word salad" produced by schizophrenics on the edge of an episode. A shiver passes down my spine. But why should it surprise me that she has picked up on the eruption of medical vocabulary in our household? Her hearing is as acute as bat sonar. At this age, she could learn a language in six months.

"And is Canka a nice friend or a nasty friend?"

She considers for a moment. "Nice."

"Really?"

"No. Nasty."

We sway our knees backward and forward companionably. "Nice. No, nasty. Nasty-nice." She giggles at her verbal audacity. The forging of new coin from old. "Nice-nasty. Nasty-nice."

I practice my breathing. "And what does Canka do?" I inquire, as if nothing whatsoever hinged on the answer.

She spreads her arms wide and imitates something planing through the air. "Flies in the night," she says. There is a swooshing sound of wind rushing past. "Through the sky. When her feet touch the roof, the house goes on fire. *Whoosh!*"

"Really?"

She nods solemnly.

"Golly, Kitty. That must be very scary."

"And you know how I know she's coming?" She turns to me conspiratorially.

I shake my head.

"Yellow dragons on the wall," she whispers, pointing at the section of wall straight in front of her bed. "Big yellow dragons. When you turn the light off."

"That sounds very frightening, Kitty. I had no idea you were having these thoughts."

She swishes her knees back and forth a few more times for good measure, without comment. And then, in that mad, manic, life-denying, lifesaving way that young children have: "Mummy? Can you read me a story?"

I nod. She flops down in front of the bookshelf and comes back with her faithful companion of the moment: *The Gruffalo*. And soon we are singing, in the gleefully lugubrious style of her recorded version of the song: He has terrible tusks, and terrible claws, and terrible teeth in his terrible jaws . . . He's the Gruffalo, Gruffalo, Gruffalo! He's the Gruffalo!

And so life is contained. To a monster with knobbly knees and turned-out toes and a poisonous wart at the end of his nose, horrible enough to generate a delicious frisson of fear, but nowhere near horrible enough to threaten home and hearth. The sort of monster you can feel a bit sorry for at the end of the day, once you've thoroughly trounced him in the deep, dark woods.

"SO HOW ARE WE doing, then?" It is Charlie Faith, Macmillan cancer nurse. Charlie has been recommended to me by my GP, Jocetta Bailey. Ordinarily, I would have run a mile. Macmillan means terminal to me. It means palliative care and the doctors unlocking the sweetie cupboard because there's nothing else they can do for you. But I trust Jocetta Bailey implicitly. She has followed me each step of the way: through the effort to obtain screening tests difficult to access under the NHS, through the dark time of testing positive for *BRCA1*, through the still darker time of diagnosis for cancer itself. Unfailingly kind and levelheaded, she has been willing to work hard on my behalf to negotiate a system often rigid and refractory, and I am grateful to her. So when she suggests that I contact Charlie Faith, I swallow hard and agree.

Charlie, it turns out, is used to rejection. "I get it all the time," she says cheerfully. "Some of them tell me straight out to bugger off. 'Is it the Angel of Death, then?' they say. And you have to smell the tea carefully to check the children haven't put something in it."

I quickly warm to her, learning on her second or third visit that her husband died young and that she has brought up three children single-handedly. She also battled her son's addiction to alcohol for several years. OK. She passes muster. She has suffered. We take to meeting on a regular basis.

"So how *are* we, then?" asks Charlie on one of these visits, looking into her cup of coffee.

"Oh, you know. Up and down."

"Yes? And the family?"

I try to describe the scenes of the past few weeks. Kitty's wetting herself at school. Her physical aggression toward R. Michaela's outbursts of anger toward me, coupled with withdrawal. The same pattern as at the time of my oophorectomy.

"Not too good, then."

"No. I suppose not."

"And why can't you talk to them? The children, I mean?"

I sigh. In front of me is a dank, rainy yard. A large mound of earth. I am Prisoner 704329. I have been issued a teaspoon. My task is to shovel this mound of earth from one side of the yard to the other. Why is it that no one ever understands anything without being spoken to? Why is it that a person can't just see into the mind of another, and view the world as they do?

But Charlie is making a genuine effort. I can see it in her face, tense with strain, as she sits on the edge of the sofa. So I pick up the teaspoon. "Because I can't make it safe for them. If I talk to them, I'll just tell them what happened to my mother. I'll leave them with no hope."

Charlie nods slowly. I know that she is understanding from a distance, just as I have understood her story from a distance, but she is making the effort. And the effort isn't comfortable. Which is why so few people make it.

But she is allowing herself to imagine for a moment what it might be like to face the possibility of dying young and leaving behind young children. She sighs. "Look, I feel out of my depth with this. Maybe you need to talk to someone."

"Like who?"

"Have you heard of an organization called SeeSaw?"

I shake my head.

SeeSaw is the brainchild of former Macmillan nurse Anne Couldrick. Having spent years working with adults with cancer, she became aware of a need for support for children with the disease. So in 2001, she set up SeeSaw, a group that included a child psychiatrist, a family therapist, and an educational psychologist. Later, they added another service: support for children in the process of losing a parent or sibling.

"The idea was that if professionals could go in earlier and help provide grief support for children and families," says Charlie, "the grieving process for that parent might not be so long or so destructive."

By the time she has finished outlining this, I can hardly breathe. The retrospective vision of our own isolation as a family when my mother died, the complete lack of support, the silence around her death that has endured to the present day, breaks my heart. That such an organization should exist now is almost unbearable. Except that it may be of value to my children.

"The professionals do a lot of 'memory work' with the children," Charlie continues. "They try to help them develop strategies for coping with their grief: they make memory boxes, that sort of thing . . ."

At the phrase "memory boxes," I am off the sofa and at the other end of the room, with so much adrenaline pumping through my system I could run ten miles at a lick.

"Now look here," I am yelling at the bookcases. "I may have breast cancer. Grade three. Invasive. Several lumps. I may be *BRCA1*. And the jury's out on how long I've got. But no one—*no one*—is putting me in any bloody box before I absolutely have to go there. Do you understand? *Memory boxes!*"

This is all the more dishonest, since from the moment of diagnosis, I have been planning the contents of the children's memory boxes as meticulously as I do their lunch boxes. What shall it be? Silver christening bangles and woolen booties, images of the ultrasound scans taken when they were in my womb, photographs of them as newborns in my arms? Their first drawings, the first teeth to fall out, a piece of my jewelry perhaps? A long letter to open when they are eighteen? But how do you write to a child whom you no longer know?

Charlie puts out her hands by way of calming the situation. "Please. I really didn't mean to upset you." She hesitates. "It's just I was thinking of the best person for you to talk to. Someone with expertise in talking to children. And Kathy Moore from SeeSaw is the one I thought of. Let's face it," she says, after a pause in which my rage abates as rapidly as it rose, "you could do with some help. If only for the sake of your children."

KATHY MOORE IS a tall woman, about fifty-five years old, with salt-and-pepper hair and an easy smile. She arrives shortly after lunch, when the children are still at school. "Nice to meet you," she says, taking my hand. "I was surprised to get parking up here. Now, shall I leave Sheba in the van, or shall I bring her in? We won't be at all offended if you don't want her. She's used to it."

Upon reassurance that Sheba is welcome, Kathy opens the back of her van, and a yellow Labrador as ample and ambling as Kathy herself bounds out and sets off for the park at the end of the road. It's clear she could find her own way there, despite the fact that you have to turn right and cross a roundabout. But Kathy gives her a whistle. "This way, Sheba. It's talkies, not walkies." And the dog falls instantly into line, returning good-humoredly along the pavement, swishing the bottom of the hedge with her tail as she goes.

She keeps up her vigorous tail-wagging in the hall, where it makes her skid on the tiles, and then makes her way into the main room, where she slumps down in the middle of the rug, her muzzle resting on her paws so that her jowls spill over them. She looks up with an expression of good-natured interest.

"I got her a few years ago. She's very helpful with the children,"

Kathy offers by way of explanation. "They like looking after her. And they like taking her for a walk with me. It breaks the ice."

A natural dog-lover, my hostility has all but evaporated. "Coffee?" and "How can you bear to do this work?" are my next two questions, delivered so closely together they run into each other.

"Milk, three sugars, please," says Kathy evenly. And when I return with the coffee, she gives an account of how she came to be doing this work, while stroking Sheba at her feet.

"My own parents died when I was in my early twenties. It wasn't easy. But I survived. Later, after qualifying as a social worker, I found myself working with children with leukemia. I felt I had something I could share with them—an experience of loss, maybe. And now I do this work with children facing bereavement. Of course, life can never be the same for them. It will always be different. There are many times when they will feel lonely, sad, set apart. But this doesn't mean they can't have a life. And a good life, too. And it's that that I like to focus on."

"We didn't have a life after my mother died. Not really," I say. "And I can't talk to my children now."

"No," she says calmly, stirring the sugar in her coffee.

And then, with the sunshine coming through the glass, the dog half-asleep but whumping her tail on the rug now and again, Kathy's salt-and-pepper hair, and the slow stirring of all that sugar, I'm off. "It's a mess," I say. "Oh, they know something dreadful has happened. Of course they do. Everything's different. Nothing's the same. I know I should talk to them. But every time I'm about to do it, I feel as if I'm going to choke. As if I'll just start sobbing. Or howling. Or worse. I prefer not to look at them. To be honest, I'm having a lot of thoughts about running away."

Later, when we go for a walk in the park, Kathy throws sticks for Sheba and we run through scenarios. "You don't have to say much to them now. They just need to know that Mummy is poorly, and that's why Mummy and Daddy are upset. They need to know that you will be away in hospital for a while, so that the doctors can make you better. And they need to know that someone will be there to look after them while you are there." She turns to glance at me sideways. "And who will that be?"

"My father. And my stepmother, Miriam."

"Good," says Kathy. "Mummy's in hospital so the doctors can make her better. She will be there for several days. In the meantime, Grandpa and Grandma will be looking after them until Mummy comes out of hospital. At this stage, that's all they need to know."

"Grandma Miriam," I correct.

"Sorry?"

"She's not Grandma. She's Grandma Miriam. My father married her after my mother died."

Kathy blinks. "Ah. Right. Grandma Miriam, then."

Sheba goes off on old legs, lolloping across the park. She scampers through patches of crocuses and beechmast, chases her tail, then picks up a branch bigger than herself and starts dragging it back across the grass, to drop it at Kathy's feet. Then she thumps her tail on the ground, looking up expectantly.

"And what if Michaela asks me whether I'm going to die?"

"You say you're going to do your very best not to."

"Just like that?"

"Just like that," she says evenly. "Children are very matter-of-fact. Given half a chance, they just want to get on with things. Besides," she adds, "if she is as clever as you say, she may already have some sense of what's at stake."

I shiver. Pick up the branch, wet with slobber, and hurl it as far as I can. "Go for it, Sheba! Go for it!" Sheba leaps in the air and twists around on herself like a much younger creature. Then she hares off across the grass, no sense of her silver hairs or the corpulence accumulated through her visits with Kathy—too many "talkies, not walkies," too many children struggling to shoulder their grief and plying her with treats. "Go for it, Sheba! Go for it, girl!"

THAT EVENING, I run a bath for the children, leaving the taps on for a while until it is unusually deep, pouring in bubble bath, and testing the temperature with my elbow, as if for a baby. "May I come in?" I ask, when the tub is full and the children are undressing.

"With us?" Michaela looks up to check she has heard properly. "Are you coming in with us?" Her enthusiasm touches me. In Dublin, the house we rented had an opulent triangular bath with gold taps and side ledges. We got in the habit of taking baths together on Friday evenings, with toys and toast. "Come on, Kitty, Mummy's getting in with us." Michaela starts taking off her clothes at speed. "You can have the hot end, next to the taps," she says to me, in cheerful managerial mode. "Kitty and I'll go at the back." And they scoot up to the other end to make room for me.

We let the warm duvet of foam lap gently against us for a while before I open the conversation: "Michaela and Kitty, there's something I need to talk to you about."

Two sets of eyes are snapped on me.

"Mummy and Daddy have been very upset recently. It's probably been hard for you not knowing what's going on. But we weren't sure what to say to you."

Silence. If I were to do a painting of this scene, it would have to be Impressionist, Degas or Monet: grey washes, luminous sails of moisture. Behind the vapor, two sets of eyes as alert as those of any hunted creature whose life, in that instant, depends on the perfect functioning of any one of its senses.

"I have a lump in my breast, where the cells have gone wrong. The doctors have told me that it's breast cancer. The same as Cousin Chrissie had."

"I thought so," says Michaela.

"Did you?"

She nods.

I take a breath. "Do you remember how Chrissie had her lump removed, how she was ill in hospital for a while? How we went to visit her when she came out? And how she's better now?"

They nod solemnly. "Well, something like that is going to happen to me. I'm going to have to go into hospital for a while. The doctors will give me an operation. And while I'm gone, Grandpa and Grandma Miriam will come and look after you. Then I'll come home again."

There is silence.

"If you want to ask me any questions, you can," I add, remembering the leaflet instructions.

"Mummy, what makes cancer?" asks Michaela. It is a typical Michaela question, blunt and focused. At the time of my oophorectomy, we had several conversations about ovaries, fertility, and cancer. It was explained to her that my ovaries were being removed so that I would never develop ovarian cancer like my mother, who would have been her grandmother. Later, she would come to me with questions like: "Does everyone have ovaries, Mummy? Why don't they get cancer, too?" Or, fitting it in with wider knowledge of the animal kingdom: "Do dinosaurs have periods, Mummy?"

My eyes are dry and gritty. "Cancer is when the cells go wrong, Michaela. You remember how our bodies are made up of millions and millions of cells. Well, these cells are always dying, and they have to be replaced. So the cells make copies of themselves. Sometimes a cell doesn't do a good job of making a copy. It makes a wrong copy of itself. Usually, the body cleans up this bad cell. But sometimes it doesn't. And then that wrong cell goes on to make another copy of itself. Then there are two wrong copies, which go on to make more wrong copies of themselves. And so on. Until you have a lump."

But Michaela has gotten the gist of this. She heard it at the time of my cousin's cancer. She's after something else now, and impatient with it. "Yes, but what *makes* them go wrong, Mummy? What *makes* them go wrong in the first place?"

"Oh." I pause. "That's difficult, Michaela. I'm not sure I know the answer to that. We do know that some things, like smoking, make the cells go wrong. But mostly, the doctors probably don't know the answer. Can I have a think about that and talk to you later?"

At this moment Kitty lifts up her hand with a large bubble in the palm. "This is a huge one, Mummy! Look! It's a spaceship." And she flies it through the misty air on her hand before bursting it on the tip of her nose. "I burst it, Mummy! I burst it!"

"Is your lump the same as Chrissie's?" Michaela asks.

I shake my head. "No, Michaela. It's a little bigger."

"How much bigger?"

"Oh, just a little."

Pause. "Does that mean they'll cut out more?"

I nod.

"Look, Mummy, look! The spaceship has had aliens!" Kitty holds up another large bubble on her hand surrounded by lots of smaller bubbles at its base. "Look, it had baby aliens. Lots of them!"

"Amazing."

"How much more?" Michaela persists.

"How much more what?"

"Of your breast? Will they have to cut?"

I touch my breast. "Well, because there's more than one lump . . ."

"More than one?" she interrupts.

"Because there are a few little lumps, they'll have to take away a bit more."

"How many lumps?"

I clear my throat. "Ugh . . . four."

I am aware that I have lost the advantage in this conversation—truths extracted under pressure are a very different thing from those freely offered.

"How much more?" Michaela asks.

"Oh. Well, the size of my breast, really."

Her eyes widen. "*All* of it?"

I nod.

"How?"

"Well, the surgeon will cut it off."

"Cut it off! *How?*"

"With a knife, darling."

Michaela's voice is awed. There is no revulsion, more a profound curiosity that such things are possible. "With a *knife?*" she presses, to be sure. "Your whole *breast?*"

I laugh out loud, glimpsing her thinking. "Not like that, Michaela. Not like that. With *anesthetic*. Anesthetic is what puts you to sleep. Do you remember in *Paddington Goes to Hospital,* when Paddington Bear is hit by the boomerang and has to go to hospital for the doctors to fix his shoulder? He goes into the operating room, and the nice nurse gives him an injection to make him go to sleep, and then the doctors put his shoulder back in place? Well, that's what'll happen to me. The doctors will give me an injection, and then they'll take my breast away. I won't feel a thing. I won't feel a single thing."

Chapter Seven

A Surgeon of the Guard

O N THE AFTERNOON of September 30, 1811, Dominique-Jean Larrey put his instruments case by the stand in the hall and reached for his greatcoat. He took his time, turning out the collar, the thick worn cuffs still bearing the mark where a bullet had singed him at the battle of Wagram—waiting for Charlotte-Elisabeth to come down if she chose. He was aware of her moving about in the drawing room above, straightening things, patting a cushion, adjusting candlesticks or a bowl of fruit. She pretended to be occupied but was in fact listening for the sound of his departure. Knowing this, he couldn't help prolonging his movements, though he was aware that the posture afforded him no dignity—and that he had no business keeping the other woman waiting.

She had great strength of will, Charlotte-Elisabeth. Boldness, tenacity, decisiveness. In another life, she might have made a fine surgeon herself. He couldn't blame her for this refusal. She had yielded so much already. His was a calling that consumed sacrifices. He had cheerfully thrown his own life on the pyre sometime in his fourteenth year, shortly after the death of his father. He had been sent from his native village of Beaudéan in the Pyrenees to live with his uncle, a surgeon in Toulouse. There he had shadowed the older man as the surgeon went about his business: a continual round of fractures, broken limbs, births, and bladder stone extractions. It was the beginning of a passion that no amount of practice ever diminished.

But what right had he to sacrifice Charlotte-Elisabeth's life? Or those of his children? She had not complained. Or only rarely. She had endured his endless absences: the long campaigns in Egypt, Italy, Poland, as he tracked his master's war machine like a hungry seagull in a bloody furrow. She had held up, been there to provide a home for him when he returned, to regret him when he left again. She wrote to him regularly, affectionate letters full of details of the children, common friends, affairs in Paris. Sometimes he felt theirs was a life in mail-coach stages. News of the arrival of his second son, born when he was engaged in the siege of Malta, reached him in Egypt two years after the event.

So her refusal now had the power to rattle him. Cannon and musket shot, a troop of cavalry bearing down on him, the management of horrific injury, quantities of death—none of this seemed to unseat him. In fact, he was of such constitution that the din of battle brought calm to his reactions, effected instant entry to a world of great stillness and focus. But this rejection by the one closest to him unsettled him. It made him hesitate in the hall, like a man much younger and more diffident than himself.

If she would only understand that these things were necessary, he thought, picking up the paw of a sea bear he himself had shot on a voyage to Newfoundland, where he had served as ship's surgeon. The fur was yellow now, and worn. But he still remembered the magnificence of that creature, the acrid stench of her filling his nostrils long before he saw her. With your back to the wall, you had to act. Better to play for life, however grim the odds, than to lose it uselessly, for want of trying.

But Charlotte-Elisabeth came from a different milieu. She had ancestors, a fine home in the Ardèche. Her father was influential, her mother knowledgeable in history and literature, fluent on the piano. Wasn't it partly this that had captivated him? He was the son of a shoemaker, after all, not so many edges knocked off him by his sojourn with his uncle in Toulouse.

They had met at a musical soirée. He was taken there by Sabatier, chief surgeon at the Hôtel des Invalides. Sabatier liked to finish a long day with a little music in the house of a friend. At first Larrey hadn't wanted to go. "I'm busy," he had said, thinking of the coveted volume of Ambroise Paré, the sixteenth-century surgeon, waiting for him back in his garret. But Sabatier had insisted: "Man cannot live by bread alone, Larrey. Not even surgeons. Change your shirt and come!"

So Larrey had gone, grumbling inwardly about being forced to smarten himself up, and taking a stand on his old coat: They can take me as I come. It was an attitude that had borne up admirably all the way through the dusky streets, up the marble staircase, and into the blazing drawing room full of officers of the Republic, and then abruptly crashed to dust when he was introduced to Monsieur and Madame René Leroux de Laville and their three lovely daughters.

It was Charlotte-Elisabeth who had imprinted herself. She was tall with dark hair, a *front bombe,* and wide brown eyes. The breath knocked out of him, he was left to wonder whether the smell of the operating theater still hung about him.

She was twenty-one years old, the second daughter of the former minister of finance to Louis XVI. She was an accomplished pianist and portrait artist. She had sat at the piano and played something. He forgot what. Haydn perhaps. The notes tumbled out fluently enough. But at the back of them was a gravity, a kind of sustained sweetness, that was far from facile. And at the end, she had looked up with a smile that seemed a challenge addressed directly at him.

The courtship had lasted two years; her parents were naturally skeptical. What was he then but a penniless provincial on the make, without even a proper post? But the couple had exchanged their own vows and bided their time. In 1792, there was the campaign in the North Rhine, where Larrey was made surgeon major to the army of the Republic. Then the horrors of Italy, where he had come to Bonaparte's attention with his invention of his *ambu-*

lance volante, the light horse-drawn vehicle designed to evacuate the wounded from the field of battle. "This invention alone will suffice to ensure your reputation," Bonaparte had pronounced when he saw the ambulance in action. In 1794, after the couple had waited two years, Leroux bowed gracefully to the inevitable, and they were married one spring evening in a civil ceremony in the Paris town hall before the sacred flame of liberty.

There had been many happy years: children, home, growing professional and social success. And through it all, Charlotte-Elisabeth, while not endeavoring to enter his world, had been a silent support, apprehending its difficulties in the way she knew how, with quiet watchfulness and a decisive, unfailing tenderness.

But the business with Madame Grignaud had made it impossible for her. He saw that now. They had been firm friends, Mme Grignaud and his wife. Their children were roughly of an age, and went up together like a set of steps. The women consulted the same physician, sat up through the same childhood illnesses. They went to the same parties and plays, used the same dressmaker. When Mme Grignaud became ill, it was to Charlotte-Elisabeth that she had turned. Suffering pain in the left side, and much weakened over the course of two years, she had finally divulged a lump the size of an orange in her breast.

Larrey had agreed to help her, though he considered the case almost certainly hopeless. He had done his best, but the patient had developed sepsis and died in delirium forty-eight hours later.

"I want you to promise me never to do such work again," Charlotte-Elisabeth had said.

"You are not responsible," he tried to console her. "Nor I. You must remember, we might have saved her." But she held up a hand as a barrier to speech: "I want you to promise."

So now he waited in the hall with Doziet the footman, Charlotte-Elisabeth motionless upstairs. In the mirror, their reflection made a comic tableau: the footman tall and thin, he an altogether shorter and stouter figure, with his wide brow, his once luxuriant dark hair scattered with grey. What a pair of booby birds, he thought, as the carriage clock on the gilt table rattled out the hour.

Charlotte-Elisabeth had outmaneuvered him in silence, her refusal of his world more implacable than his desire that she should acknowledge it. He put the severed paw tenderly back on the table. In all conscience, he could not keep the other woman waiting. "Eh, Doziet?" he said with a wry smile, taking up his surgeon's case. "Time waits for no man."

IT WAS DUBOIS who had brought the woman to his attention. As he was chief surgeon to the emperor's household, his path crossed frequently with Larrey's: at the Hôtel des Invalides, in salons across Paris, on the long, bitter days of campaigns. They discussed treatments and outcomes, and shared a passion for the design of hospitals, which they compared throughout the empire. From time to time, Dubois would pass along cases in which Larrey took an interest.

He had first mentioned the Englishwoman at the opera, where they had gone to see *Don Giovanni*. "A writer of renown," Dubois had said. "An Englishwoman. Married to a certain Colonel D'Arblay. I should like you to meet her."

In the neighboring box, in an interval, Larrey found himself before a short, slight woman of about sixty years old, wearing a large black hat with a wide brim and a shawl. She met him courteously enough. But when she offered her hand, he noticed a stiffness in her right shoulder, which seemed to retain the elbow at the waist. It gave the gesture an odd, contradictory quality, making the hand seem both proffered and withheld at the same time.

"An abscess," said Dubois when they were back in their seats. "In the right breast. Quite large, I believe. She's on some regime of ass's milk and caustics. Useless, of course. The thing is just growing, and she's in a deal of pain. It's bad enough now to prevent her writing."

Through the next act, Larrey found himself wondering about her. It could be a simple case of bursitis, freezing the shoulder. Or it could be that the scirrhus had traveled into the glands under the arm, as sometimes happened, causing them to swell and stick fast. If so, there was little to be gained from surgery on the breast itself without addressing the wider dissemination of the disease. Either way, speed was of the essence.

So when Dubois approached him a few days later, saying that Mme D'Arblay had expressed an earnest and humble desire for his opinion, he found himself in a cabriolet halfway to Rue de Miromesnil before he remembered Charlotte-Elisabeth's prohibition.

Rue de Miromesnil was in a shabby part of the city, occupied by a motley group of aristocrats whose property and fortunes had been seized in the Revolution, and who spent their days in vain efforts to recover them. The colonel and his wife had rooms on the first floor, filled with dark, heavy furniture of a type Larrey recognized as belonging to the last century, and which contrasted greatly with his own gleaming surroundings—all mirrors and stenciled gilt—courtesy of Charlotte-Elisabeth.

The most striking thing in the apartment seemed to be a life-size portrait in the hall of the colonel in full military regalia. It was one of those glossy productions that flatter the sitter with a passable likeness from a heroic template, and serve only to record in detail a certain fashion in military attire and fill a space on a wall. But the colonel seemed well pleased with it, and stood in front of it as if inviting comparison.

D'Arblay's story was one familiar to Larrey. Dispossessed by the Revolution, the colonel had fled to England, where he spent several years in the company of a group of exiles gathered round the once powerful figure of General Narbonne, minister of war to Louis XVI. There he met his wife, a writer of romances by the name of Frances (Fanny) Burney. They returned to France in 1802 so that D'Arblay could apply for a procuration to recover his estates in the Yonne. This had been unsuccessful. With no other income than that earned by his wife from her writing, he then sued for a pension from the Grande Armée on the grounds of military service completed before the Revolution. Strenuous string pulling on the part of influential friends looked fair to secure this. But in a rash moment, on the outbreak of war with England, he had thrown it away, dashing off a letter to the emperor to the effect that his loyalty to his beloved wife's country prevented him taking part in any aggression against the English. This was something against which Larrey himself could have counseled him. The emperor took a dim view of any loyalty other than to him. The pension had been canceled forthwith.

Now D'Arblay had a lowly paper-pushing post in the Ministry of Interior. Larrey had met many such: fine, affable fellows without the wherewithal to make the transition to a new world. In the past, he might have looked harshly on this. As a young man, after all, he had been among the leaders of the first groups in the assault on the Bastille. But the Terror had instilled a different way of looking at things. It had taught him that certain kinds of change could be accomplished only gradually, across generations.

And D'Arblay seemed a kindly enough fellow, with a genuine affection for his wife. "Can you help her?" he asked, taking hold of Larrey's sleeve and peering anxiously into his face. "She really is suffering horribly."

When Larrey entered the drawing room, leaving D'Arblay behind, and the woman herself came forward, he was struck again by the odd black hat and the hand proffered stiffly from beneath the shawl. At first, he suggested examining her, but this made her flustered and he relinquished the idea. When he reassured her that a verbal history would suffice, she came roundly out with an account that was quite as clear and to the point as any he could have produced himself.

The abscess had first appeared seventeen years ago, she said, when she was nursing her son. Two weeks after his birth, she had developed a milk fever and pain in her right breast. At the time, this was attributed to the baby's thrush, which was supposed to have communicated itself to her breast. She had been advised to wean the child, a circumstance she found extremely distressing. At age forty-two, this was her first child and almost certainly her last. However, the fever had subsided and the abscess disappeared. But years later, and on two separate occasions, it had come back. Each time, she had followed a strict regime of fasting—avoiding meat and rich foods—and it had gone again. But six months ago, it had reappeared. And this time, nothing she did seemed to have any effect, neither the ass's milk she consumed with each meal nor the caustics she was applying twice daily, under instructions from a physician in the Marais. The lump just continued to grow. The pain was severe. Latterly, it had even prevented her from writing.

"The case is grave," said Larrey. "But quite possibly curable. However, it may be necessary for you to undergo a small operation."

At this, she became extremely pale, reaching out a hand to steady herself on the back of a chair. For a moment he thought she might faint. But no, she held up.

"I should prefer to risk all for a quality of life," she said quietly, "than to conduct a longer life in suffering and incapacity."

He issued instructions to her rapidly, in a low voice, before the husband returned. She would receive notice by telegram on the morning of the surgery, to spare her the torture of suspense. He would perform the procedure himself but would be accompanied by Dubois, chief physician to the emperor, and several other men, all surgeons of the highest caliber. She would need to prepare herself in advance: an armchair, bandages, quantities of old but clean linen that could serve as dressings. She might like to think of a way of securing the absence of her husband, at least until evening, and instead retain a female servant in whose strength of character she could trust. And she would need to sign a letter of consent. It was not a complicated procedure. But no surgery was without risks.

Three weeks later, arriving at Rue de Miromesnil at a little after 3:00 p.m., Larrey noted with satisfaction the stout middle-aged woman who opened the door to him. She looked like the type to hold up in a crisis. And there was no sign of the husband.

The surgeon Moreau, acting as his deputy, was already waiting for him in the drawing room, surrounded by stacks of lint and dressing. An armchair, covered in a sheet, had been positioned in the middle of the room. There were signs of recent turbulence. On the far side, there was an open bureau, with sheaves of paper scattered about it. His telegram would have arrived at breakfast that morning. In the interim, Mme D'Arblay had been writing letters, as was proper in such a circumstance. Now she stood by the bookshelves in the corner, wearing a housecoat, her face the color of ash. Next to her was a young maidservant.

Bowing briefly, Larrey went over to the trestle table that had been erected for the occasion, and began to set out his instruments. First, the straight-bladed amputation knives; then scissors, suturing cord, and needles; sponges of all sorts; and the little moxas, or metal cones of flammable material he had designed himself to seal minor blood vessels. These were more precise than the cautery, which got the job done but could cause savage burns in the process.

Soon there was the sound of the cabriolets pulling up outside, scrapes of metal wheels on cobbles. One, two, then a third. There were quick steps on the staircase. And suddenly, the room, which had seemed fairly spacious until that moment, was filled with men in dark coats. *"Messieurs?"* said Mme D'Arblay sharply, as if querying the breach of decorum, the fact that they had entered without knocking.

Dubois bowed gravely to her and cast his eyes round the room. "We need a bed," he said. Two assistants immediately left the room in search of one, accompanied by the housekeeper. Mme D'Arblay herself seemed too shocked to move. After a few moments, she turned to Larrey with a profound reproach. *"Vous m'avez dit qu'un fauteuil suffirait!"* You said an armchair would be enough!

Larrey ignored her and continued setting out his instruments. What he had or hadn't said was not the issue here. What was at issue was the work at hand. Dubois was right. With an armchair, it would be messy. The body would slump forward with any loss of consciousness. And the field of action was limited. There was scarcely room for one person, let alone others, to move in and apply pressure, sponge away blood, tie ligatures, and so forth. Far better a bed. It was an indignity, but actually more merciful. The wine cordial Moreau had given her would make very little difference. She might be an old lady of sixty, but in a fight for her life, Larrey gave her the strength of a bullock.

When it was done, and the iron bedstead had been dragged into the center of the room and raised to working height with the addition of two mattresses, Larrey bowed to her again.

"Please," he said.

For a moment, he thought she might bolt. She stared wildly round at the windows and at the door. Then she took herself in hand and began to approach the bed. She walked a little stiffly, with a dip in the left hip, probably due to arthritis. At the last minute, Moreau came forward with a small stool to help her. But she had already gotten there herself and was lying back, utterly rigid, and slowly unfastening the housecoat on her right side. They watched in silence. If there was a way she could have been spared what was ahead of her, he believed several of them might have offered to endure it in her place. They were not without feeling. They all had mothers, wives, sisters.

It was immediately clear to Larrey that the whole breast would have to go. The abscess was large, in the upper right quadrant. It had that familiar granite hardness of a tumor, quite distinct from the slacker flesh surrounding it. And the surface was scored with dark lines, which had probably been caused by the repeated applications of the caustic, possibly some kind of nitric acid.

Just as he was considering where to start, a scuffle broke out. Dubois had told the two women, waiting behind the surgeons, to leave. Mme D'Arblay, until this point absolutely still, now raised herself up. "*Qu'elles restent!*" she cried. Let them stay!

There was a short conference in which it was agreed that one of them should be allowed to stay. The housekeeper stepped forward. And the younger maidservant melted from the room as quickly as if she had been given personal reprieve from the guillotine.

Now Moreau leaned forward and covered the patient's face with a cambric handkerchief. As a blindfold, this device seemed near useless. For when Dubois held up his hand and silently drew a vertical line in the air, followed by a cross, which he then proceeded to surround with a circle, indicating that the whole breast was to go, she raised herself up again in horror. "You're taking the whole breast?"

Larrey held up a hand for silence. Bending down, he looked straight into Mme D'Arblay's eyes and spoke slowly and emphatically, as if to a child. "The lump is too large," he said. "We must remove it in its entirety. There is no way of doing this without taking the breast. Do you understand?"

Normally, there was no time for such considerations. There was brute restraint and tourniquets. There was the hope that your comrades loved you enough to make a decent job of holding you down. But in this situation, he could allow the lady a little leeway. Finally, she lay back.

"Please tell me when you're about to begin," she said dully. The housekeeper, who had been crossing herself during this exchange, now moved forward to take up a station behind her mistress's head and began fluttering at Mme D'Arblay's cheeks with chapped hands, whispering a torrent of tender expressions in a dialect Larrey couldn't understand. Moreau reapplied the handkerchief.

From this point, the tempo was assured. The operation took seventeen and a half minutes. It was not difficult. He had only done a handful in his life, but the anatomy was familiar to him from the dissecting room. And the technical challenges were minimal compared to, say, the amputation of a leg, where you had to go through a major artery, or the attempt to disengage a bullet from the abdomen, where any false move might result in damage to a vital organ.

The breast is a gland composed largely of fat. It sits upon the chest wall, held fast by the pectoral muscle on the one hand, the latissimus dorsi on the other. There is no major artery. Care had to be taken not to puncture the chest wall or the intrathoracic organs beneath. But that shouldn't be too difficult. These were luxurious conditions, after all. Six men to keep her still and help with ligatures and dressing. Very different from the battlefield, where he might find himself sawing through bone, nothing but a rough board for a workstation, someone holding a greatcoat over him to protect against driving snow, the ground rocked by the explosion of cannon.

He nodded to Moreau, who held the breast taut, and went in at the base with his amputation knife. He met with little resistance. The flesh was slack and lacking in density, as was natural in an older woman. It made the job easier, in fact. And it took him only a couple of minutes' concerted effort to sever the gland, which he then passed to Moreau to discard.

Management of the blood vessels was the only thing that posed any serious challenge. He knew their rough geography, but there were always surprises. At first, the surgery was relatively bloodless. A few vessels sprang up here and there, but were easily managed by a little pressure from one of his assistants. Then, all of a sudden, near the sternum, they were awash with blood. Sponges, compresses, lint, and wool, everything came away sodden. Moreau stood ready with the ligature cord. But Larrey couldn't find the damned thing.

Finally, he got ahold of it, there between the junction of the second and third ribs and the sternum, a severed stump of artery the width of a nib. A branch coming off the internal mammary artery, itself hidden behind the breastbone. More of a force than he had reckoned on. Gripping it between thumb and forefinger, he nodded to Moreau, who tied it, two tight knots, until the flow was stopped. Then Larrey wiped his forehead and leaned back. It was no match for one of the main arteries in the leg, certainly, but powerful enough to give him a few unpleasant moments.

Next, he wanted to track the tissue up into the axillary region under the armpit. The female breast was not a discrete organ. It was like the milk line in a pig, reaching down the chest wall toward the abdominal muscle, and up in a long tail toward the axilla. He felt firmly for nodules or swelling beneath the armpit. As far as he could tell, there was nothing. She was fortunate. It seemed that the disease had confined itself to the breast.

When he had finished, he invited the other men to examine

the area and pronounce on whether they saw any remaining suspect tissue. Dubois leaned forward and, with his index finger, indicated a spot here and there. Larrey moved behind him, not questioning his judgment, easily stripping away the whitish yellow fat from the darker fibrous muscle beneath.

Finally, it was done. The chest cavity was in front of him, scattered with clipped ligatures as neat and orderly as the nets of a Brest fisherman. It only remained to put her back together and apply a good dressing. He set about stitching the ragged edges of skin and muscle, lashing them roughly with long sutures. The flesh would probably never meet again over this raw hole. But in time, a skin covering of sorts would grow back.

As for the woman herself, the scream that she started to emit from the first incision had no more human existence in it than that of a fox being torn apart by hounds or a soldier being disemboweled by a bayonet. Now and again it deepened to a low growl, a kind of unearthly rattle. From time to time, she lost consciousness altogether. Then the surgeons would relax their grip. But no sooner had they done so than she was coming to again, waking with a wild kicking, and they would move forward to a man to pinion her.

As he held his knife over her flesh and invited the other surgeons to pronounce on whether the job was sufficiently thorough, Larrey felt the agony of her whole juddering body beneath him. But he allowed nothing—not her unremitting howls, the clock on the mantelpiece chiming the hour, sounds from the street outside— to interrupt his purpose. Surgery was a form of wrestling, fast and furious. In the interests of the patient, he must be the victor.

When it was over, and she had been taken from the bed, she hung lifeless between two surgeons, unable to support the weight of her own body. She had lost blood, but there had been no serious hemorrhage. The wound was clean, the vessels so neatly secured that he would be surprised if any blood seeped through the dressing by the following morning. If she got through the night, and the cancer made no return, he gave her many more years yet.

"You will need to be careful," he said to Moreau, who was to pass the night watching over her. "She'll be twitchy. Feverish. The dressing must not be disturbed. You may need to give her antispasmodic potions. And watch out for vomiting."

Once they had gone from the room, Larrey began to flush out his instruments in the basins of hot water that the maidservant had brought. Only when they were sitting snugly back in the crushed blue velvet of the case did he transfer his attentions to his own person. A mirror showed him gaunt and streaked with blood. He removed his apron, wiped himself down, taking care over his hands and his face. And there he was, transformed, a fine, stout gentleman of the French bourgeoisie—not nobility; you would never have given him that. He had too many rough edges for that, his vigor too implacable. They had this in common, he and his master the emperor. A force of restlessness, ambition that overrode the natural human desire for a soft bed. "Sometimes I think that it is to *him* you are married!" Charlotte-Elisabeth had said once, in a rare moment of bitterness. "To that *butcher!*"

Picking up his case, he bowed to Dubois, nodded his thanks to his assistants, and set off down the stairs. The housekeeper, torn between following her mistress straight upstairs and showing Larrey due courtesy, hurried ahead to open the door for him. As he passed through, she dropped a deep curtsy in which awe and horror were finely mixed.

The September sunshine fell on his face like a revelation. The street was warm. It was full of carriages, carts, women emptying pails in the gutter, children playing. He wouldn't go home, not immediately. Better a separation. What the eye couldn't see, the heart couldn't grieve over. He had never been any good at deception, particularly where Charlotte-Elisabeth was concerned.

No, he would go to the Invalides. There were boxes of reports waiting for him, on military hospitals he had helped to design in Syria, Palestine, Egypt, Sudan, and Italy. After that, the Café Procope. There would be gossip about the new front. Troops were already massing on the border with Prussia. It wouldn't be long now. That woman had been fortunate to have the crème of the emperor's medical corps attending to her. A month or two later and they would all be gone. The city would be emptied.

He would be much needed. A continent of snow and ice. Hardship and hunger. But such things to discover. The mysteries of the East. All the treasures of the Czars of Muscovy. The opportunity to perfect certain systems and techniques. At Wagram, for example, by dint of treating the wounded within twelve hours of injury, and evacuating them far down the lines so that they did not succumb to typhus and other diseases of the field hospital, he had achieved a survival rate in excess of 90 percent! Could that be repeated? There was also the business of freezing the limb prior to amputation, which they had chanced on in the Spanish campaign, in the mountains of the Sierra de Guadarrama. The reduction of pain was remarkable. Packing the stump with ice afterward also seemed to have great effect. If Bonaparte spared him from the slaughterhouse, he might have time to connect with Korotkin, the Leipzig anatomist whose books he had read. And he had heard great things of the Foundling Hospital in Moscow. It would be interesting to see how the Russians looked after their own.

Chapter Eight

The Happiest I've Been

I'M IN INTENSIVE CARE, with two nurses to look after me. There is a young one, Chinese, with a slender waist and hair so thick the ends seem burred with electricity, and a middle-aged Caucasian one, with rounder, softer features and dyed blond hair. I am in love with them both. They come and go with electronic thermometers and blood-pressure cuffs, entering their observations on a large chart to the side of my bed. Sometimes they lift a glass of water to my lips or lean over with softly whispered questions: "How are you feeling, Mrs. G? How would you describe your pain level on a scale of naught to ten?"

This was not a question anyone asked me when my mother died. The world moves on, on rails of steel. You stay on them, or you come off. Steam engine Percy, what is your destination? Busy little engine, off to Tidmouth or York. If you haven't got one, no one wants to know. You rust away in some dank yard. Slumped off on a siding. Pain is a very private disgrace.

The clock on the wall says 1:00 p.m. When I open my eyes again, it says 3:00 p.m. Where has this gap of time gone? If Time can fall down a crack and vanish from consciousness in amounts of two hours or more, can it be said to exist at all? And if it can disappear in this way, tumbling through a tear in space, is the passage of Time an illusion? If you could just find a way of toppling into the cracks behind it, would you have discovered a place where All Time was eternally present, like History in the Mind of God?

I am busy contemplating this when I realize that the woman in the bed opposite is in trouble. Head sunk forward on her chest, propped up on pillows, she is opening and shutting her mouth noiselessly. Whether to take in air or in response to some horror going on inside her is not clear. Whatever it is, it's not working. Her face is colorless. There is a sense that if someone doesn't do something fast, she won't be around much longer. A curtain skids round her bed; nurses and doctors dive behind it. There is a shadow puppet show, all very sotto voce, but urgent nonetheless.

"Hemorrhage," says one of the nurses in response to my query as she hurries past. "Back in a minute."

I smile beatifically, wrapped up in my bales of bandages. It doesn't bother me. Life, death? It's all one. I've got bigger fish to fry. If only I can get back to those Cracks in Time, I might be on the brink of something, a major discovery. Illness, finitude, death: how might they appear from such a vantage point? Mere punctuation marks in the elaborate fiction of chronology . . . a bagatelle? Now that would be something to get ahold of. I make an effort to focus my mind, with a sense that my opportunity is limited. But just as I am approaching it, great waves of tiredness come over me, and I doze off again.

When I wake up, R is there, standing at the foot of the bed, in his leather jacket. It is his damp kiss on my forehead that has woken me. "How are you, sweetheart?" he asks.

"Great!"

"Really?" He frowns anxiously.

I beam at him. "Wonderful. I feel wonderful. I'm so happy it's all over."

The bed opposite me is calm now. They've got that woman under control, or she's gone somewhere else—back down to the operating theater, perhaps, or off in a body bag; at any rate, the curtains are quite still, and the cloth is hanging in white pleats with the light shining through it like something from William Holman Hunt's *The Light of the World*.

"How are you *really?*" R repeats, leaning toward me.

My temple begins to throb. "Wonderful," I say, indicating the board to the side of my bed, with its precise handwritten measurements, the lovely nurses moving to and fro, the freshly laundered sheets. "Wonderful. I love it here. I never want to go."

R looks tired. The stress lines that have appeared in the last few years never really leave his face now. How can that have come about? I wonder. Is it the strains of work, young children? Of our marriage—long years linked to a depressive? Is that the end of the marital road, when you look at what living with you has done to the person you love and are so horrified by the sight that you have to turn and run? And he's wearing that old seersucker shirt I've never liked. And his collar is squashed under the lapel of his jacket. Why is it that R can never seem to manage his appearance by himself?

"And what about the . . . wound?" He hesitates. "Is it sore?"

Wound? What's he talking about? Wound. I'm beautiful as a bride, wrapped up in my fresh white dressings, my gleaming sheets, the stacks of laundered pillows behind me. I'm perfect. Resplendent, even. Floating on air. And I'm very busy at work on a theory about the Cracks of Time.

My frown seems to trigger his clumsiness. He takes off his leather jacket and, looking round for a seat, drapes it over my feet, which instantly feel suffocated. Seeing the effect of this, he picks up the jacket again hastily and, still looking round for a chair, kicks the metal frame of the bed by accident. This sends a sudden shooting sensation into the chest area, which up to this point has been so detached from me, it might have floated off to form a new continent with a name something like Gondwanaland.

"Ouch!"

"Sorry."

"You kicked the bed!"

"Sorry."

"I mean, if you're visiting someone in intensive care, you should . . . "

"S, I said I'm sorry." He holds up his hands in self-defense.

We fall silent, a little shocked by the fact that we can't even seem to do the scene in intensive care without an argument.

He stands at the end of the bed, holding his jacket awkwardly and looking miserable.

I take pity on him. "How are the children?"

"Fine. Or rather, I don't really know. I haven't talked to them since breakfast. I think your father and Miriam were going to take them swimming."

My father and stepmother have come down from the west coast of Scotland to take care of the children while I am in hospital. It is a big event, as it has been each time they've come south to see us or help with the children. For many years after my mother's death, my relationship with my father was difficult. It had foundered on strains that had developed before my mother's death, on the wound of his rapid remarriage with Miriam, on his silence about my mother. But at the birth of my first child, we were both anxious to make an effort. The fragile relationship grew, reinforced by annual summer visits to their home in Tiree, where my father and Miriam were generous and committed grandparents. Now, in the event of cancer, my father has stepped forward again to offer help. It will be critical to our ability to cope.

"And how are *you*?" I ask.

R seems taken aback. Not since diagnosis have I asked him such a question; he's out of practice. He launches into a long story about parking the car in Onslow Square opposite the hospital; overshooting the deadline on the meter; running back to find the traffic attendant in the process of writing him a ticket; having an argument with him, which he won ("I got my point across, I got it across," he repeats, as if he can't believe it himself); taking the car to East Putney, where someone has told him you can get free parking; getting stuck in East Putney tube station because of a problem with the District Line; phoning the nurse in Ellis Ward to find out whether I'm out of surgery; getting lost on the way to visit me in the recovery suite, because the lift let him out in the basement at the wrong end of the hospital and there seemed no way to get to the suite except by going all the way back up to ground level and taking the stairs down again. By the time he's finished, there's a dark ache in my chest and my eyes are wandering about anxiously in search of a nurse. Who let *him* in? Have they forgotten me? But no, here she comes, the middle-aged mumsy one with the warm smile, intuiting my distress. "Perhaps you're tired, Mrs. G?" she says, giving me a welcome prompt.

You bet I am. You bet Mrs. G is tired. And she's very busy, too. She's got a lot of work to do. There's been another Crack in Time. The clock on the wall says 4:30 p.m. An hour and a half. Now, if Time can disappear at that rate when you close your lashes for a moment, who knows what might happen if it started coming back again at the same rate? Is this what the Buddhists mean by Nirvana: My selves are scattered like leaves, my soul is abroad on the air? This is what Mrs. G would say out loud if she could. And traveling this fast toward Enlightenment, don't they realize, a husband can be a major distraction, if not an active impediment.

"Do you think it's time for a little more relief?" suggests the nurse kindly. "It's always much better to get *ahead* of the pain curve."

What a lovely phrase, getting ahead of the pain curve. Now that's a concept I can appreciate. This is a world I can inhabit. I have been wasted on the old, rackety, messed-up mortal world. All those visits to the GP over the years for antidepressants, antianxietants, counseling, cognitive behavioral and psychoanalytic therapy. I should have been here all along, in intensive care, with two whole nurses to myself and open season on the drugs cupboard.

She comes back with a small plastic beaker of clear liquid, which she lifts to my lips. Ah, the prince of pain relief: morphine. I know it by its sweet, faintly syrupy taste. Now where was I? Those Cracks in Time . . .

*   *   *

BACK IN ELLIS WARD, my father is sitting in a chair beside the bed. I glimpse him from behind, a darkly rounded shape, like the ridge of a mountain seen through clouds. As the porters maneuvers the metal crib back into its space, he gets up. He doesn't sit down again until they have finished. "How are you, S?" he asks, giving me a kiss on my forehead.

He is wearing his Aran jumper, the one with the heathery flecks, and carrying a bunch of sweet peas, which he places carefully on the bed beside me. "Beautiful," I say, my eyes suddenly full of tears.

"I got them from a flower seller on the Fulham Road, just down from the hospital," he says proudly.

"Yes." That would be the Kurdish flower seller at the corner of Fulham Road and Ebury Street. He stands there rain or shine in his parka with the ratty fur-trim hood, pulling up the long stems of English flowers from their cool buckets and twisting them into poetical arrangements, which he sells to the well-heeled residents of Chelsea at £100 a throw.

My father is not given to extravagant gestures. He brought up five children of his own and had a major hand in raising Miriam's two, on limited finances. Money was always an issue. The fact that he has permitted himself this gesture touches me, not just its lavishness toward me, but its lavishness toward himself, as a father.

"They had all sorts of things. But I liked the sweet peas best," he volunteers.

"They're beautiful," I repeat. "Just beautiful."

My father. The earliest memories are smells. Soap, clean skin, shaving foam. There is an old brown leather sponge bag, given to him at the time of his honeymoon with my mother, with a sturdy rectangular shape. For as long as I can remember, this sponge bag has stood on the ledges of different bathroom sinks, its zip open to the same bare range of contents. A bar of Imperial Leather soap, the waist wearing thin; a wooden shaving brush, the bristles coarse and stiff; and a shallow black dish, in which a new tablet of shaving soap is inserted annually. His clothes have an equivalent economy of ritual. There is an Aran jumper, and a set of brown-and-white-check flannel shirts from Marks & Spencer, so similar across the years that each new member of the family might have been cloned from the previous one through the preservation of a small piece of cloth. Now and then, the bounty of Christmas or birthdays brings a new texture or color, even a whole new style, in which case the garment is worn respectfully until its day is done, whereupon his wardrobe drifts undeviatingly back toward its default mode: Aran jumper, check flannel shirt. The background smell of these clothes is air. Wind and woodland, small, brown peaty rivers, heather, sawdust, grass.

To this day, if I pass a decorator's van, topped by a bundle of ladders, I can't stop myself going over to have a look. Something about the cheerful guddle of the interior, paint pots in ascending size, trays of brushes and rollers set out on the big tarpaulins, gives me a lift. It reminds me of my father, the one from earliest childhood, whom I was free to love. The one who was always shinning up a ladder with a pot of paint, in a pair of canvas dungarees, or on his knees with a hammer, building something, fixing something, repairing or securing.

My father is not describable except by movement. His is a life in verbs. A few slides inserted into the lightbox my parents had when they were newly married—the type of handheld plastic device where you peer down the luminous interior at the image—reveal him always active. The first image is Parsonage Farm House, Kent, the garden with the wide beds and espaliered apple trees. My father is pulling down a wall, at the end of this garden, that is overgrown with ivy. My sister and I are watching him. I can still feel the furious energy with which his short, square fingers tore at the bricks, bringing them down in crumbled chunks, along with mortar and brambles. Why is he doing this? I don't know. It is a Sunday-afternoon project. On Monday, he will put on his black coat and take the train into London for his job in the civil service. We are not sure what he does there, but we know he doesn't like it very much. He comes back in the evening with a dark face and takes the dog for a walk. On weekends, he's got a lot of energy.

In the next image, he is sawing up planks to make a tree house. We are standing round him in an enraptured circle: four of us now, a fifth on the way. In a few short years, my parents have determined the shape of their lives. Whether this is what they thought they were doing is another matter. They are full of hope, full of promise. Nothing in life could weigh them down. Children are like the largest, shiniest parcels under the Christmas tree. Young and beautiful as my parents are, they deserve many of them. It is 1968. The rhythms of Nina & Frederik are playing on the gramophone. "Come Back Liza." "When Woman Say No She Means Yes." "Little Donkey." The needle bumps lazily over each track of the record, laboring over a particle of dust like a drowsy beetle, while the seductive rhythms flow out into the English summer garden. My father has seen a picture of a tree house in a Peter and Jane book and thinks he can do better. He is hurling himself at the wood in a fury; clouds of wood shavings fly up behind his plane. The blond curls scatter through the air like Rumpelstiltskin's gold. They cast a sweet, resinous smell. When he's done, he wedges the house in a crook of the apple tree, lashing it fast with rope. A stretch of chicken wire ripped from an old henhouse serves for walls, some overturned crates for table and chairs. And there we are, in our jubilant green world, way above everything, hardly daring to breathe.

The third slide is more troubling. It's mottled at the edges, where the cardboard frame encloses the transparency; my parents couldn't keep up with their growing collection of photographs, and in one of many moves, some crates would have gotten flooded. Peering in, I see my father in his black coat, the one he used to wear to work, with the mulberry silk lining and the little brass chain. This is my handsome, matinee-idol father, with a big smile and more charm than is good for him. Right now, he is hopping over a stile, in search of the Pilgrim's Way, which he is sure must be nearby. He has a map in one hand and a dog lead in the other. There are five children trailing behind him. His palm on the post is light as he lifts himself effortlessly over. He turns and waits to see the children over the stile. There is a flash of impatience as their Wellingtons drop heavily to the ground one by one. But he quickly bends over and stuffs them back onto their feet, then sets off again at a cracking pace up a chalk escarpment. The children can't keep up. They are wailing now. But my father doesn't hear them. He is talking energetically with another man in a stylish black overcoat, a little older than he is. An important person, we have been told, who is to stay for Sunday lunch. My mother is at home right now making roast lamb and chocolate mousse. The man is from the Labour Party. He is there to discuss strategies for pushing up the Labour vote in certain key constituencies in rural Scotland.

The last image is frankly disturbing. 1970. My father's hands are gripping the metal handle of a lawn mower. He is heaving it from side to side over a large area of coarse grass in the village of Killiemore, Aberdeenshire. His face is grim. Now and again he bends down to pick up a stone that is in his way, tossing it effortlessly to one side, or yells up at us over the roar of the mower to stand back. A lot has changed in the meantime. He has resigned from his job in the civil service to enter politics. We have moved up to Scotland so that he can run in an election for the Labour Party. The house in Kent, with its ruddy brick walls and peony beds, the house where I learned to read, side by side with my mother, back pressed to a radiator, the smell of the lilacs coming in at the open window, is gone. Instead, we are living in rented accommodations: a gloomy granite cottage at the edge of a wood. My father has bought an old manse next to a churchyard—cheaply, because it was due for demolition. The beams are rotten, the slates are falling off. But he is hurling himself at the renovation. With his implacable drive and appetite for work, he makes the place habitable in short order. But I am struggling at school, where I am bullied for my English accent and my unhappiness. The nocturnal rows between my parents, intermittent before, have become protracted and bitter. Childhood, as I had known it, was over.

"Can I get you anything, S?" asks my father. "A glass of water, some grapes, another pillow?"

I shake my head. "No, I'm fine, thank you. Very comfortable."

My father sits back in the armchair, hands clasped in his lap. At age seventy-two, he seems to have learned a kind of stillness. It is far from his dominant characteristic. But it is present often enough, and deeply enough, to form part of one's sense of him.

I encountered it first when Michaela was born, when he flew down to be with us at the hospital. I remember him sitting in the chair by the bed in the overheated room, in his Aran jumper, the new baby in his arms. She was wrapped in a stiff cocoon of hospital sheets, a lick of black hair at the top. My father doesn't touch her, he scarcely looks at her, but all his attention is focused on her nonetheless. It is as if he is inhaling her. Brand-new baby. Joy. Either age has slowed him down, or life has taught him the risk of movement—that when you move, you have an impact on things, and that this may be both for good and for ill.

Now, at my bedside, he is in this mode of stillness once again.

"How are you feeling, S?" he asks gently.

I nod, with a delightful sense of expansion. How are you? is not a mode that can happen when someone is hopping up a ladder with a paint pot; hurling himself at a log with an axe; lashing slates on a roof; running in an election; fixing a cesspit; or roaring at an adolescent child because he has neither the time nor the emotional apparatus to deal with the child's problems, which make him feel wild with anxiety. How are you? is a question that depends on just enough inward stillness to invite, or listen to, a response.

"Great," I say. "I feel great. Life on morphine is very doable."

He looks a little startled, but accepts it, which startles me in turn. This is my father, whose mother had an addiction to drink, who never saw a daughter take a second glass of wine without looking uncomfortable. And now he is allowing me morphine.

"Well, long may it last," he says.

The children come with cards and flowers, their faces peeping shyly round the door.

"What's that?" asks Michaela with quiet focus as they approach the bed, indicating the long plastic tubes that travel from my chest down to two plastic bottles on the floor. They are filled with a pus-colored liquid streaked with blood.

"They're called drains," I explain. "When the surgeon cuts you, there is a lot of liquid, blood and so on, which has to drain away. It's like when you cut your knees, except more. When it's stopped, I'll be able to go home."

"That's disgusting," she says tonelessly, her face pale.

For a while, they are shy of going near the bed. But then they discover the hospital technology. Michaela gets hold of the remote-control device for the bed and, with her swift mastery of how to make things work, delights in sending it up and down, up and down, and bending it at the knee. "Look, Mummy's got a whole television to herself!" she says, pulling round the screen on its adjustable arm and running through the channels. Kitty discovers the hospital trolley. "Mummy's got a table on wheels!" she says. "And a cupboard. With chocolates in it!" Just when my chest begins to develop a dull ache, and white noise starts scattering through my head, a nurse comes forward. "Perhaps Mrs. G is getting tired now?" And my father gets up to take them away, gathering their bits and pieces and bending stiffly to fasten the straps of Kitty's shoes. "Bye-bye, darling," I say to each of them from my lovely impregnable bed. And I listen to the sound of their sweet, high voices, breath syncopated from time to time by a skip or a hop, a counterpoint to my father's deeper, more even rumble, disappearing down the corridor.

THE NIGHTS ARE DELICIOUS. With no pressures of any sort, I wander the wards in my pajamas, trailing the IV drip behind me, drain bottles inserted into little embroidered pouches, which some kind person has sewn especially for women like me. I have a sense of being on holiday, as if someone has presented me with the keys to an ancient Florentine church. I delight in the long, heavily waxed corridors with their subdued glint, in the iron filigree of the banisters, and in the portraits of famous physicians. I wander to Wiltshaw Ward, dedicated to gynecological cancers, where I had my ovaries removed. And then all the way back again to the other end of the hospital, where I find a corridor decorated with charts of nasal and facial reconstruction. Cancer, I am beginning to realize, is a disease of life itself. Wherever the process of a cell's reproduction can go right, it can go wrong, too. The wonder is not that it happens at all, but that it doesn't do so more often. From the sash windows of the third floor, I look down into the Fulham Road, where the traffic runs through the night, thinning out but never stopping altogether. I look across to the jeweled beacon of the NatWest Tower, which appears like an urban annunciation. And sometimes I see the dawn come up, the lilac flush tearing at the young leaves, as it reaches up over the rooftops.

I become close to my fellow sufferers, with that rapid bonding of people in difficult circumstances. At the end of the ward, close to the bathroom, is Dani, aged thirty-five, a banker in the City. She had just had her second child when she found a lump in one of her breasts, in the bath one evening. "I was so tired. Just dog tired, all the time. I kept having conversations with personnel, putting off going back to work. And then I found it. It was almost as if it was meant to be." We weep together, sharing the particular pain of going through cancer when you are a mother of young children.

In the corner near the nurses' station is Jeanette. She is small and elegant, about sixty years old, and she sits up in bed in mulberry silk pajamas with a newspaper. She has lost two daughters to the *BRCA* gene: the elder at thirty-five, the second at twenty-eight. Now she is in hospital for breast cancer herself. It means nothing to her. She talks about her daughters, both of them, over and over again. They start to live for me, the beautiful, brilliant girls growing up in a big house in London, the elder sister with a gift for mathematics and politics, the other, artistic and creative, putting her parents through hell as she recovers from anorexia. Each time Jeanette talks of them, she weeps. Her tears are not violent or demanding; they are a gift, as natural as rain. This is how she bears such grief: by continually letting it go.

In the bed next to mine is Vinny, who is dying. Tall and very thin, with haunting eyes and graceful arms, she is propped up on the pillows—the cancer is in her lungs, and pleural effusion means she can no longer lie horizontally. She spends most of the day drifting in and out of sleep. I learn from her daughter, who visits daily, that she is a former actress, known for her striking portrayals of Lady Macbeth and Hedda Gabler. Now and again Vinny opens her eyes to greet a friend, some vivid acquaintance from her old acting days. There are a few snatches of dialogue, a little soft laughter, before she disappears into sleep again.

There is nothing anyone can do for her, but from time to time she is taken in a wheelchair to some other part of the hospital for a scan or an X-ray. And three times a day the catering staff brings her a tray of food, which they place on the table, adjusting it carefully over her bed before lifting the aluminum lid that keeps the food warm. Three times a day they take it away again, untouched. But on the table next to her is a little cut-glass sundae dish, like a child's ice-cream dish, filled with small colored sweets. Every now and again, her long, graceful arm reaches out to take one of these sweets, which she pops into her mouth and sucks meditatively, before drifting back to sleep.

During the day, Nicky Perrone comes to check up on me. "Lovely clean wound!" he says, peeling back the sticky-backed dressing to examine his handiwork. "Healing up nicely. Have you looked?"

I shake my head.

"No?" He raises an eyebrow and smiles. This is the woman who came to each interview with a tape recorder and a typewritten list of questions, who wanted answers backed up with statistics and references to the latest articles in leading medical journals.

But my instinct is clear. My appetite for reality has dwindled to zero. I am here to enjoy myself. Every morning, I take out a different pair of freshly pressed pajamas. I do my makeup carefully and arrange my flowers. I study my visitor list for that day. Brigid is coming, whom I used to share an office with when I worked as a secretary. And Judith, an old college friend whom I haven't seen for years. How lovely. I read the little blue menu sheets carefully and tick my preferences. How can anyone ever complain about this?

And then, on the fourth day, it all comes crashing down. A nurse comes to my bed to measure the fluid levels in the drain bottles. Squatting on the floor, she enters the results on a chart at the end of the bed, and then peeps up over the side with a smile.

"It's below fifty milligrams, Mrs. G. Both of them. We should be able to remove the drains tomorrow, and then you can go home."

And I burst into tears. Which turns out to be extremely painful, affording me the first image of what might have happened under-neath, as each suture, lashed tight across the lip of the wound, seems to be stretched.

"But what is it, Mrs. G? Don't you want to go home—to be with your husband? Your lovely children? Be in your own bed?"

I think of the small, battered house with its shaky floorboards, of the rickety bathroom with no lock on the door, of the children bouncing up and down and making the bed shake. I think of the anguish of looking into their faces fifty times a day and wondering what will happen to them if I'm not here. And I think of R, with his tired face and anxious ways and his habit of kicking the bed. "I just don't feel ready!" I sob. "I need to rest."

"Well, isn't there somewhere else you can go?" She sits on the edge of the bed. "To your mother? Or an aunt?"

This sets off renewed sobbing. Don't you realize? I want to say to her. That's what this gene does. It kills the mothers. And then, when the daughters get cancer, there is no one to look after them. That's what this is all about. The collapse of the mother line. The great edifice of matriarchal support—grandmothers, mothers, granddaughters—that others take for granted for me is broken. So that I stand in space, a door without a hinge, an arch without a key-stone, while the cold wind whistles through.

WE TAKE REFUGE in the Rockingham, a four-star hotel a few miles outside Oxford. It is an old Knights Templar building whose central medieval hall has been converted into a plush lobby. I used to despise its padded luxury, the thick-pile carpet and maple-veneer bar, the baronial-style chandeliers and the little swimming pool steaming with chemicals and dubious Roman statuary. But now I am in desperate need of it.

The exit from the hospital has been frightening. How can people survive the speed of the crowd, the sudden cut and thrust of traffic? Each brake at a traffic light, each surge of acceleration at a roundabout, however carefully R tries to drive, causes pain. I sit crouched in the passenger seat, a pillow strapped to my chest to protect against the pressure of the seat belt.

By the time we reach the hotel, I'm exhausted. Clutching the shoe box of painkillers that the nurses have given me, I hobble along the padded corridors to our room. I feel like a hunted creature, looking for a spot under a bush where I can crawl in and die. Only when I am lying on the solid bed, with its expensive, well-sprung mattress, watching R pull the heavy curtains on their silent track to shut out the day, do I begin to feel safe. Walls, I think. I need walls, curtains, and counterpanes, thick-pile carpets. Bandages, dressings, and quilts. I need so many surfaces between me and the world that nothing could ever break through.

In the morning, the phone rings. The noise is piercing and insistent in the darkened room, and we wake groggily. Our night has been disturbed and we have slept late.

"Ah, Duncan!" says R, jumping out of bed and standing to attention. My father is not someone you would naturally take a call from lying down.

"I'm not sure," he says nervously. "I think she just feels she had to leave hospital too soon. I don't think she's up to the children just yet. She needs a bit more time to recover. If you could hold the fort a bit longer?"

My father and Miriam had offered to look after the children while I was in hospital. The term of their stay was left vague. While I seem to remember the phrase "for as long as you need us," my father has become anxious about arrangements. Particularly, he doesn't understand why I haven't come straight home to be with my children. It's making him uneasy. "Megan Dacre said it's not an enormous deal," he says of a cousin in Australia who had a mastectomy. "She only spent three nights in hospital. Then she just discharged herself. Her husband taught himself how to do the drains." This story, which my father has already told me once in hospital, and which he is now rehearsing on the phone to R, is intended as inspirational. But I experience it as prescriptive, a statement of how I should be handling things. Megan Dacre didn't have young children, I think resentfully. Her husband could do a decent job of nursing her because he had no one else to care for. They lived in a great big house in the Australian outback with buckets of bathrooms. And anyway, what does it matter what she did? I just feel differently.

In the deep murmur of my father's voice, pressing home his point, I sense judgment, the all-too-familiar quality of disapproval. Still woozy from anesthesia and morphine, made vulnerable by shock, I have regressed. It is my child self that emerges now, or rather, a flimsy, gimcrack adolescent self not yet safely moored in adulthood. Ducking, weaving, parrying, defying, I am back in the old dance, the endless dodging dance of opposition with my father. My skin starts to prickle.

"I think she just needs a bit of peace," says R defensively, the pitch of his voice creeping higher. "She's not feeling that strong."

I am not behaving according to the script. I am supposed to have picked up my drains and walked. I should be at home right now in the bosom of my family, telling jolly stories of how I fought the doctors to make good my escape. Instead, I am malingering in a highly suspect four-star hotel, avoiding my children and mourning the loss of the nurses and my fellow patients.

As my father talks, R's posture becomes more tense. His shoulders start to sag, his neck stoops. "Yes, Duncan, yes," he says, rubbing the back of his neck, as if trying to relieve pressure. "I think she just feels . . . I think she . . ." But each time he starts an explanation, he falls silent again as my father's more emphatic murmur breaks in. Soon he gives up altogether and settles into a groove of assent. "Yes . . . yes . . . Of course . . . of course . . ." My father's is a forceful personality; his will has a tendency to exert itself upon those around him. Such people are creative, dynamic, courageous. They shape the world and make things happen; they give everyone a standard. But the reverse side is turbulence. They are not peaceful to live with. There is too little space for autonomy, a calm exploration of the world. And the wills of others may often present themselves as an obstacle, to be overcome at all costs.

I have worked hard over the years to try to parry a tendency to diminish in my father's presence. Hours on the couch have been devoted to it, among other things. But under pressure, I can still disappear. My voice goes silent. I lose myself, or else flare up in ugly defiance. Worse still, R sometimes seems to disappear as well. Now I watch him diminishing before me, shrinking and shrinking until he is no higher than Mrs. Pepperpot to a chair leg, while my father looms larger and larger, his colossal presence launched irresistibly on the room. My chest starts to throb; my mouth becomes dry. I get up and go into the bathroom. But even here, sitting on the side of the bath with the door shut, I can't escape the dark dynamics: the dim, emphatic murmur of my father's voice, R's anxious, conciliatory assents. "No, no, I'm sure it's not for long," I hear R say eventually, feeling a stab of utter betrayal. "I'm sure she'll probably be home by tomorrow."

We visit our own house the next morning for coffee. It is a friendly arrangement that allows us to see the children, and to show my father and Miriam that we are grateful to them, that I am avoiding neither them nor the children: it is simply that I need quiet and rest, and had to leave the hospital too soon.

But when my father answers the door, my confidence evaporates. He is in a state of anxiety. His face seems to be set in a grim expression. The square rims of his glasses reflect the light coldly. And perhaps I'm imagining it, but there seems to be harshness in the tone with which he greets me. "S?" he says stiffly. "I hope your night was reasonable?"

*   *   *

I AM SEVENTEEN years old again, sitting on the granite step outside
our house in Victoria Road, Aberdeen. It is midnight. The door is
locked. I have spent the evening with my boyfriend, a gentle man a
decade older than I, who works as a roustabout on the oil rigs and
plays folk songs on the harmonica in his free time. We have had
dinner together and spent a long time kissing in his hotel bedroom.
And now I am late back. I have no key. And the door is locked. And
I am hurt because it seems that my mother must have acquiesced.
I knock quietly, do not dare to ring the doorbell. No one comes.

The long marches of the night come and go. I walk up and down
the front path, along the lane at the back of the terrace, round the
monument of Queen Victoria at the end of the road to stop myself
from freezing. I push my hands up my sleeves, hunch the thin cotton coat round my neck. I hear the racketing of the first starlings.
The milk lorry arrives, with its trembling load of bottles. There are
little streaks of satin light in the east.

Somewhere toward dawn, my father unlocks the door. There is
the sound of different chains being released, laborious, censorious.
The door opens a crack, and there he is, a dark, forbidding figure in
his green tartan dressing gown. "S?" he says grimly. There is a long
pause, in which I feel that I am invited to consider my moral tur-
pitude, my outrageous excesses, my conditional status within his
house. "Your mother is waiting for you."

INSIDE OUR OWN HOUSE, Miriam is bustling about in the kitchen,
anxious to make coffee for us. "Milk, sugar? Have you eaten? Can I
get you some breakfast?" She is smiling, polite. But the atmosphere
is tense. We're in trouble now. Benign Daddy seems to have disappeared, the one I remember from earliest childhood, the one who
leaped a stile in a carefree manner and wept when the dog died. Also
gone is the white-haired man of seventy-two, loyal and steadfast,
who despite his stiff knees has made all these journeys, by ferry,

train, and bus, to help us through our ordeal. Before my eyes, or through them, he is turning into the ambivalent figure he became for me through the long years of adolescence and early adulthood.

"How are the children?" I ask, seeking instinctively for our common ground: the next generation.

There is a pause. "Well, as you will see for yourselves," says my father stiffly, "they miss their mother."

At this moment, Michaela comes running down the corridor, plunges her head into my stomach, and flings her arms around my waist. I lean my head on hers and we stand in clumsy joy, like the figure of the father blessing the prodigal son, by Rembrandt.

"'Lo, Mama," says Kitty, twisting round the side of a doorway with a shy smile. She examines the tableau for a few seconds and then leaps the last two feet like a tree frog to clamp herself to one of my legs, pressing her face into my knee. I lean my cheek down next to hers and keep it there for a long while.

We go through to the main room, where Miriam brings a tray of coffee and biscuits. We chat about the weather, the children, the hotel, before my father mentions something about homecoming. "I'm not feeling strong," I say in an attempt to claim a space for myself. But my voice comes out wobbly and pathetic, as if in a self-piteous whine. Why is it that any claim of weakness before my father must seem like standing trial for murder in the Old Bailey? Is it the culture, a fierce, proud Scottish culture that puts its shoulder to the wheel without complaint? Is it the distilled wisdom of my ancestors coming down to me now, that fetched them through wars and hardship, the pain of childbirth, separations, poverty, and unremitting physical labor? Is it my grandmother's particular twist on it, her bold and brilliant personality not shaped for statements of weakness, which would have seemed a poor "party piece," to be booed offstage? Or is it my father himself, who, with all those children and all that drive, scarcely knows the meaning of rest? I don't know. What I do know is that I find it almost as impossible to say "I'm not feeling strong" as I do to take a phone call from him lying down.

And in any case, he's not listening. He's got his own point to make. "The Children need their Mother," he says. "And one would have thought that the same might be true in reverse."

Michaela and Kitty look up, a little startled at this description. They don't recognize these august personages. Could the "Children" in this narrative possibly refer to them?

"And Miriam has put sheets on the bed," he finishes emphatically.

It's going now, the ground beneath my feet. There's not a lot left to stand on. Whatever adult self I have fashioned over the years, patched together out of feathers, wastepaper, and pins, it's coming unstuck. How could I explain? Even before my mother died, home was an unsafe place. After she died, I found it unspeakable. I'm falling back down there now, down, down, into the long chasm of childhood, where there were no kind arms to hold me, no kind voice to rescue me.

"I'm not feeling strong," I repeat in a renewed effort to claim space for myself. "I'm really not feeling at all well."

"Of course you're not," says my father in a sudden strategic concession. "How could you be expected to?" I blink. Is he going to change shape again into Benign Daddy, the one with the newfound capacity to inquire how I am and to listen to the answer? But no. He is simply gathering his strength to press home his point. "Of course you're weak," he repeats. "It's perfectly natural. You've been through a lot. That's why you need to come Home, isn't it? Home is the Right Place to be, surely. And Miriam has put Sheets on the Bed."

Miriam. First appearance: 1978, two years before my mother's death. Divorced, two children, teaching art in the local state school. "A very fine painter," said my father one morning over breakfast. "You should take an interest in her, S, if you're planning to be an artist. If we're very lucky, she might even accept a commission to paint the manse."

My father was back working for the civil service in Aberdeen and unhappy there. With a natural talent for building, he was renovating in his spare time some old agricultural steadings to turn them into holiday cottages. Later, he bought a remote manse a thousand feet up in the Cairngorm Mountains and began to renovate it, too. It was this building that he wanted commemorated in paint.

The whole thing jangled. My parents' marriage was not easy. It lurched forward in magnificent tumbling harness with five children, several dogs, horses, cats, a good leavening of financial insecurity, and my father's disappointed political hopes to contend with. Nor did his restlessness confine itself to the world of work: it was a sexual force as well. There were attractions, flirtations, humiliations. They may not have been very serious, but to my adolescent gaze, this slighting of my mother seemed unbearable. Any love and affection in their relationship were invisible to me at that time, and I came to reject my father. I could scarcely bear his perfunctory kiss each night, but suffered it in silent fury. I felt the complex rage of the victim-predator: the daughter of a mother whom I believed scorned, whom I myself scorned because of her subordination to my father. It was against this background that Miriam made her entrance.

The commission was accepted; the portrait went ahead. My father talked about its progress from time to time, ventriloquizing excitement. I think the atmosphere on these occasions was strained. Then the day came for its delivery. My parents went out to Miriam's cottage together to pick it up. "I thought at the time your mummy didn't look well," said Miriam casually, many years later when we came to talk more openly about this period. It is thus, through a torture as exquisite as it was unconscious, that I discover the other woman's gaze on my mother's failing body. "But I didn't realize what was happening."

The relationship began shortly after my mother's death. My father took to going out to Miriam's cottage on the weekends. On one occasion he insisted that his five children, aged eleven to nineteen, accompany him. There was opposition, which was overruled. I remember the low white building with its semicircle of green grass in front of it, demarcated by little granite posts looped together by a fine chain. I remember Miriam standing in the doorway, short and dark and watchful, her two children, the elder just about to enter her teens, not far behind. I remember the main room, decorated with her paintings, landscapes in watercolor. I have no idea what we said to one another. I have no idea what we did, or what we ate. What I do remember are the nights.

My father shared Miriam's bedroom, which lay behind a thin partition to the main room. Miriam's children occupied a room at the rear of the house, while we slept in sleeping bags, laid out one after the other on the floor of the main room.

We lay awake, rigid, as the darkness quickened with the sound of their lovemaking, frozen in horror at the dim rustlings beyond the wall. Why so motionless? you might ask. Why would we not turn on a light? Reach out a hand and gently touch one another, whisper a few words of consolation in the darkness? But we could no more have moved than we could have flown. The prohibition was total. This is the pity of children: their sorrow, their shame. Adults determine their world. They decide the words that shall be spoken and the words that will remain unsaid. In such abandonment, shame is an immutable law. My mother was ten weeks dead.

"Miriam has put Sheets on the Bed," my father repeats obdurately. "She ironed them especially."

Certainly, she has done this. Miriam has worked hard; she always has. Each summer in our visits to Tiree, she has made us more than welcome. She has put wildflowers on the table of our cottage, has cooked for us all, and has helped to take care of the children. There have been many happy days spent combing the beaches, searching out driftwood and shells to paint later at the long table, going for swims, climbing hills, having picnics. It is Miriam, and not my mother, who has held the children as babies and pointed out a flower or a tree; Miriam who has taken the trouble to teach them to sew or to knit, to make a cake or to celebrate a birthday. My children love her as their grandmother and make no distinction between their biological and nonbiological grandparents.

But at this moment I struggle to receive her kindness. A relationship between stepmother and stepdaughter is necessarily complex. There is diffidence, hesitation, conditionality. There is a need for forgiveness on both sides. And right now, I have no resources for such complexity. My needs are primal. They are for a mother.

More significant perhaps, as my father talks, I hear instructions. I feel forced, as I was forced after my mother died. My heart beats faster. It does a squashy syncopated kind of beat, in which the muscle fails to contract properly. The blood seems to fall back on itself, bubbling up a flabby ventricle, like fluid backing up a drain. "I'm not feeling strong," I say. "I'm really not feeling that strong."

IN THE HOTEL, I wake up with a nightmare. Something is squatting on my chest, an apelike thing, large and hairy and monstrous. Its haunches are so heavy I can't move. It leans forward from time to time and inserts a long finger into my mouth, from which it picks out crumbling teeth, one by one, inspecting them as a monkey might inspect a seed or a piece of dried peel. Until this moment, I had no idea my teeth were in such a state. But the minute the creature reaches its finger into my mouth, I know that they are done for. The roots are all rotted, even the bone beneath them is decayed. I wake up drenched in sweat, my chest in pain.

In the bathroom, I drink a glass of water in front of the brightly lit mirror and breathe carefully. I am still there: two eyes, one nose, a mouth. The teeth are all there in my head. I have my hair. The only thing that's different is the shape under the pajamas, a kind of collapsed asymmetry on my left side. My gaze keeps wandering to it, and veering off again.

Three o'clock in the morning. The hotel is silent. Only the hum of the ventilation system, so well regulated you hardly hear it. At this hour, there seems to be something of the luxury abattoir about this bathroom, with its slabs of veined marble, its stainless-steel towel rails, the batteries of spotlights slung along the mirror. Something about the clinical light prompts a sudden urge to get to the bottom of things. "You haven't looked?" I hear Nicky Perrone's voice clearly, see his quizzical smile in front of me. I lean forward and start peeling back the clear plastic edges of the dressing.

"R! R! For God's sake! There's something badly wrong!" I am wailing, beside myself with horror.

He appears in the doorway in his striped pajamas, his face slack with sleep. "What's going on? What is it?"

"There's something badly wrong here. It's not the way it should be. There's masses of liquid under the skin. It's horrific. I don't know what it is. It's as if my chest is trying to grow another breast!"

R bends over to examine it. He prods the skin round the wound cautiously with his long, square finger. The liquid gives to the touch and bounces up somewhere else. "It does seem a bit odd," he says, swallowing.

"Odd!" I scream. "For God's sake, I've got a bloody water bed growing on my chest. And you're calling it odd!"

He phones the receptionist at the Marsden, who phones the nurses on Ellis Ward. Within half an hour, the night registrar has phoned back. When was the surgery? Is there pain? Is the wound inflamed? Do I have a fever?

R relays these questions, to which we give careful answers. "It's probably just a reaction to the surgery," says the registrar finally. He sounds weary. Goodness knows what other horrors are assailing him in the middle of the night. "It's probably fine. But without having you here to do a physical examination, I can't say for sure. If you're worried, why don't you get yourselves to the emergency room? You've got the John Radcliffe Hospital right on your doorstep, haven't you?"

The ring road is almost empty at this time of night. We glide past the huge metal storage hangars that line the edges, past the industrial complex of the Cowley car works, ever dwindling, and on through a succession of traffic lights that are all at green. There is a last twisting rise before we see the hospital ahead of us, its vast blocks pale and shining, the modern version of the City upon a Hill.

After parking in a near-empty car park, we duck in and out of the jets of hot air sent out into the night by the vents of the heating system. The automatic doors spring open just as an ambulance draws up and some men in green scrubs start unloading a stretcher from the back. There's an old man on it, wrapped in a green blanket, his face bloody and bruised.

It's Saturday night, rush hour at the ER. We give our details to a woman protected by a glass partition and take our seats on the bucket chairs. Two hours later, we are seen by a young Scottish doctor. With her hair pulled back into a ponytail and her alert, cheerful manner, she has the air of a teenager about to go out and thrash someone on a tennis court. "Oh, that!" she says, prodding at the water bed on my chest. "That's nothing to worry about. It's just a seroma! My auntie had one after her mastectomy." She giggles. "She got a bit of a scare, too. Phoned my mum in the middle of the night. So my mum phoned me. They can be enormous. You can get *liters* draining off them."

I look at her dazedly.

"It's the body's natural defense." She settles into tutorial mode. "It has to get a lot of white blood cells to the site of the trauma to fight off infection. That's quite a big cut you've had there. And because the wound has been stitched up, this fluid builds up under the surface. Did no one tell you about it?"

I shake my head.

"Did no one give you a leaflet? Not one of the nurses?"

"No."

"Oh well." She gives a shrug. A wry smile. "They probably didn't want to frighten you. If we told you everything that could happen, you might never have treatment at all, eh?"

"SMILE, MUMMY!" says Michaela, pointing in my face the digital camera my father has given her.

We are back at the house. We had promised to drop in again for coffee that morning. And while part of me just wants to go back to the hotel and collapse into bed, another, bigger part craves comfort and reassurance, the blind immersion in the warmth of family.

"Smile!" Michaela repeats. But all my optimism, the blithe detachment from my own body that has sustained me over the past week, has drained away, vanished as if it had never been. I have suddenly become what I am: a wounded creature, lost, maimed, and scared. In the narrow hallway, with Michaela's camera on me, I feel close to collapse.

My father appears in the hall. All of a sudden, he is his kind and gentle self again. "Mummy's not feeling well," he says to Michaela. "Now, you go and arrange some cushions on the sofa and make it comfortable for her."

Michaela goes off happily to do this, while Miriam makes coffee. "Goodness me. How dreadful. What an awful night. Thank goodness it has all sorted itself out. Sugar, milk, biscuits?"

She doesn't want to know details. She doesn't want to know facts. There is always a distance between us, a politeness pronounced enough to feel recessive. Sometimes it's hard to tell who is holding whom more firmly at arm's length. But I know that there is genuine concern for me. And for this I am grateful.

We go through to the main room to have coffee. The atmosphere is better today. The children are playing with a jigsaw puzzle. My father sits peacefully, with an air of taking things as they come.

"I can see your plaster, Mummy," says Kitty shyly. Her little owl eyes are wide.

I nod.

"It's very big."

"Yes."

"It's white."

"Yes."

"Is it sore?"

I shake my head. "Not really."

She comes over to the sofa. "Can I touch it?"

She strokes the edges carefully, avoiding the center with instinctive delicacy. Having touched it, she seems to decide that it's all OK and she can forget about it. "Will you read me a story, Mummy?"

We settle down on the sofa with a book of Bible stories illustrated by Jane Ray. Kitty chooses the Christmas story. We lose ourselves in the rich and beautiful illustrations: Mary stirring a pudding bowl in a kitchen in Nazareth when the Angel of the Annunciation appears; the long journey to Bethlehem; the donkey leaning over a stall. And then the point to which all other things lead, the image of mother and baby. It is beautifully done, Mary, with her long black plaits, breast-feeding the baby. She proffers him a nipple, flushed rose on the almond skin. It hits me with the force of a slap. So this will never come again. Fertility, pregnancy, breast-feeding. Most of the time I had it, I had no use for it. Most of the time I had it, it brought me difficulty and pain. But what a world I am leaving behind! At this moment, I realize that Kitty has leaned her head on my chest. For her, it seems, it makes no difference whether the breast is there or not. I am still Mummy. I can still talk. Read. Cuddle. Smile. And I *have* breast-fed her. It is the ground of our being, a candle of joy between us.

"Herod doesn't get the baby!" she comments with satisfaction. Understanding the strand of the narrative that involves Herod did not come easily to her. She had to work hard to follow the systems of empire, the displaced cruelty, the overweening urge to power. But now that she has got it, she delights in exhibiting her grasp of the story, the triumph of good over evil. "The wise men tricked him," she says. "They go home by a different way. Herod doesn't get the baby!"

At this moment, my father's mobile phone rings. It is Callum, the manager he has left in charge of his business, reporting a failure in the computing systems. Despite the backup system, which should have functioned to prevent it, some bookings have been lost. Suddenly my father is standing up dictating things in a loud voice. His IT systems are the bane of his life, causing him countless hours of anxiety and stress. However hard he works at them, with a freelance programmer who comes over from Glasgow, there are glitches. It is April, the start of the holiday season—not a good moment for them. His anxiety threatens to well over.

When he has finished giving instructions to his manager, he

turns stiffly to me and R, sitting in a chair nearby. "And yourselves?" he inquires in a voice that suddenly makes me feel we are a pair of fare dodgers on a railway. "Are you any clearer about your intentions?"

"I'm still not feeling strong," I begin, surfacing from the image of the breast-feeding Mary. "Could you give us a bit more time?"

There is an oppressive pause. "Is this wise? Is this in your best interests? As you can see, the *Children* need their *Mother*." He indicates Kitty with her head on my chest, Michaela playing with a puzzle at my feet.

"I really am not feeling strong . . ."

My father interrupts. "You would have thought, under the circumstances, you would draw strength from being at home with your children."

We should have been able to find a way round this. We are grown people, in our middle years, with resources. But weakened as we are by shock, frightened and disorientated, it seems to be beyond us. And suddenly I can't cope with it.

I hear a tide swell of capitalized instructions from my youth. Women Are Equal but Different . . . Symmetry of the Sexes . . . Instinctive Nature . . . Born to Care . . . Greatest Fulfillment . . . Helping Others . . . The Nature of Women . . . The old battlefield; my helpless revolution all the years under his roof.

My chest is throbbing. The raw obliteration of the wound is so vivid now, I can't understand how it could have been invisible to me all these days. The walls of the hospital have gone. And with them, so many other protecting walls. I am back where I have always been, the blind creature in the spell that cannot be broken, the spell of my father's judgment. I am also wincing with pain caused by the pressure of Kitty's head on my chest.

"Just leave me *alone*, would you! Leave me *alone*! What do you *know* about what I need? Why do you always have to tell people what they need! Why can you never *ask* them? Did this happen to *you*? What can you possibly know about what it feels like or how to cope with it?"

I rush out of the house, down the path, and take refuge in our car, which is parked on the curb just outside. "So now you've done it," a voice says bitterly inside my head. "Now you've blown it." Rifts and division, we're good at that. We've had a lifetime's practice. So will I find myself tossed into an outer bowge of hell, the reviled daughter, the ingrate child? I won't be able to rescue myself, and no one will do it for me. I don't *care,* I tell myself furiously. Not if he's going to tell me what I am, who I am, and how to feel. If that's the price of selfhood, I pay it willingly.

A tall shape appears in the doorway, hesitating. There is a long pause. My father's steel-rimmed glasses reflect the light strangely. Then he turns away again and disappears into the darkness. So that's it. Neither of us will know how to bale ourselves out of this one. Our conflict-resolution skills are zero. And I have to go through cancer in the meantime. I don't *care,* I repeat to myself furiously. He can think of me what he likes, judge me as he likes—Bad Mother, Good Mother—with my maimed body, my dressings, the water bed swilling about on my chest. I am what I am. This thing is too big. I can't be told how to go through it.

But then, miraculously, he reappears in the doorway: white haired, slightly stoop shouldered, I notice. He looks out hesitantly. There is another long pause. Then he comes down the path, crosses in front of the bonnet, and appears at the side window of the car. "May I?"

He climbs in carefully and sits next to me in the rear seat without saying a word. He stares ahead of him, hands resting quietly on his knees. He is wearing his Aran jumper. There is the familiar smell, that warm, faintly oily smell of sheep. There is something else, too. A trace of mustiness, of close warmth, as of trapped air. The smell of skin that is old. Rubbed worn like a flannel. My father has the smell of an old person! I have difficulty accepting it. He is still the mythic one in my mind, like Father Chronos, astride the universe, implacable and all-powerful, consuming his own children to defeat the curse of generations.

It is a quarter of a century since we have sat like this, side by side, on a seat. The sensation of friendly companionableness, of undemanding togetherness, is so unusual that I am dazed by it.

The last time we sat like this was in Victoria Road, Aberdeen, 1980. We are sitting on a bench in the kitchen, and my father is telling me that my mother is dying. I have just made the terrible journey home from Oxford and have gone upstairs to my mother's room. I have seen the truth of what he is telling me. It is spelled out all over her body. But I can't accept it. I am knocking my head against the whitewashed brick wall behind me.

In the wicker basket at my feet sleeps my dog James, a cocker spaniel. I remember being confused by the state of his fur. His eyebrows are white. There is white tracery over the bridge of his muzzle. His paws, which once scampered across cornfields and heather, through snowy woods in winter, gathering snowballs like burrs in the thick glossy fur, are toothed with silver. It is as if a sea mist had just come in and tossed itself over him. What has happened to him in the short space that I have been away at college? And what has happened to my mother?

"It is cancer, Sarah," my father explains. "The doctors thought they had dealt with it. The surgery seemed to have worked. We were all hopeful. But now it has come back. There is nothing . . ." He clears his throat, looks down, looks up again, and forces himself to continue. "There is nothing anyone can do. Mummy is dying."

So my father sits beside me in the car, saying nothing. It is the middle of the morning. A neighbor comes down the garden path to wheel back the empty green bin; a cat slinks along a hedgerow, ducking under a stray branch, before hopping down into the street; a skinny mother with an anxious expression pushes a buggy ahead of her, with a toddler so fat and blooming he seems to have siphoned off all her nourishment.

It is twenty-five years since we sat like this. Life supervened. It went forward on rails of steel, my father atop his revolutionary train, hurtling into history. Within months of my mother's death, the house in which she died was sold. Miriam and my father were to be together. He moved the two families to the remote manse he had renovated in the Cairngorm Mountains. This had been used for holiday letting and already had its own furniture—there was not space for everything. So, while valuables were retained, and cherished items, much of the accumulated contents of my parents' marriage was fire-saled in what my father grandly called a "rowp"—a term used in the area to denote a sale of agricultural machinery. Farmers came from far and wide. Their sharp-eyed wives couldn't believe the prices. The weather was appalling. Driving rain turned the ground to mud. Everyone slipped around in it, while these remnants of my parents' life together were broken up. I remember a mattress tied to the top of someone's van. I remember someone else lowering the sides of his truck to accommodate my mother's wardrobe, wedged in beside some hay bales. I remember Miriam coming round the side of the granite house with a set of crystal glasses on a chased silver tray given to my parents as a wedding present, when a dog bounds toward her. "Oh no!" she says as the whole lot falls to the ground. This was not the part she meant to play. This was not what she intended. Her own mother died of cancer when Miriam was nine. She suffered not only the loss of her mother but also the intrusion into her family of a stepmother, with whom relations were never easy. But life is complex. And it is cruel. It has a way of finding out a blind spot—there, where you least expect it, where you are most vulnerable—and moving in to apply pressure. *Smash* go the glasses! They fly up in a thousand fragments. "Oh no!" says Miriam. Such is happiness. Such is home.

"I miss my mother," I say experimentally into the silence of the car. The speech has a quality of fiction. It is all so far away. It is all so long ago. Can I really be said to have feelings anymore toward her? Or am I just imagining them?

When she died, my sisters and I fought over her clothes. There were handmade suits from the glamorous early days of her marriage; a beautiful blue wool coat with floral silk lapels and lining; a chiffon ball gown that dated from the time she was a student at Oxford; a gorgeous apricot silk dress made by my grandmother, after a pattern from *Vogue,* and stitched all over with crystal beads.

We had no interest in the dowdy fallen clothes, dating from the move to Scotland, financial troubles, the difficulties with my father. Oppressed, unlovely clothes: beige skirts and pastel twinsets from Marks & Spencer, a dark brown dressing gown with embroidered yoke. We left these to the side. It was the early clothes we fought over, wearing them day after day in inappropriate situations and contexts, spying on one another jealously, until the seams frayed and the cloth was worn thin. My feelings are like these clothes. They are worn to a fray, and I am jealous of them. They have suffered years of mistreatment and disrepair. I don't know whether I can reclaim them. I don't even know whether they are real anymore. But I know there is anguish. It has a shape. It is a missing at the heart of things. A lost place the foot keeps stumbling over.

"I miss my mother," I say, not something I have felt able to mention to my father in twenty-five years. From the point of his marriage to Miriam, my mother's name seemed taboo. My father talked about her with what felt like extreme reluctance. It seemed to me that her image, her property, any shared memories of her, the narratives of a life, all were expunged. A great silence was cast over them. So my heart is thumping as I speak her name. What do I expect? For the ground to open? For the car to blow up? For the sun's chariot to fall out of the sky, pulling the planets behind it like a trail of paper bunting? But my father is quiet. His hands rest in his lap. They are still as a wooden dish gathering rain. Eventually he gives a sigh. The quality of this silence feels very different from the silence that prevailed before. In it, I experience assent, allowance. In a spirit of experimentation, I find myself leaning my head on his shoulder. Not since I was very little would this have happened. The wool of his jumper is warm and scratchy. It is comforting. "I want my mother," I repeat. "It's very hard to get through this without a mother . . ."

Chapter Nine

Therapeutics

IN 1943, an American ship called the *John Harvey,* carrying a hundred tons of mustard gas, was attacked and sunk by German bombers in the port of Bari, Italy. When the ship's doctor, Peter Alexander, came to make a record of the catastrophe, he noticed a strange phenomenon: the bodies of the survivors all showed a dramatic decrease in the numbers of their leukocytes.

It was already known that leukocytes, the white blood cells in the lymph system that fight off infection, were bound up with the processes of cell proliferation. In the laboratory, a reduction in these cells had been seen to inhibit the growth of certain kinds of tumor. Alexander's report was read with great interest by scientists in the U.S. Department of Defense. If mustard gas could bring about such a startling reduction in leukocytes, what might it do for lymphomas, or cancers of the lymph system?

Scientists extracted a derivative of mustard gas, mustine, and gave it to the first patient, a man with non-Hodgkin's lymphoma, in 1946. His tumors regressed significantly. The effect lasted for only a few weeks. But it was a medical milestone, leading to the development of the alkylating agents, of which cyclophosphamide is one. One year later, Dr. Sidney Farber, at Harvard Medical School, produced the first remissions in acute lymphoblastic childhood leukemia with a drug called aminopterin. Finding that folic acid stimulated the production of these particular leukemia cells, he was hopeful that suppressing it might do the opposite. Aminopterin was the first of a new class of chemotherapeutic agents known as antifolates.

Since then, hundreds of new agents have been developed, some a variation on existing compounds, others launching a whole new class of drug. In the 1970s, there were the taxanes, based on the bark of the Pacific yew tree, used for the treatment of ovarian cancer and advanced breast cancer; then the camptothecins, derived from a Chinese ornamental tree, used for the treatment of colon and lung cancer; later the platinum-based agents cisplatin and carboplatin, used for the treatment of several cancers, including testicular, ovarian, lung, and advanced breast cancer.

Along with the discovery of particular compounds were breakthroughs in how to use them. One of the most important was the launch of combination chemotherapy in the mid-1960s. It was argued that the use of different drugs concurrently would make it harder for the tumor to develop resistance. If a tumor was made up of millions of cells, of many different types, replicating through different processes and at different intervals, chemical attack on it needed to be multipronged. Then came adjuvant chemotherapy in the 1990s, designed to mop up the invisible micrometastases that had been shed by the tumor into the blood or lymph system and that could not be tackled through surgery alone.

Chemotherapy has always been a high-wire act, a balancing act between the attack on the cancer and the limits of the human body. Why can't you hit the cancer harder, and for longer, and with a wider mix of toxins, to be sure of killing it? the patient not unnaturally asks. Cancer is a complex disease, the doctor replies a little sadly. You might kill millions of tumor cells, while millions of others escape. And chemotherapy is toxic. It can cause heart failure, damage to the kidneys, even another cancer, such as leukemia. In high enough doses, it can wipe out your immune system altogether, so that the common cold might carry you off.

Cells are ordained to proliferate. It's what they do. You can put the body in suspension for only so long. Nails, hair, teeth, skin, gut, heart, lung, all must grow themselves anew each day. How much of this process can you put a stop to before the body is technically dying?

For dying is what it feels like. Or death-in-life. A contradictory, paradoxical state, like the word *chemotherapy* itself, derived from the Greek words *khemeia*, the art of transmuting metals, and *therapeia*, healing.

Only our age could have produced it, this word, with its "yoking of incompatible elements," as the *Oxford English Dictionary* puts it. An age of industrial warfare and pollutants; the invention of plastics, robotics, informatics, astronautics; the returning terrors of the hygienized psyche. With nowhere to go but to little couches in suburban houses on a Monday afternoon. A box of tissues. A sympathetic ear. How can a chemist, trained to isolate the infinitesimal processes of which material life is made up, be a therapist, in the old Greek sense of the word? A word warmed by sunshine, born in a stone cradle at Epidavros, made clean by the crystalline air.

Subjectivity can't catch up with science, and we're back in leaflet territory again. The little grey booklets are everywhere. *Chemotherapy: Your Questions Answered; Coping with Hair Loss; Nutrition for Chemotherapy; The Chemotherapy Survival Guide*. The familiar colorless prose unfolds. *You may experience sickness . . . you may become tired during treatment . . . You may find that treatment affects your ability to concentrate or think clearly, which may be frustrating . . . You may have a sore mouth or gums . . . which may become ulcerated . . . your finger- or toenails may fall out . . . It is possible you may lose interest in sex during chemotherapy . . . you may lose your hair, which may be distressing . . . you may experience feelings of low self-esteem . . . these may persist, in which case, do not fail to consult your doctor.*

How to define this language? Neutrality. The studied expunging of the personal. It is in the gaps—the "chasms of consciousness," as Fanny Burney called the parts of her mastectomy that escaped recall—that you find them out. For what is so unspeakable that not a ray, not a photon, of light is allowed to escape?

"Chemotherapy . . ." says one woman I consult who has been through it, and falls silent. She has been enthusiastic to the point of boisterousness in her recommendations as to how to cope with surgery, as if I am preparing for my first term at a distinguished girls' boarding school. But on chemotherapy she has nothing to say. I go to someone else. "Chemotherapy," says this woman with a small shrug. "You get through it."

A distant relative sends a get-well card, with the following statement: *Our thoughts are with you at this difficult time. Surgery will be a challenge. Chemotherapy will be unpleasant. Then you will be back to your normal, happy self.* I spend weeks, and energy I don't have, hating her for this, particularly the word *unpleasant*. It's she, the one who's been authoring the NHS leaflets! I've tracked her down. She's got a samizdat press in the basement of her eighteenth-century manor house in Sussex. The one with the perfect garden, where her daughter, who went to all the right schools, got married in a big white dress under a pitched marquee.

She writes the leaflets for all the girls who lost their mothers when they were young and were too unsavory to take home. Upstairs, there's an endless production line of marbled Battenberg cakes and raspberry pavlovas. Downstairs, in the cellar, there's an ancient printing press half-hidden by an oilcloth. She steals down there at night (we've all got to add a bit of spice to our lives) and, unbeknownst to her family, stays up till all hours churning out sage advice: how to behave when being poisoned within an inch of your life; how to talk to your children when you might be about to die; how to have sex when your breasts have been cut off.

Listen to her. Because she knows the score. Nice girls don't. They just don't. They don't do it in back alleys. They don't do it in cars. They don't do it with the wrong type of men, in dirty bedsits, without enough money to power the meter, and get their faces rearranged by a broken bottle. And they don't inherit filthy diseases that require treatment with buckets of poison so they spend all day chucking up, their children turn feral, their hair falls out, and they can't make shepherd's pie or Victoria sponge—or even baked beans on toast. And if by any chance they do, they'd better maintain a well-bred silence on the subject. Or they'll really be for it. The ice will crust over them. You'll see them thrashing around beneath you, green handprints pressed up against your feet. Society can tolerate only so much dirt and disorder. Let's face it, we've all got to get up in the morning, put one foot in front of the other.

THE CHEMOTHERAPY DIVISION is in the roof of the hospital, up a flight of stairs from Outpatients. I think of it like Bertha Rochester's attic. You never see her, mad Bertha, but you know she's there; there are strange routines: trays of food that disappear, the doctor's unexplained visit in the night, the housekeeper's silence. I haven't been there yet. But I've seen them coming from there. Baseball caps and bandannas, wigs, turbans, Kylie-style kerchiefs, and scarves. A catwalk of chemo chic. But underneath the jaunty headgear, the skin gives it away. Sallow, ashen, or puffy with steroids. And the gait. Especially the gait. As if each step costs effort, simply to maintain balance and forward motion.

There is a smell, too. It meets you at the end of the corridor on the ground floor, the one with the royal blue carpet that is always being vacuumed. You go up a flight of stairs at the back of the hospital—linoleum now, with a brown swirling pattern, like those seaside buckets you had as a child—and there it is, under the laminated sign saying OUTPATIENTS.

The heart rate quickens. There is a gastric fluttering, yellowish, sour. You might think it was reassuring at first, this warm, faintly sweet smell. But by the end, when you have stayed the course, there's no confusion. Your body has come to know it absolutely. It works like carbon-monoxide poisoning, binding the receptors on the hemoglobin, which aren't free to absorb anything else. The body can't get enough oxygen to flush the blood red. Your lungs knew it long before you did. They have pushed up the volume—there they are, under the Outpatients sign, rasping away inside you, trying to extract enough juice from the sweetly poisoned air to power . . . what? Not a life anymore. We're way beyond that. Simply a movement, a breath, a thought.

"YOUR PATHOLOGY SHOWS six tumors, three of them malignant," Professor of Oncology Don MacBryde had said in the meeting that followed my mastectomy. "Grade Three. Estrogen-receptor negative. You aren't eligible for hormone-based therapies—tamoxifen, Arimidex, and so on. There is no point cutting estrogen in the body if that's not what is making the cancer grow. So our best line of defense is chemotherapy. The standard schedule that we use in this country is one called FEC: fluorouracil five, epirubicin and cyclophosphamide. So that's what I would recommend." He's perched on the edge of a Formica table in a cubicle off Outpatients, arms akimbo, in a suit the color of fine Highland rain. R and I have been waiting for him for over an hour. First we waited in the Outpatients area, studying the electronic board flickering with the delay times of the various clinics. Then we waited in Bloods, taking our ticket from a device like that of a supermarket deli counter. Then a nurse ushered us into this tiny cubicle, where we sat broiling in our bucket chairs, bickering over spelling errors in our list of typewritten questions. Finally, unable to stand the stuffy atmosphere any longer, I leave to fetch a cup of water. No sooner have I done so than R rushes out to fetch me. "Hurry up, S! He's here!" We get back to find the professor, flanked by registrar and breast-cancer nurse, on the point of whisking from the room again. "Ah, we thought you'd run away," he quips.

I am beyond smiling. I sit down on the chair and pass him our list of typewritten questions in silence. I have given up trying to talk to doctors. The bigger and more important your questions, the more evasive the doctors' body language. From the moment you are diagnosed with cancer, there is a big black bell tolling, like the one in Hitchcock's *Vertigo*. Pressing engagements, groaning clinics, weighty decisions. There's a lot of very sick people out there, don't you realize? I've got to get through them all before teatime. Doctors, like most people, may be free with emotional engagement in inverse proportion to need. It's a human instinct. It is so easy to give when the going is good, so much harder when the person in front of you is disintegrating in terror. So I have taken to typing my questions. It's as if the existence of a row of print puts a screen between them and you, the medical equivalent of the confessional box, enabling reengagement. Clearly formulated questions are a courtesy; they allow everyone a chance to behave decently.

"Why FEC and not other agents such as cisplatin or Taxotere? Good question," says MacBryde, with the cheerful air of a six-year-old boy going off to fly kites on a windy knoll. "You could try other agents. But nothing is proven. The taxanes are effective against advanced breast cancer, also against hormone-receptive cancer with node involvement. But so far the evidence suggests that they may not be particularly effective against early-stage *BRCA1* breast cancers. There's a trial going on at the moment about which is better, FEC alone, or FEC in combination with Taxotere. But we won't know the results for a while. Now, cisplatin has certainly shown great promise for *BRCA*-type cancers in the laboratory situation. But that's *in vitro*. *In vivo*, we don't know how it will behave. It might be better, it might be worse. If you had nothing to lose, and were very keen on having it, we might be able to get you on it. But in your case, there is a lot to lose. I think it's safer to put you on something tried and tested. As soon as you get into new routines, which the team is not so familiar with, the security and safety system is tested to the limit."

Next there is a batch of more personal questions. "Sickness and fatigue? Well, impossible to say. It's like pregnancy: different people have different responses. Maybe you should plan for being pretty ill in the week following each cycle of chemotherapy. Then if you're not, it's a nice surprise . . . Hair? Most women lose their hair on this protocol . . . Prognosis?" He comes to my last but most important question. "Mrs. G's pathology, please."

The registrar passes over my notes, two inches thick and growing. MacBryde pushes his half-moon spectacles up his nose, reads for a few seconds, looks up again. "Three invasive tumors: one point two centimeters, one centimeter, six millimeters. The consensus now is that you add the diameter of the lumps. Total tumor size: two point eight centimeters. Grade three. No estrogen or progesterone receptors. Tamoxifen isn't going to be effective here, and that would make a difference. With chemotherapy, which adds about twelve percent to your chances, I would give you eighty percent survival odds at ten years, give or take."

"A one in five chance of dying," I murmur.

"A four in five chance of living," he corrects.

He pauses for me to digest this, then turns to his registrar, a young Asian with a quick, alert manner and a brilliant smile. Tariq Dhanjani, says his name tag. "Now I'm going to put you in the very capable hands of Tariq to get teed up for chemotherapy. The evidence suggests that with *BRCA1* women, the sooner we get on with it, the better. We'll give you six cycles, one every three weeks."

But I'm not ready to be teed up. A question is burning in the back of my mind, though it doesn't appear in the printed list. I was too ashamed to write it down, and there has been nowhere to ask it.

"I need to talk about whether there's any point in this," I blurt out, leaning forward in my chair.

He studies me through narrowed eyes, perched on the side of the desk. I have broken the deal, departed from the printed list, become emotional. But he doesn't seem fazed. "What do you mean?" he asks directly.

"This gene killed my mother when she was forty-two. Now I have full-blown invasive cancer myself, even after oophorectomy, which was supposed to reduce the risk of breast cancer by half; even after all the screening. I feel doomed, as if there's nothing I can do to escape it. As if it will get me whatever I do. I would rather not put myself and my family through it all—more amputations, sickness, hair loss—if there's no point. If I'm doomed, I would rather face it and die with dignity."

There is a pause. The room is filled with an expectant hush. For the very first time since diagnosis, I feel that I have fully captured a doctor's attention. The black clock has stopped ticking.

MacBryde looks me straight in the eye and answers in the same undeviatingly optimistic manner. From anyone else this might be jarring. But from someone who has spent his life on the front line, measuring his progress in a graph that records the extra weeks or months of survival granted by each new therapeutic agent to a woman living with terminal breast cancer, it is strengthening. "You are not doomed," he says. "You have cancer. OK. It's not cheerful. It's got to be dealt with. But on the plus side, you have had your ovaries removed. Good. Very good: you can't get carcinoma of the ovary if there is no ovary. You've had one breast removed. Good. And you will have the other removed prophylactically a year down the line. Excellent. That takes your risk of getting another primary breast cancer down by ninety percent. So what you are left with is the cancer you have. And we're going to do our best to deal with that. OK, so it's not a hundred percent. But it's not a disaster either. Go away, be optimistic!"

THE FIRST SESSION is on May 18, one week before my mother's birthday. We turn up in good time and are shown to a waiting area to the right of the reception desk, manned by a young New Zealander called Catherine. She is so unfailingly kind and gentle through the process that I never once resent her her long glossy hair and clear skin as I am transformed into a balding, middle-aged witch.

The style of the waiting room is midmarket hairdresser: there are rows of easy chairs, magazines, and the odd print on the wall. There's not much talking, though. Mostly, people leaf through their magazines or stare into space. You think twice before getting into discussion with your neighbor and discovering he is on his third or fourth course of chemotherapy, with no perceptible impact on his liver cancer, or that the young woman to your left, who can scarcely be thirty, has a breast cancer too widely disseminated to be operable.

We have a meeting with MacBryde's clever sidekick, Tariq, who has a level cheerfulness, like his master. He could be making preparations for a tug-of-war at the village fete, or adjusting the icing nozzle to decorate a cake with the children. "FEC!" he says with a smile. "Wonderful! We will start you on twenty milliliters of dexamethasone intravenously for the sickness, along with oral medication to take home. If you have any problems, we can increase the dose. Chemotherapy is a work in progress. By the time you get to the end, you are just finding out what you need."

There is a last-minute flurry of phone calls to the hematologist at the John Radcliffe Hospital when Tariq spots on my medical records that I have Factor V Leiden, a condition carrying a slightly higher than average risk of blood clotting. Chemotherapy raises the risk of strokes, and the question is whether I should be given a blood-thinning agent such as warfarin to get it back down again. This has to be balanced against the risk of hemorrhage, which is also higher when on chemotherapy. The risk in each case is about 5 percent. Which to go for? After neatly setting out the parameters of the decision, Tariq smiles and shrugs. I have come to recognize this shrug. It's the same one that Professor Wiesbach gave when discussing different types of reconstruction. It translates roughly: you pays your money and you takes your ride. We're not looking for the perfect solution here: we're looking for the least nasty.

"Good luck," says Tariq, shaking us both warmly by the hand, which we appreciate.

Outside, Catherine tells us that we are free to leave while Pharmacy prepares the drugs, which will take about two hours. We might like to go and have lunch. She asks us to keep the mobile switched on.

It is a beautiful spring day, the sun shining liberally on the elegant stuccoed houses, the interior design shops, and the Kurdish flower seller, with his buckets of peonies and delphiniums. Momentarily, it seems big-hearted enough to bless even us. We head for a noodle bar on the Fulham Road. With its low wooden benches, parchment screens, and geometric place settings, it gives me a lift. I feel safe for the first time in weeks and start ordering food as if there were no tomorrow. "Tempura?" I say to R. "A plate of dim sum? And what about that Thai curry with the king prawns and lemongrass?"

"Are you sure? I'm not really that hungry," says R. But I'm unstoppable. "Oh, come on. Have another look. Let's see what's on the Specials. Let's try something *new*."

Back in the hospital, at 2:30 p.m., Catherine looks anxious. "We tried to get you on your mobile," she says. "But I think it must have been switched off. Your drugs have come up from Pharmacy."

"Oh, I'm sorry," I say, suddenly feeling foolish and ashamed. What was I thinking?

"Don't worry. I'm sure it'll be fine. We just wanted to get you done in good time. It's Friday, with the rush hour, and you said you had to get back to Oxford to pick up your children?"

I have a sense of déjà vu. When has this happened before? Here it comes. You open the trapdoor; you fall down the stairs. I am nineteen years old. Another moment of great pressure and jubilant denial.

IT IS 1980. I am standing under the clock in the porter's lodge at University College, Oxford, the one with the ivory face and the Roman numerals. The porter, whose name is Douglas, has just pressed the receiver into my hand to take a phone call from my father, who is telling me that I must come home. "Mummy is ill," he says. "You need to come home." I don't understand. My mother had a hysterectomy about a year ago. But there was no word of any illness. What does he mean? What is happening? My father repeats himself. And then he says the word that makes all the difference, the word that no one has mentioned to me before: "Cancer," he says. "You need to come home, S. Now."

Getting a train at that time in the evening is difficult, and I have to wait in Birmingham for a couple of hours for my connection to Edinburgh, where I will take another train on to Aberdeen. It's past midnight in Birmingham New Street; they've switched the heating off and it's cold. I curl up on one of the bucket chairs in the waiting room in an effort to stay warm. The only other person is a cleaner, an old man with a tin bucket and a mop, who looks at me oddly. After that, everything goes smoothly, and when the train draws into Waverley station in the morning, I feel a sense of exhilaration after the dreadful night. Sun floods the station platform. There is just time to go and see my grandmother, as I always do, before catching the train on to Aberdeen. I hop up the steps and along the cobbled street to sit in her kitchen drinking pink gins, as we have always done, chatting and pretending to help her with the *Times* crossword. Somewhere in the middle of this, my grandmother mentions the fact that my mother is dying. "What did you say?" I am shouting as I jump up from the table. "*What did you say!*"

"You may have to face it," says my grandmother without turning round. She has her back to me. She is stirring something on the hob. I am out of the flat, down the stairs, along the cobbled street, under the sooty vaults of Waverley Bridge, and on to the next train without another word. *What does she know? What does she know? Nothing! Nothing! Nothing!* pounds in my head, keeping pace with the violent rhythm of the train as it rattles over the iron girders of the Forth railway bridge and up the long loop of the northeastern coast. *Nothing! Nothing! Nothing! She knows nothing!*

When I get to the house, I burst into my parents' bedroom. I see my mother in the bed in front of me. She is very thin. Her eyes are as blue as the glass in cathedral windows. I know instantly that what my grandmother said is true. I fall to my knees and press my face into her hand.

After a few moments, she reaches for a white enamel bowl on the chest beside her bed and is sick into it. I watch her shoulders under the skimpy cloth of her nightdress. They are as frail as a bird's wings; she is racked by the effort.

"She just got a bit upset," says my father by way of explanation. "The waiting. She was expecting you on an earlier train."

"I'M SORRY," I bleat now, on the point of tears. "I lost track of time. I'm so sorry."

"Hey, no worries," says Catherine kindly, in her easy voice. She is giving me the benefit of the doubt, because that's the kind of person she is. Also, she sees a lot of suffering in her work, and it's taught her to be slow to judge. "I'm sure it'll be fine. We'll get you out of here before the rush hour."

A Czech nurse called Magda with curly brown hair and a warm smile takes me through to the main chemotherapy suite and invites me to sit in an armchair. She puts a fresh pillow under my right arm and starts trying to insert a cannula into the vein in the back of my hand. "Got small veins," she says. "We gotta be clever."

She brings a tall, thin yellow bucket of warm water and invites me to place my arm in it to open the veins. After a few minutes, she tries again. This time, with the arm supine on the pillow, the needle slides in effortlessly.

She pulls up a metal trolley covered with transparent plastic syringes. They are about ten inches long by two and a half inches in diameter. Two are filled with a colorless liquid, the third with something so intensely scarlet it looks like stage blood. She proffers us a printed sheet and begins to read off the amounts of each drug from her own control form: Cyclophosphamide: 960 mg; 5-Fluorouracil: 960 mg; epirubicin: 120 mg. She looks up interrogatively at the end of each one, inviting us to check the amounts with her. The process must be completed with care; errors in drug calculations can be fatal. R enters into it with enthusiasm, grateful to have something to do. I am too dazed to concentrate. Those syringes; they are huge. They look like something for injecting a horse.

Next, she returns with a blue rubber cap steaming from the freezer. The cold cap is designed to shrink the hair follicles during chemotherapy in an effort to minimize hair loss. It's a long shot: 90 percent of women on FEC will lose all body hair. She draws the rubber tightly over my scalp, before inserting little wedges of cotton wool over the tips of my ears and at my forehead to minimize the impact of the cold. "OK?" she asks gently. The delicacy of this touch—its gratuitous tenderness—confuses me, so that I nod dumbly, eyes pricked with tears.

Pulling up her mobile chair, she attaches a tiny syringe to the tube running from the cannula before injecting something into my vein. There is a cold stinging sensation. "Flushing," she explains. "We gotta be careful. If the drugs leak, they can damage the tissue."

She unfastens the tester, then picks up one of the large syringes—*Cyclophosphamide* says the blue print on the side—and attaches its nozzle to the cannula. She pulls her chair still closer to mine, so that our knees are almost bumping. "Ready?" she murmurs, looking up at me gently. I nod. With the syringe resting in her lap, nozzle pointed toward me, she begins to pump the fluid steadily into my vein.

I remember the tales of certain Indian yogis who have practiced meditation for so many years that they can slow their heartbeat to zero. I have no such skills. My heart is an involuntary muscle; within two seconds the clear liquid has been pumped to liver, kidneys, lungs, and brain.

"Are you OK?" murmurs Magda from time to time. "No pain? No burning?" I shake my head.

In fact, I register very little during the process. There is a faint sensation of warmth, of brimfulness, as if the skin were expanding to accommodate the liquid. There is also a feeling of separation, as if I were both here and not here at the same time.

I don't want to talk to anyone. Except with Magda, I avoid eye contact. I don't want to know about the other women in the chairs opposite, not the one with the ill-fitting auburn wig and the expression of strain on her face, or the one next to her, supine and bald. I especially don't want to have to look at the man right next to me, with his yellow complexion and sticklike arms. When an attendant comes round with a food trolley, this man chooses an egg sandwich, which he unwraps with a slack hand before starting to eat it straight from the package. How can he do that? I think with revulsion, and close my eyes to block out the sight of him.

During the next hour, I would have said that nothing at all is happening except that the plunger within each syringe steadily passes the blue numerals printed on the exterior. And Magda quietly exchanges first one syringe, and then another. Also, the little air bubble in the bend of the tube running into the cannula squeezes itself from time to time, and does a kind of queasy somersault, before lying still again.

"There!" she says at the end, wiping the site of the cannula injection with a sterile strip and pressing a prescription form into my hand. "Now you will need to go to Pharmacy and collect your antinausea medications. You've had twenty milliliters of dexamethasone intravenously. You'll also need to take dexamethasone orally—two tablets every four hours—for the first few days. You can have granisetron as well. And we'll give you some domperidone for backup."

It is only halfway back to Oxford that I know something has happened. We get through Kensington, with its snarling traffic; past the Shepherd's Bush roundabout, with its swirling water tower; past White City, with its straggle of car dealerships and dirty pubs. We even get to High Wycombe and the cutting where the Ridgeway is bisected by the M40, and ancient chalk escarpments rise on either side. We are almost at Oxford itself when the traffic slows. Taken unaware, R swoops up on the back of a truck and curses. It's a long tailback, several miles perhaps: two rows of glittering metal, expelling carbon monoxide into the summer air.

The world has been turning for some time now. I've transferred to the backseat in an overwhelming urge to lie flat, and I have been counting my breathing. But at the Forest Hill truck stop, where there is often a line of big lorries (a dogging truck stop, someone once told me), I can master it no longer. Getting out, I deliver the contents of my stomach into the verge. Through the hedgerow, I see there is a green knoll with a stand of oak trees, tinged in gold: a Samuel Palmer painting, a perfect piece of English pastoral. The prawns are distinct in the mess of yellow broth. They look like little embryos in the fresh green grass.

"HOW *ARE* YOU? How *are* you? I only heard last night. I was *so shocked*." It is a woman called Katie, with long brown hair and an

English-rose complexion. I have not been introduced to her but have seen her often at the school gate. She is pushing a large pram downhill with a baby inside it. On a rollerboard attached to the back is a two-year-old girl with cheeks as red as a Russian doll's. A little boy of four or five plods along beside it.

How does she know? I wonder with a jolt. My policy has been to tell no one, except family and a few close friends. It is not a policy so much as an instinct, the instinct for self-protection. Trying to explain inheritance of the *BRCA1* gene was a painful experience even before getting cancer. "We all have risks; you could be run over by a bus every time you cross the street," said one woman of my 85 percent lifetime risk of contracting breast cancer. "Perhaps you should talk to my husband, who practices evidence-based medicine. He might help you get it in perspective." (The lifetime risk of being run over by a bus in Britain stands at roughly one in ten thousand, or 0.0001 percent.) Other people I talked to said nothing at all, which was painful in a different way. They simply blanked it, never returning to it, as if it were an error of taste they were willing to overlook. "Don't talk about it," said someone else, at the time of my surgery, holding up her hands in a barring gesture. "You'll just upset yourself." In the end, I gave up trying to communicate. There was a glazed air to people's reactions, a kind of numb horror that I found profoundly unhelpful. It seemed that few people were simply willing to inform themselves about this strange territory of risk that I had been forced to inhabit. It made the experience of going through oophorectomy, with its debilitating physical and mental consequences, one of great isolation.

But now the news of my breast cancer is doing the rounds. Two nights ago, someone turned up unannounced at my doorstep with a bunch of flowers. "I've just heard. It's *terrible*. But you were part of that clinic, weren't you? How did they *miss it*?" Her gesture is kindly meant. But the emotional pressure—she is too distressed simply to deliver the flowers and go—is overwhelming. I lean against the doorjamb, fighting tears. By the end of her visit, I no longer have the strength to make the children a meal and crawl upstairs to bed.

Now Katie is clearly shocked, too. Her cheeks are flushed and her eyes dilated. "It's *terrible*," she says. "I felt so upset when I heard. I couldn't sleep properly. How *are* you?"

In truth, in the weeks since diagnosis, I have lost over seven pounds. My legs are tottery. But whenever possible, I am determined to take the children to school. I don't know how many times it will be given to me to do this: each one feels precious. But what I don't have strength for is this type of interaction, however well-meaning.

"Fine, fine, just trying to get to school on time," I murmur. Her children have gotten tangled up with mine, and what with the pram and the scooter, the lunch boxes and jackets, it is a bit of a squeeze on the narrow pavement and I feel light-headed.

"Oh yes. Well, you must tell me if there's *anything* I can do," she says, rushing off so that suddenly, irrationally, I feel abandoned in the chilly updraft from the pram. "Anything at all."

"*So* sorry, S!" a woman calls out of the front window of a red people carrier. "*Terrible*. You must be *devastated*."

We have reached the bottom of the hill, crossed at the traffic lights, and taken a left along a side street in an effort to go in at the rear entrance of the school and avoid further interaction. But as we turn, the people carrier turns, too, slowing to a halt alongside us.

"Have to take each day as it comes, eh?" continues the woman, Karina, through the rolled-down window. I don't know her well, but we have mutual friends and someone has told her my news. "Got to be positive. That's my philosophy. You'll get it licked."

Karina is in fund-raising. She is managing a hectic work schedule, with young children and a husband who is often away. She has the bipolar mood pattern of so many working mothers, alternating between a pumped-up energy that might tick a few boxes on a questionnaire for mania, and a caved-in black humor that tells of exhaustion in the effort to cover too many bases at once.

Now she is lost between these two modes. "You can beat it, eh!" she repeats, punching the air in front of the steering wheel with her fist. "Just got to stay positive. My mother had a friend who . . .

Years ago . . . Strong as an ox now. She'll probably outlive us all." Her words are bright. So is the laughter that accompanies them. But as her fist punches the air, it has a dying motion. And the glance that flickers over my chest is dark and anxious. "Well, if there's anything I can do, you will tell me, won't you?"

"Thank you," I say, gripping the children's hands tighter. "Thank you so much." And she moves off. I see her children strapped in the rear seat, their faces as round and empty as moons.

Suddenly, I am aware of complicated networks of gossip, of the force of my news as it takes on independent life, goes up and down these narrow streets, to be chewed in the mouths of people to whom I have never been introduced, who do not know me, or my dead mother, or my children. I am not strong enough simply to extract the kindness from these gestures. I feel violated, as if the last shreds of force have been sucked from me by an enormous impudence, the invasion of this world that presumes to know my business.

"Look, Mummy, it's a weeny snail," says Kitty, breaking away from me to extract a tiny creature from a crevice of brick and holding it up between two fingers. "A weeny weeny baby one."

"Yes, yes," I murmur, unable to concentrate, gripping the children's hands for support.

"That's sore, Mummy," says Michaela finally, detaching her hand from mine as we reach the back gate of the school. "You're holding me too tight."

In her classroom, Michaela moves away from me. She puts her lunch bag on the little rack by the door, fills her water bottle at the tap, fetches her jotter, sits down in her seat, and begins to copy down in a large, careful hand the sentences written on the blackboard. She seems relieved to be among the orderly rituals of her class. She does not look up at me.

I watch her carefully. There is something pale and fragile about her, too set. It is not just I who has been violated, I realize. She has been violated, too: in her need to be a normal little girl with a well mother who can take her to school without incident.

Momentarily, I am filled with such tearing rage I can hardly breathe. The cancer has not attacked just me. It has, perhaps more devastatingly, attacked my child. For this I need to fall upon it. I need to tear out its liver and lights, to bite out the ventricles of its heart, to feast on its blood.

Someone is looking at me and I turn round to find myself staring into the wide brown eyes of Francesca. Francesca is Michaela's best friend. The girls spend their time in and out of each other's houses playing schools; climbing the apple tree; making pop-up books, dens, and magic potions. Normally, Francesca would hardly spare me a glance. But now she can't take her eyes off me.

Her mother will have talked about me. The word *cancer* has been mentioned. Even to a child who has never heard it before, it has the power to terrify.

I smile at her reassuringly. What I really want to do is take her hand and put it in my daughter's and say: "Look after her, please. She's so very vulnerable. Look after her." But I can't do this. It would frighten them both. Francesca smiles uncertainly back at me and looks away.

I lean clumsily toward Michaela, who holds up her hands as if to defend herself.

"Bye-bye, Michaela," I whisper to her with aching love. "Bye-bye, my darling."

Needy Mummy. A frightening phenomenon. "Bye-bye, Mummy," she says in a small, pale voice without looking at me. "You can go now."

It's easier with the nursery school. Kitty is just three. Her sense of dignity does not depend on any convergence of her own behavior with notions of normal. There is no carefully constructed edifice that my sickness, and the behavior of other mothers in respect to it, threatens to pull down. She knows that something is the matter. She knows that I am frightened and sad. Her response to it is to need her mummy all the more. "Don't go, Mummy!" She throws her arms round my neck and clings.

I sit cross-legged on the floor while she climbs into my lap with a book. At first, I can't concentrate. I'm too upset to follow a line of print. But gradually the act of reading exerts its spell. Images and snatches of narrative begin to come into focus. I am behaving like the other mothers, I think with satisfaction. There they are, in a circle, each with a child on her lap. Kitty's hot body becomes heavier with relaxation. Her feet are crossed, the little plump soles curved inside each other as they would have been in my womb. It is still easy and natural to her, this resumption of her prebirth shape. She has not yet fully stretched out. That I carried her thus is the sweetest thing in the world to me. Nothing and no one can take that away: not cancer, not idle talk, not death itself.

The bell rings for start of class. "I've got to go now, sweetheart." She reaches her arms up for a kiss.

I almost get out in one piece. But just as I am clambering over the slurry of jackets, cardigans, and Wellingtons that gathers beneath the pegs, a teacher with a long embroidered skirt and straggled hair comes up to me in a state. "It's awful! Awful! You must be so upset. Are you *coping*?" At the same moment, I become aware of someone else looking at me intently from the other side of the hall, a woman in her late thirties with a mane of curly black hair—Saskia is her name.

Saskia is a theater director at an alternative playhouse. She puts on avant-garde plays from Eastern Europe and is married to an opera singer. We met once at a drinks party. When I told her I wrote business pieces for a trade magazine, she closed her hooded eyes and drawled, "How interesting," before moving off sharply. We have not exchanged a word since.

But now her gaze crawls over my face like a fly feeding on a corpse. *Is she? Is she not?* Dying, that is.

This time, I know exactly how it happened. It is her friend Josephine, or Josie, a professional musician, leader of an organic vegetable delivery and the Walk to School campaign. The conversation would have taken place in Josie's kitchen, at the long table heaped with musical scores at one end, children's beakers and tomato seedlings at the other. Like me, the women have had their children late.

Their training does not easily reconcile them to long afternoons tending to the toileting needs of toddlers, stirring shit-filled nappies in buckets of ecologically sound detergent, waiting for husbands to come home and lecture them on the intricacies of a day at work while failing to notice the sinkful of dirty dishes. There is often a current of frustrated rage, of envy. My tragedy falls aptly into the middle of this, answering several needs at once.

Looking at her, I hear the conversation. "Mother died of cancer. Leaving five children. Terrible business. And now she's got it herself." Josie is generous and loyal; she will make soups and casseroles for friends in need, and look after their children. But she also has a taste for the dramas of others. "Got to have a mastectomy," she says, tying string round a joint of organic lamb and glancing sharply at her friend. Saskia has only ever heard this word in relation to elderly aunts or friends of her mother. It belongs to that great terrain of unmentionable female experience that you ardently hope and trust will never happen to you. Until it does. Her jaw falls open slightly. "Not just one, either," Josie continues, pausing for effect, while slashing the sides of the meat and pressing in pieces of garlic. Saskia stares dazedly at her mug. Finally, her friend flips the joint the right way up and bangs it into the oven. "Yep," she says. "Both of them got to go. And chemotherapy. Will lose her hair. Won't like that at all. Always was very fond of her appearance, that girl."

Now, with all this intoxicating material whirling in her head, Saskia is staring at me across the hall. *Will she? Won't she? Is she? Is she not? Dying, that is.* Her gaze is as blunt as a Gestapo border guard's. I am it for her, her first taste of mortality. The black fairy at Sleeping Beauty's birthday party. I look up at her, trying to make her avert her gaze. But curiosity overwhelms common courtesy, and she uses the opportunity to devour my face further. Her gaze quarters my face. I think of the chart of the side of beef in the local butcher's shop: rib, neck, chump, loin.

Meantime, my knees won't hold up. I am trembling with rage at this invisible assault. It appears that I no longer even have the strength to repel an arrogant woman's gaze.

"She *looked* at me!" I stutter later to R on the phone when I have staggered back up the hill and locked the front door. "She *looked* at me!"

"Yes, S?" he says in bewilderment. "I'm not sure I understand."

"In such a *way*!" I begin. "She would *never* have looked at me like that if I didn't have cancer!" Then, realizing that it's hopeless, I put the phone down and burst into tears.

Other people's reactions. There's not a person who has cancer who doesn't have to deal with them. Sometimes they can be as overwhelming as the cancer itself. What you crave is a kind hand, a kindly voice, simple understanding. You crave those close to you to draw closer, with the minimum of fuss. It seems so simple: to hold your hand, to permit your grief, to share your hope. What you so often get is other people's fear.

It was only thirty or forty years ago that cancer was the disease that dared not speak its name. You might be treated for and even die of it, without knowing you had it. This was for your own protection. It was not thought morale-boosting to be told you had a disease that would almost certainly kill you.

"When I was a young doctor and doing ward rounds with the professor, I remember he would stop to have a word with everyone—except the man in the corner with cancer. I was struck by that. Didn't the man with cancer need it most of all?" says a friend who later died of the disease himself. "I think it was fear that did it, the fear of not being able to do anything."

We live in a different age, or so we like to think. Big, bold, blinding light has been shone into all these dusty places. We have dismantled the old paternalist model. We train our doctors to be truthful. We are truthful ourselves. And why wouldn't we be? Half a century ago, cancer killed the majority of people who got it. Now some cancers, such as childhood leukemias and lymphomas, are largely curable. Although others, such as stomach and lung, remain stubbornly intractable, the basic trend is upward. Over two-thirds of those diagnosed today will still be alive five years later. And as more cancers become curable, the disease becomes more mentionable.

But cultural attitudes die hard. They have an afterlife, like radio-active isotopes. And the newly diagnosed patient still navigates a mixed and ambivalent world. In our busy lives, full of careers, mort-gages, children, pensions, cars, holidays, life insurance, gym mem-berships, plumbers' visits, kitchen extensions, meals out, and trips to the dentist, how welcome is serious illness, really?

When you enter the kingdom of the sick, you are taking more than a stimulating city break on an open return ticket. You are crossing a frontier to that other country—the night side of life. And if you think you can come back from there and talk about it, think again.

Don't be surprised if the civilian army is a little rough with you. It's got its own job to do; its own state to defend. "The important thing is to be positive," it says. "One foot in front of the other. That's the ticket." Rough translation: just because *you're* facing life-threatening illness doesn't mean *I* have to face it, too. It's very unpleasant. And anyway, what's the point when the worst might never happen?

"*Do* tell me if there's anything I can do," it says with brittle enthusiasm. "If there's any way I can help, do just *ask*."

People are often able to give things practically: a visit in hos-pital, a bunch of flowers, a card. They may be startlingly generous with their energy, their time, their money. But emotional demands they may find harder to cope with. If the sick person makes the mistake of responding to the question "How are you?" by begin-ning to vent even a tiny portion of the grief or fear they feel, they may be startled to see the silhouette of their friend on the horizon, running away as fast as they can. And with good reason. Because in the kingdom of the well, the grief of the sick person threatens the fragile structures of self by which we live.

So you get the stories. In the support groups, on the telephone hotlines, on the bulletin boards of cancer Web sites, or by talking at length with anyone who's had it. There is the woman who came down her front path after her diagnosis to see her best friend pull her hooded anorak down over her face and cross to the other side of the street. The friendship never was repaired. By the time the hooded friend thought she might like to see a little of her old friend while she was sick, guilt had confused the situation, and she let it go. There is the man dying of lung cancer whose siblings don't come to see him even though they live just half an hour away. "Always was a bit of an attention seeker, Jimmy. Needs to develop a more positive attitude. Get out of the house more." Jimmy's bed has been moved to the ground floor of his council flat because he can no longer climb the stairs; his oxygen tanks are delivered by the hospital.

There is the woman who has to have a stem-cell transplant for her aggressive breast cancer. She will be in isolation for twenty-eight days as she is taken as far into death as medicine will allow and then snatched back from the brink. She tries to talk to her mother and sister about her fears for herself and her children. Her prognosis is poor: a 10 percent chance of surviving two years. She would like the consolation of making plans, of knowing how her children might be cared for. But her mother and sister consider it their duty to give her pep talks. "Now, Mary, you've got to stop this morbid thinking. The doctors wouldn't be treating you if they didn't think they could cure you. You know you always did have a tendency to look on the dark side of life. You've got to be positive, or you'll make yourself ill."

As her hair falls out, her teeth come loose—as she vomits by the hour and is too weak to go to the toilet by herself—Mary longs for a visit from her mother and sister. She needs to hear those voices, those presences from earliest childhood, as she does this work of dying and yet not dying. But they do not come. "She's got a husband, hasn't she?" they ask, safely upholstered in daily routines in Louisville and Tennessee. As long as they don't come too close, they don't have to see that treatment has turned Mary into a five-stone ghost whom her husband carries to the bathroom like a child.

The loneliness of cancer. It spells itself out in so many different ways. For me, it is written in the intractable grammar of mother-lessness—who takes care of the motherless child with cancer? She is an object without a subject; she hangs in an evolutionary vacuum. "There are few overlapping generations with mutation carriers," as one *BRCA1* woman put it. The dizzying frailty of my situation, and that of my children, is brought home to me each day at the school gate, where I watch the other mothers' mothers come to support their daughters and their daughters' children.

It is spelled out, too, in the experience of serious illness within a community largely blessed by youth and health, orderly families, living parents. It's a liberal-left, *Guardian*-reading, right-thinking sort of community, with its organic deliveries, antiwar posters, and car abstention. It likes to think of itself as caring, and in many ways it is. But it has little experience of mortality. Under threat, it reacts with the robust reflexes of the well world, to protect its state, defend its order.

"It must feel terrible to lose a breast!" says one friend emotionally. "It's so much a part of a woman's femininity. I don't know how I'd cope with losing mine." She fingers the base of her throat in horror. "I just don't think I could *bear* it."

Well, it's a good job you don't have to lose *two*, then, I think savagely. And your ovaries. And your hair. That might seriously challenge your femininity.

"Well, with your job, I suppose . . ." mutters someone else. "All that stress. All those deadlines. Very bad for the immune system. A woman has to make choices."

This woman gave up work after her first child and is an inveterate attender of cranial osteopathy sessions, ashtanga yoga, toddler groups, and PTA meetings. Every now and again, while sweeping the colored rice grains off the floor for the thousandth time, or getting out her great pots to make marmalade in Seville orange season, she has a flicker of doubt about the life she has chosen. "How would it have been if . . . ?" Then a darker matter enters the turbid, sweet-smelling stew of her marmalade, adding the pungency of envy, of schadenfreude. "A woman has to make choices."

She doesn't mean to be cruel. She doesn't mean to insult those less fortunate than she is. She is just working out an orderly cosmology in a random world. We all do it.

My friend Gina is convinced I got cancer because of the HRT I took for three months after the removal of my ovaries. "It was a big mistake," she says. "You should never have done it."

Gina has never read a book about cancer in general. She has never read a book about breast cancer in particular. She has not been to my medical appointments to hear the specialists discuss *BRCA* mutations and their role in the formation of cancer. But she *has* read an article in the *Guardian* women's section. And another one in *Marie Claire*. And she does talk to her friends.

"No, Gina," I say. "The professor said the cancer must have been growing for at least a year. It couldn't have been the HRT."

"It was a mistake," she continues, not listening. "They should never have prescribed it."

I give up. What is at stake is not Gina's understanding of the etiology of my disease; it is her own protection against the same thing happening to her. She is painting a big red cross on her front door so the Angel of Death will pass over. We are talking at cross-purposes.

"You've heard of the cancer personality, I suppose." It is a Jungian analyst at a party.

Yes, I've read about it. Sad, repressed, prone to resentment and rage. Does he realize how rude this is? Not to mention cruel, misguided, and plain wrong: there is no evidence linking personality type with incidence of cancer. But it suits people to think so. We don't like depressives, and we don't like the cancerous. Insisting that depressives get cancer is the perfect way of expressing our latent hostility for both under the guise of righteous wisdom.

"Sounds like trying to punish the person with cancer for getting it," I say grimly. "Are you saying my mother got cancer because she was sad, repressed, miserable, and secretly wanted to die? I don't think so. She had five children to bring up. She was in the middle of life. I believe she was terribly unlucky."

But who wants to know about unlucky? It's messy. It's not edifying. It doesn't answer to our deepest needs for shape and order. Unlucky means the universe is out of control. And that's scary. Even to a Jungian analyst. "Well, there's a lot in this mind-body connection, you know," he says sententiously. "People who have a positive attitude get better faster. You can't deny it."

In the Middle Ages, if a woman was accused of being a witch, of having put a spell on her neighbor's corn or a child, she was tied up and thrown over a bridge. If she sank in the water, which had been blessed, she was innocent: the water had accepted her. If she floated, the water had rejected her and she was guilty. It was that simple. Well, I've got news for you: for many people, it still seems to be that simple. Cancer is a contemporary version of trial by ordeal. According to the majority of people, I got my disease because I failed to be positive. If I die of it, it will all be down to the same thing.

There is strenuous approval when the correct attitude is exhibited. "You're so *brave. Magnificent*! I don't think I could cope," says someone rushing past in the street.

Am I brave? I wonder, contemplating from outside this heroic, armored vision and whether I can allow myself to lay claim to it. I don't think I can, not in the sense in which she means it. The word *bravery* carries a sense of choice, a voluntary component. But what choice was there for me? As for being brave in the other sense, so often implied, that of enduring what is painful and difficult without complaint, I am definitely *not* brave. I *want* to complain. I *want* to bother people. And it is there that I get myself into trouble.

"I don't think I am brave, really," I say uncertainly. "I do feel . . . very frightened."

A hunted look appears in the woman's eyes. A shadow clips the sun. I notice with a pang that she has crossed her arms in front of her chest. "You've just got to be positive," she says in a high-pitched voice. "You'll be fine. I know you will. It's been caught early, hasn't it? Treatments are very good nowadays. I know a woman who . . . a friend of my mother's . . . amazing fighting spirit."

Everyone's mother has a friend. They all got breast cancer and they all survived. It was always down to their amazing fighting spirit. And if you don't exhibit enough of it, and publicly enough, you're in serious trouble.

I get to recognizing when an attack is coming on. Someone has been told I have cancer. (People are very helpful that way: I've lost track of the number of times I was told that Professor Leahy at the end of the street had cancer, despite the fact that I've never met him and he seems a gentle, rather reserved man who might not like his business being bruited about.) Milly or Mandy or Meg is in shock. She goes pale. A hectic spot appears in her cheek. This is soon followed by a dredging-about, helpless sort of look, which might make you want to put an arm around her shoulders. "Don't worry too much—I'm sure it'll all be fine. And anyway, it doesn't have to happen to you—it was all in my genes."

But then, bang, whack, eureka, she's got it: the solution! I can see it in the gathering glint in her eye. And whatever it is—coenzyme Q10, daily divided doses of buffered vitamin C, Bach Flower Remedies, acidophilus tablets, milk thistle, shark's fin powder, or putting your children up for adoption to go to Mexico and do Gerson Therapy (taking hourly juices of calf's liver extract and coffee enemas)—if you're not on top of it, you're not doing all you could.

"Please excuse . . ." I murmur. "I really must go."

But there's no stopping them. My cancer has put the fear of God into them. They're in an altered state. You can't just do that to someone and walk away as if nothing has happened. So now they're going to let me have it.

It's like standing at the bottom of a landfill site and watching a large truck back up to off-load. "Stop!" You put a hand up feebly to signal to the driver. "Please, stop!" But it's too late. He's already released the lever. And the whole lot—a gigantic slurry of organic potato peelings, rooibos tea bags, eco-nappies, colored healing crystals, cartons of vitamin pills, used sex manuals, textured UVP soya mince—is coming right down on top of your head.

Chapter Ten

The Beast Is Born

A FTER THE SECOND SESSION, my hair begins to go. I cling. I cling. But it falls away from me. I confront evidence of my own dying. There is hair on the pillow in the morning, in the brush, clogging the drain of the bath. I buy a wide-toothed comb and wash my hair infrequently. But it is going. It has its own rhythm. Like everything else, it is falling away from me.

I think of Dani and her three-year-old daughter. "One day, she found a photograph of me with my old hair and said: 'Who's this?' When I told her it was me, she didn't believe me. I used to have long black hair, you see . . . it was a feature." She underscores this with a glance from very blue eyes to check that I have understood. I have. With long glossy black hair and those eyes, she must have been stunning.

I think of Ruth Picardie, whose cancer was advanced when it was diagnosed, whose two-year-old twins watched their mother lose her hair, puff up with steroids, die. Toward the end, as described by her husband in a postscript to her beautiful and painfully brief memoir, *Before I Say Goodbye,* she is determined to read her children a bedtime story. She climbs the stairs on all fours, stopping frequently: the cancer is in her lungs; breathing is a challenge. But after a few sentences, the twins remove themselves quietly to the other bed, seeking the cradling arms of their father. She is left alone, a bloated silhouette against the light from the landing. They know; children know. A dying creature is not safe harbor.

I think, too, of a little girl I knew when we lived in Dublin: Anna was her name. Her mother was having treatment for breast cancer. We would see Anna and her brother at the swings in the local park with one teenage au pair after another. "It's the home situation. It's hard for a girl that age to cope with," said one woman. One day at school I saw Anna's mother, a slim woman my own age, with a head scarf on. She was kneeling beside her daughter with an arm encircling her.

Following her out to ask if I could help in any way, I had a sense that she was avoiding me. But then, on the pavement outside the nursery, she swung round and held her hands out to me, palms down. I peered at them in the Dublin dusk. Where each nail should have been was a charred mess. "It lays waste to everything, you see," she said. "Hair, nails, mouth. It's like a medieval sacking of a village. The lump was over five centimeters, in lots of lymph nodes. I'm on a trial. The moral is: do those self-examinations."

Later, we receive an invitation to Anna's third birthday party. We enter a lovely home in one of the city's finest suburbs: rugs and pictures, a real coal fire, elegant bookcases. At one end of the room a table has been laid out with platters of little sandwiches and sausages. There are balloons and decorations. A horde of three-year-olds dressed as fairies and pirates romps through the house, exhilarated by the space and music. But Anna just sits in her mother's lap, her legs wrapped round her waist, sucking her thumb. Her mother smiles and rolls her eyes at a friend next to her as if this were just a normal attack of separation anxiety. At one point, she tries to unpick her daugher's tiny fingers one by one from her body to get her to join in a game of pass the parcel. Nothing doing. Anna spends the whole of her third birthday party clinging to her mother like a newborn spider monkey. It is her day; she can do what she wants. What she wants most is to hold tight, and never to let go.

Meanwhile, my own children come looking for a mother. "Look,

Mummy, we did negative numbers in school today!" Michaela runs upstairs and opens her jotter on the bed. "It's really interesting!"

She lies on the bed and shows me a chart with an *x* and a *y* axis, numbers distributed evenly along the horizontal. "Look, you take four away from two and you get minus two, see?" She points to the numbers to the left of the vertical axis. "You take eight away from five and you get minus three. See?"

I nod.

"Now, this is really tricky. Listen to this. What do you get if you take minus four from minus four?"

I shake my head. "I can't think."

"Oh, come on, Mum, you can do it!" says Michaela. "It's not that difficult. You just have to concentrate."

But each time I try to focus on the numbers, they blur and ripple off. There is a logical crux at the center of the problem that I can't get ahold of. It's like trying to climb a castle staircase in a dream: the stairs spiral ahead of you, but the steps in front of you are missing. "I'm sorry, darling. It's the chemotherapy. It makes you stupid."

Kitty tramps upstairs with a children's cookbook, which she bangs down on the bed beside me. "I want to cook."

"Can it wait until another day, Kitty? I'm very tired."

"When?"

"Maybe next week? I don't have the energy right now."

"*Please,* Mummy!" she says. "You *never* cook with me. Everyone else in my class gets to cook with their mum."

I drag myself out of bed with grim determination. "OK, then, Kitty. But only something *very* simple."

But on chemotherapy, there's no such thing. Bending to fetch a mixing bowl makes the room sway. The tin baking cases are hidden at the back of the cupboard, which is full of junk. Kneeling on the floor to grapple in the dirty interior, I think of my mother. Her cupboards would never have been in this state, grimy and unused. Then I hear Kitty behind me, ladling out sugar and flour. "Uh-oh!" she says, and I turn to see the contents of a flour packet shoot past the edge of the table and onto the floor. I am not going to have the strength to clean that up. Right now, the terra-cotta tiles of the floor look so inviting. If I could only curl up on them, lay my head down, and sleep.

WE HIRE A CHILDMINDER. Bessie is in her late fifties and comes with one grubby reference consisting of two curt and guarded sentences dated from seven years ago, and plenty of gaps in her CV. But we are desperate and she is available. In the interview, she tells us that her mother died of cancer and that she nursed her to the end. Together with a warm smile, that does it for me.

Bessie does her duties with a good-natured slapdashery. A few jabs at the front teeth serve for teeth cleaning; a queasy swipe with a bacteria-ridden flannel to clean their faces; a quick scurry over the surface of the hair with a brush. Sometimes, a sign of neglect— a little cloud of fetid breath, lank hair, dirty fingernails—stirs me into action. What's going to happen to them if I die? My heart begins to thud between my ribs. Will their teeth go bad? Will their hair be matted? Will they have the look of *neglected* children? I stagger downstairs. "Bessie, I thought I *explained. This* is how I want you to clean the children's teeth. *Bessie! Bessie,* I don't think you're hearing me."

"Now, S. We mustn't get ourselves in a state. Must she, children? It's not good for Mummy, is it? Now, you go back to bed, and I'll bring you a nice hot cup of tea."

In the six months that she is with us, she never does quite get the children's names sorted out. "Michaela! I'm Michaela. And that's Kitty!" Michaela is still doggedly correcting her toward the end. Instructions to cook a particular meal tend to end in a stalemate of burned saucepans and confusion. We return from hospital appointments in London to find them tucking into a TV dinner of jam sandwiches and Mars bars. "They need a treat now and again, poor loves," says Bessie cheerfully.

On the plus side, Bessie is reliable and flexible. She is willing to stay late when we are held up by the hospital, or in London traffic. She is honest. And she is affectionate.

And I am in no position to complain. So they spend a summer watching daytime TV with the curtains drawn against the sun, eating ice creams, and feeding the ducks in the park. They bump up and down the narrow streets that surround us in Bessie's Fiat Uno, heading for the manicurist or the hairdresser, with the windows rolled down, "Lady in Red" blaring out of the sound system.

THE CHILDREN'S BIRTHDAYS come and go. They are bittersweet experiences. There is a clutching triumph: She is six; I am still here! And then the terror: What if this is the last one? We had planned to take Michaela's friends for a trip on the riverboat that runs from the center of Oxford to Abingdon, some seven miles downriver. In a meadow by the water, we would have games and a birthday picnic. "It's too much," says R. "We can't manage." But I am determined that nothing will be less for them because of my cancer. So the night before the outing sees us staying up late to fight furiously about quiz games, cakes, and party bags.

When we all meet at Iffley Lock the next morning, the weather is perfect: the sky cloudless, the air bright and clear. The children run from bridge to bridge in their party dresses, like a cloud of young butterflies, spying along the sleepy green bends of the river for a sign of the boat. Michaela runs with them, dress flying up, legs long and golden. When she sits on a painted bench to catch her breath, her friends offer their presents. I watch her face as she opens them, dazed, her gestures shy and happy. Perhaps she will be OK, I think. She has a capacity to inspire affection, to return it. Perhaps . . . even without me.

I lose myself in the excitement of the children as the boat arrives. They track a speck in the distance, flickering between the willows, then swoop to the lock with screams as the great metal hull draws nearer. We pile onboard with rugs, scooters, baskets, coolers, hats, presents, games. The children run about the silvered planks of the deck, and then go below, where they throw themselves on their backs to study the green water, higher than themselves, flowing past through the portholes.

We float downriver, past the dappled shade of the willows, the lock at Sandford, the boathouse at Radley; past the sandy coves where the herds of stout-legged cows come to drink in the evening; past a patient heron in a reed bed and the fishermen with their elaborate tackle and cabinets of maggots.

But then I come unstuck. It's the other mothers. At first, they chat idly about their children's progress at school, different teachers, a yoga class, a holiday they are planning. But then the conversation turns to secondary schools. It is no longer a leisurely passing of the time; there are things at stake here, the tempo has quickened. There is a fierce flurry as they exchange information: details about schools, private and state, feeder primaries, catchment areas (down to the nearest half a street), together with details of recent government reports on the schools, chunks of which are reported verbatim.

"Oh no, you can't go there!" says Josie, whose husband is a head of department at a famous private school and who knows about these things. "Failed its last inspection. Doomed by its catchment area. Forty percent English as a second language, you know. All very well at primary, but at secondary it's a serious handicap. At secondary, I always have believed, it's worth paying for teachers who are passionate about their subject."

The green-gold light of the water, which filled me with such pleasure just moments ago, turns dark and bitter. The stiff reeds look forlorn. The heron's cry is harsh. Secondary school . . . it seems so hopelessly far away. And the conversation of these mothers, seamlessly spinning the web of their children's future, stitching it with bright protective threads, fills me with desolation. Where will I be? What will become of my children?

By Kitty's birthday, I am no longer pretending that I can control anything. R and Bessie organize the food for her party. There are fairy cakes from Tesco, with slabs of icing so thick they look like colored Polyfilla, and wrinkled grey sausages. There are pirate plates and Barbie cups and a nasty pink cake with a pornographic fairy on top, which Kitty has been coveting for months. I sit on a plastic stool in the garden in my wig while the children tear round the garden in their summer dresses—trampling the food into the grass—and jump on and off a small inflatable bouncy castle in the rear. Their motion makes me nauseous; the bright sunlight makes my head ache; the lurid colors of the bouncy castle trigger hot flashes.

"Are you here to help?" asks a pregnant woman with long blond hair. I have met this woman before. We had a whole conversation about phonetic versus orthographic spelling. But she doesn't recognize me now. And there is something about the torpid way I am squatting on the plastic stool that makes her think of hired help. I grunt noncommittally. She waits for me to explain myself. But I don't have the energy. She would be shocked. There would be exclamations of concern and horror, the pressure to give an account: the Tale of the Lump, the Tale of the Wig, the Tale of Treatment. So I say nothing. She will make inquiries; it will be simpler that way. Eventually, she turns away with an odd look. "Well, it's a lovely day for it anyway."

And then it's over—party bags distributed, separation tantrums endured, children's clothes recovered—and I drag myself back to bed.

"Where's Mummy?" I hear Kitty ask in the kitchen. "I want to show her my new glitter-glue set. And my bead kit for making bracelets from Selma. And my mermaid book."

"Not now, darling," says R. "Mummy's gone upstairs. She's very tired."

"She's *always* tired," says Kitty suddenly, with unwonted ferocity. Something about its being her birthday, the day when she is supposed to be given whatever she wants, has triggered this protest. "She's *always* in bed. She *never* has any energy. It's not *fair!*"

One morning, I wake to find Michaela fully dressed and looking down at me. "I hate you, Mummy," she says with chilly precision.

"What?" I struggle to surface. I must have slept through the alarm, through R getting the children up, through the whole of breakfast, and now they're on the point of leaving.

"Let's fight!" says Michaela. "I bet I can beat you."

"I'm sure you can. But that's not a very good idea, is it?"

"I'm really good at fighting. I can beat Florence and Miranda and Aisha, and sometimes I can beat Daniel and Jamie, too."

I feel a surge of panic. Is she getting into fights with her friends? Has she become disturbed because of my cancer?

"What do you mean, Michaela? Do you have problems at school?"

She flops on the bed and lifts her arm into the wrestling position. "Come on, silly. Try it. I bet I can beat you."

"I'm sorry, Michaela. I just don't have any energy. The chemotherapy."

There is a flash of hostility in her eyes. Then a wash of exhaustion, the turbid eddy of a strong tide that has nowhere to go. She is not happy, I think, looking at her pale, intent face.

"Come on, it's time to go and clean your teeth." I struggle out of bed.

"I'm not coming!" she says.

"Come on, Michaela. You've got to . . ."

She appraises me through a narrowed gaze. "You can't *make* me. Can you?"

Downstairs, there is the sound of R scraping the chairs on the tiles as he sweeps up after breakfast, the cupboard doors banging shut. I need him to back me up. But I'm too tired to go and fetch him. I'm also too tired to call out to him. My lungs don't have that kind of strength anymore. We are at cycle four now. The impact of the poisons is cumulative, and speech and movement must be rationed.

"You mustn't do this to me, Michaela," I say, panting slightly. "You really mustn't do this."

We look at each other on the landing. "You can't *make* me," she repeats.

Light-headed, I begin the slow crawl back to bed. She stares at me in disbelieving silence.

"I hate you!" she says. "I *completely completely* hate you!"

How I remember it, that hatred. My loathing for my mother if she exhibited the least sign of weakness knew no bounds. I hated her for each greying hair that appeared on her head, each hesitant or evasive gesture. I hated her for her drab clothes as she grew older and lost sexual confidence: those pastels and beiges, those timid cuts, those cheap, unlovely materials. I hated her for her hesitancy, the way her persona outside the home grew sketchy and worn, as if rubbed out by long years of domestic submission.

Most of all, I hated her when she became ill. I wasn't to know that I was hating her for her dying. I just knew I hated her for her weakness, her loss of vitality. But her biggest crime, the biggest wound to my young psyche, was her withdrawal. The immense and catastrophic withdrawal. In the place where a mother should be, there was nothing.

ONCE A WEEK, I make the journey across a triangle of wasteland—hotly contested by developers—over a dirty rivulet by the name of Boundary Brook, and up through a building site for the new oncology center to a scuffed green prefab building in the grounds of the Churchill Hospital. This is where Maggie's has its home.

Maggie's was the brainchild of Edinburgh landscape gardener and author Maggie Keswick Jencks before she died of breast cancer in 1995. On a grueling drugs trial, she conceived of a place where a cancer patient might be offered support as well as treatment—a gentler and more humane path through the disease than was available within the existing medical system. The first center was opened by her husband, Charles, and a group of friends one year after her death. Now there are nine across Britain, offering a mix of relaxation and meditation classes, art therapy, support groups, nutritional and financial advice. The centers are known for their glamorous architecture, aimed at boosting the spirits of those entering them. But the Oxford unit is in an interim state, busily raising funds for a new building. In the meantime, it occupies the prefab on the site of the Churchill Hospital, itself a conversion of wartime Nissen huts.

This is fine by me. I did much of my primary education in just such a building, with its hastily assembled concrete foundations, its jerry-built windows, its bulging green walls. I feel at home here.

One half of this building is devoted to overspill from the Churchill's oncology department. There is the regulation format: laminate reception desk, rows of chairs against the wall, a grid of cubicles with examining beds. There is the regulation smell, too: noxious and chemical. At the other end is Maggie's. It's a small space, but friendly. There is a round table covered by a patterned oilcloth, a vase of flowers, and a few bookshelves with a motley collection of cancer-related books. Someone welcomes you with the offer of a cup of tea or coffee. In a room off the main area is a circle of brightly colored armchairs. Made of blond wood, each upholstered in a different fabric, they look like something parachuted in from a Swedish design magazine or a smart advertising agency. They are a donation.

Every week, I take a seat in one of these armchairs with a group of other patients and try to share a tiny part of the confusion that is cancer. Despite our mix of age, race, and gender, we share a fundamental vulnerability. We have had our bodies taken apart like a cat's cradle and put back together again. We are frail and forgetful. Physically, we are not what we were. As for our mental health, at the back of the mind, or at the forefront, or some unspecified middle region, we have all had to consider that we may not have that long.

The group facilitator, a clinical psychologist who has spent many years working with people with cancer, leads us in some breathing exercises. He encourages us to breathe in to a count of three, out to a count of four; to let our minds go blank and allow the little tugging anxieties that cloud a consciousness to drift off. I try to do as he suggests. Sitting next to the other patients, whom I scarcely know but feel so close to, I register small sounds: the flutey stakeout of the birds beyond the window, the snarl of the diggers laying the foundations for the new cancer hospital, the subdued roar of the vacuum next door. For a while, I truly try to consider the view—so often mentioned by cancer patients and those working with them—that life itself is a terminal condition, that past and future are an illusion, that all any of us has at a given moment is the breath we are taking right now.

For a few hours after this session I feel almost normal, as if I might manage. But the feeling never lasts. Reentry into civvy street puts too much pressure on it. For the other pole of my social existence during this time is the school gate, which is toxic to my mental health. As fast as Maggie's puts some well-being or poise back into my failing mind and body, the school gate seems to use it up again.

"The builders are coming next week to do the new kitchen. We're going to have maple floorboards, a central island. French doors to the garden, of course. And upstairs, in the en suite, we're going to have a wet room, can you believe it?" The woman's lips go in and out, painted scarlet. "I've got my installation accepted in a great new gallery in Hackney. Have you heard of it, the O-Zone? Made from a converted bottling factory. So great. The launch is next Tuesday. Would you like to come?" "What costume is Michaela wearing for World Book Day?" trills someone else. "Freddy is going as Superman. We had such a crazy time last night making his outfit from an old school tunic of my mother's." "You'll never guess what I've been up to this morning," says a third. "Booked a holiday. Tuscany. Two weeks. The villa has its own little pool. We can't afford it, of course. But hey, you're only young once!"

It's hard to listen to someone's kitchen-extension plans at length when your own preoccupation is with whether you are going to live to bring up your children. You don't want to know about their holidays if you're struggling to get yourself to the end of the street. And as for children's costumes, which you never manage to make, the mention of them makes you feel desperate.

But worse than any of this is the appearance of other mothers' mothers. For years, I have worked hard to screen them from my awareness. At university, you don't have to think about them that much. Your friends are still emerging from adolescence and in a mood to pretend that mothers don't count. They might express exasperation about them now and again, while disappearing each holiday to be cooked for, cared for, and driven back with freshly laundered clothes and that emblem of care: a new winter coat. In the long years establishing work, an adult life outside the home, it's almost possible to ignore them altogether. But then there is a flurry of weddings, which puts them back center stage. The sight of all those functional families and mothers-of-the-bride proves too much for you. So you cry sick. As long as you don't go near any of the normative business of being a woman, you don't have to confront it.

But having children puts you right back at the heart of the matter. There they are, the everlasting dyad, mother and daughter, everywhere. They are browsing the aisles in Marks & Spencer, buying baby clothes together. They are sitting in the hospital clinic waiting for a pregnancy checkup. The mothers return with a vengeance at the birth, to help their daughters with housework, cooking, caring for the baby. At the school gate they are there in force. Gradually, of course, you realize that they've been there all along: that that's why Jinny or Jessica or Janet is so stable and calm, got herself a proper job at the correct time, writes thank-you letters that are respectful and mature, seems to be able to manage, to know how to behave. No wonder you weltered about for years in depression, addiction, serial unemployment, fragmentation, futility. They had it all along, the secret weapon, the secret ticket to the female future: a mother.

Other mothers' mothers. I devour them more jealously than a wife devours the anatomy of a husband's mistress. Their thickening waists. Their sensible footwear. Their silvered hair, cut expensively in stylish bobs or plainly chopped. I study their skin, which menopause has turned parchment thin or plump and glabrous. How would my own mother have been? I wonder. Her hair was just beginning to grey. She had a tiny silver widow's peak. But she was way too young for menopause: no aching joints and memory lapses for her. She is preserved forever in my mind at forty-two, so old as she seemed to me then, so young as I know her to be now. So I stand in the playground studying the other mothers' mothers. I catalog the stiffness of those grandmaternal knees as they bend to pick up a child's book bag or scooter. I recognize the faint irritation when they are trying to do too many things at once—short on estrogen, parallel processing is an issue—and get flustered. I listen to them as they express pride in their grandchildren, which they do not try to hide, as they express pride in their involvement in their daughters' lives, which they also do not try to hide. Afterward, I have auditory hallucinations of their voices.

I could tell you their movements: the day of the week when one comes to stay with her daughter to help out; when another takes her grandchild swimming; when a third cooks for her daughter who is struggling to combine parenting and work. My senses seem tuned to a single precise frequency: Radio Mother Envy. "The transition back to work has been a lot better than I expected," says one young mother happily. "I'm only working two days a week. And my mother is looking after Georgie. It makes such a difference, doesn't it, to have child care you can really *trust*?"

"Oh, my mother cooked for me every day through pregnancy," runs another's happy boast. "When I was finishing my PhD she came and stayed with us for weeks. Just to take care of the house. She did the same when I was finishing my first book. And now she gives the baby a massage every day and looks after the older one twice a week. Yes, you can do a lot with a mother. Everyone ought to have one, really."

Someone else explains how protracted pressure at work has given her a bout of flu. "So my mother's coming to stay for a few days. She'll bring some homemade meals with her. Oh, I know all the stuff about mothers and daughters and control via food. But sometimes it's just so *nice* to be cooked for. I don't know what I'd do without her, really. And of course, the children just love having her."

They don't mean to be cruel. They don't mean to trumpet their good fortune in the face of another's deprivation. I have told each of these women that my mother died young. Each has felt and expressed surprise, concern. But there it stopped. It is just another world, a world where you don't have to imagine what it's like to go through life without something as essential as a mother.

AT ABOUT THIS TIME, the Beast is born. He appears one morning after the children have gone to school. The house is quiet and I have crept along the corridor to clean my teeth. Dental hygiene is very important when on chemotherapy; all the leaflets will tell you.

I have just snapped a length of floss from a carton when I catch sight of it in the mirror. Brown eyes. Ashen skin. Grizzled head. Bald, or almost. Hard to tell its age—somewhere out on the long road between forty and sixty. As for the sex, you wouldn't say it has one. It has a repulsive kind of androgyny.

"Get away from me! Get!" I start pulling the thread vigorously between my teeth. "You can't haunt me, with your scurfy head and your rotten breath. I've got friends. There are people who love me. I've got their names and addresses. I've even got numbers."

"Sssss!" it says with a soft rattle.

I put out toothpaste and start brushing my teeth systematically: twenty strokes on the upper left, twenty on the lower, twenty on the upper right, twenty on the lower.

Beast isn't impressed. It watches me with a cool gaze, in which there is something mocking. There is something else, too, something worse—that makes me start up in fury—a wet gleam of pity. "Get away from me! You can't touch me. I've got twenty thousand pounds of savings in a Virgin tracker fund. I've got a job. Or I did, before I got cancer. I've got an e-mail account. I've got a husband. And a house. I've got all my teeth."

The thing you need to know about Beast is it's not savory. Beast spends most of its time in bed. Wakes lethargic in the mornings, heaving its sweating body up through a mess of dreams. What are they? Something shameful. Something dishonorable. Sex, is it? Beast had a childhood, too. A youth. And all its old friends are paying their visits. Old lovers. Old houses. Dead mothers. Dead pets. It's a real processional in there. Beast wakes up exhausted every morning from this traffic with the past.

Downstairs, there's the rock and swell of family life. Beast used to be a part of this, but has long since dropped out of it. There is someone Beast used to call a husband—God knows how it secured itself one of those—struggling to bring up two children single-handedly. He doesn't find it easy. There's a lot of shouting and banging as they get themselves out of the house in the morning. Wailing, scraping, shoving, and thumping. It makes Beast's head throb.

Finally, a patter of footsteps on the stairs. "Good-bye, Mummy," says a creature with a chaste oval forehead and golden hair that looks as if she has just walked out of a quattrocento painting. "Bye-bye, Mummy," says another with the face of an angel. They seem to want something from Beast, and linger by its bed. "Ggrbyye," says Beast, struggling to get out some phonemes with its thick slab of tongue and twisting its head in an effort not to tarnish the little angels with its stinking breath. "Ggrbyye . . . ggrbyye . . ."

Sometimes Beast gets up. "Musssh gedup. Frsssh. Air. Goodfer. Musssh," it mutters to itself, pushing back the duvet. No throwing back for the Beast, nothing so dynamic. Everything is slow now, very slow. The molecules of poison are reaching into the heart of the cells. Nothing is growing; nothing reproducing. We are approaching ground zero.

Beast pads heavily over to the cupboard to find some clothes. But when it opens the doors, what it sees there is baffling. There are all these little colored things, chic and pretty. Tight jackets and wraparound cardigans. Skinny jeans and ruffled blouses. Dresses and belts and boots with a heel.

Beast couldn't wear any of this. That white blouse next to its skin would look macabre, like Death and the Maiden. That fresh print smock on its collapsed chest would be too sad. And maybe someone else could do the little cardigan with the animal print col-

lar when bald on top, but it isn't Beast. *Gross* is the word that comes
to mind. The way teenage girls say it, sashaying down the street
with their little headphones on and their hipster belts. "Truly *gross!*"

Beast could weep for itself. To all its humiliations, does the act
of clothing its broken body have to be added? It fetches out some
old maternity slacks with an elasticized waist, and pulls on a jumper
without registering the color. It would like the simple dignity of
escaping this room without having to look at itself again in the mirror. But not so fast: there's the question of its head. If it goes out
like this, people will stare. Baldness has never been a neutral act.
It's a symbol: of religious dedication, wartime humiliation, sexual
subversion. Female baldness is more freighted still.

Sick person. Dying person? How long before . . . ? they will
wonder. Before it's halfway down the street, Beast will be felled
with emotional exhaustion from all that interrogative horror. So it
reaches for its wig. The beautiful real-hair wig that a friend brought
to the hospital in the wake of diagnosis. Beast draws the nylon cap
tight on its head, fans out the lovely blond tresses. But no, that
won't do either. "Probably came from some Russian or Polish girl
selling her hair to feed her family." Someone's sharp comment
rattles in its head. Is this what it's come to? Beast, who *was* once
young, who *was* once beautiful, turned into a sexual vampire, an
elderly monster decking itself out in a young woman's hair?

When Beast reaches the street (in a blue kerchief with a bold
design of lozenges to draw attention from the face), it is quiet. It's
midafternoon and children are at school. Able-bodied adults are at
work. Housewives are at home or browsing the aisles at Tesco. This
is a relief. Latterly, interacting with the human race has become too
difficult for Beast, who avoids it at every opportunity.

It sets off for the park, with its shambling, rocking gait. Rock,
squelch. Rock, squelch. Its overriding concern is to reach the end
of the street without bumping into a neighbor. It manages that
without mishap. But then there's the question of crossing the wider
road to the park.

It stands on the pavement watching the cars. They come so fast.

Beast can't get the hang of them. There are two close together, one straggling behind, then a long interval and three in close succession. After a while, Beast realizes that several people have crossed while it's been standing there waiting. There is a sudden cry from a toddler descending a slide; Beast thinks someone is yelling at it to hurry up, and steps off the pavement.

But it's all at the wrong moment. A car whoomps to a halt, another behind it. There is the blare of a horn. "What the fuck!" the first driver mouths into his windscreen. Beast's heart is pounding. It feels a surge of adrenaline. And it lurches forward. Or it would if it could. But the problem now is that the muscles won't work. There is too much poison. The neural firings have gotten clogged; the messages can't get through. So Beast lurches to the left, in a panic, trying to get away from the car with the angry driver.

The driver can't see why Beast has gone off to the left like that, rather than crossing the road directly. So he keeps his fist down on the horn. The blare of it echoes out into the day. Some crows flap up from the trees. The toddler, back at the top of the slide, turns round to stare. Beast reaches the central island, the one that is always full of daffodils in spring. Truly, it thinks to itself, things have reached such a pass, it needs a companion to get across the road.

In the park, an old man is walking a dog. A couple of teenagers are playing with a football, tossing it back and forth to each other across the sloping green. Beast takes the path that runs along the top of the park, the one that gives you a swooping view of the spires of Oxford: St. Mary's, the university church, the icing-sugar pinnacles of the Bodleian, the handsome lantern of the Radcliffe Camera.

Beast comes to a halt in front of a stand of oak trees. It looks up at a particularly fine one, with vaults of green leaves and ribbed bark. As Beast watches, a breeze lifts the leaves on a lower branch. There is a stiff rustle. This spreads from one branch to the next, from that one to the one above it, and so on, until a climacteric of sound, springing from a thousand sources, possesses the tree. Formerly, this would have been a source of wonder to Beast. It might have felt a corresponding movement in its own body, a kind of internal dance. It might even have tried to find words for it. But now it stands in front of the tree without sensation. Nothing.

This tree could be wrapped in cling film from head to toe, each individual leaf sealed in it. Beast cannot touch it. Cannot feel it. Cannot smell it. There is no connection.

On the green, the boys run after the football. They chug up and down, legs whirring in a mechanical motion, like strips from a comic book. Why do they do that?

Before the oak tree, unable to feel a thing, Beast acknowledges that something has broken. Beast has come adrift from life itself. In this beautiful midsummer day, with grass and sky and leaves, it has no place. It turns away and begins to shamble back down the street. Rock, squelch. Rock, squelch. Halfway down the road, it hears the scrape of a neighbor's door. Oh, horror! Beast scuttles along the hedge, up the last bit of path, slams shut its own front door. Thank God. In its bedroom once again, it peels off the kerchief, the unlovely clothes, and eases its body between the sheets. The ash branch taps familiarly on the window. Beast closes its eyes. For it all to go away . . . the world, and everything in it. As if it had never been.

"I can't do this anymore," I say one morning at breakfast. R is busy doing the children's lunch boxes. He is cutting crusts off sandwiches, washing apples for snack time, filling water bottles. He is finding shoes, cardigans, book bags, jackets. He is filling in the form allowing Michaela to go on a school trip to the history museum, along with finalizing my self-assessment tax returns for the previous year; marking several boxes of essays that have arrived by recorded delivery; scouring the Internet at night to research survival rates of *BRCA1* women with Grade III 2.8 cm tumors; and planning when to get the plumber in for the broken boiler, which we can't afford to replace. "I just can't do it," I repeat.

"Oh, don't worry," he says without looking up. "Just another couple to go. You'll get through it."

"I don't think you heard me," I say icily.

"I know it's awful, S. I know it's really hard," he says. "But there are only two more. Really. We'll get through it."

"Excuse me. I would be grateful if you would listen. *I. Can't. Do. This. Any. More.*"

He blinks at me with soft brown eyes—Michaela's eyes, enormous, flecked with gold—in which a reluctant pain formulates itself. He looks at me as if I have done him personal injury. "S," he says, shoveling the tide of lunch boxes, book bags, helmets, and scooters ahead of him down the narrow hall before unlocking the front door. "Have you been taking your antidepressants recently? We can't *afford* for you not to take them. I can't stay on top of *everything*."

"NO ONE CAN force you to have treatment," says GP Jocetta Bailey quietly, sitting in the blue-painted chair in my bedroom, the ash branch tapping on the pane behind her. "It is your own free choice."

This idea is both shocking and seductive. It is like being told that you can run away from school or an unhappy marriage.

"I have never felt I had a choice," I say. "Not really. Because of the children."

Bailey sighs. Checkmate. I have seen a picture of them on her desk, three sturdy little boys in football jerseys, as full of life as she is herself. She wouldn't have a choice either.

She tries a different tack. "A few months ago you were clear about your decision. You knew it was going to be hard, but you were clear. Is there any particular reason for this change of heart?"

Well, there was the incident at three o'clock that morning, which saw me defecating in my own bed, having succumbed to a virus picked up from the children, R rushing along the landing with the shit-smeared sheets, while I stood in the bathroom on trembling legs, trying to clean myself up.

But more generally, my complaint is that I don't exist anymore. Everything that makes me *me* is gone. I can't read, think, work, talk, swim, run, dance, laugh, look at a tree, interact with a friend, cook, do a basic act of care for my children, or get to the end of the street. "This isn't me," I explain. "I can't live with not being me anymore. The degradation. The nothingness of it."

She nods. "You know, I have made home visits to two other women this year at roughly the same stage of chemotherapy. They said very similar things."

"Really?"

"Yes." She nods again. "You are not alone. No one says this is easy." There is a pause. "But there are only two more cycles."

"If it comes back, I would have to do more of it. Except that this time there would be no chance of a cure. We would just be buying time. And I'm so frightened of it coming back in my brain or my bones. I don't want to be mentally degraded. I don't want to be physically crippled. I don't want to be puffed up by steroids, unrecognizable. Hobbling about on sticks. I can't bear the idea of the children having to watch that. I can't bear the idea that that's what they would remember of me."

There is a long silence. Unlike almost everyone else I have talked to about the subject, Jocetta Bailey doesn't rush in to tell me the cancer is not going to come back. She doesn't assure me that I won't die, that I am going to be fine, and that all I have to do is think positively. She is careful not to tell me what she doesn't know. And for this I am immensely grateful.

"I have researched Dignitas," I continue. "The assisted-suicide organization. I am determined that if it came back, I would take things into my own hands and go to Switzerland. But I'm frightened that by that time, I might not have the strength to do what was necessary."

"You wouldn't have to go to Switzerland," says Jocetta Bailey firmly.

I lean back on my pillows. "How do you mean?"

"I mean that if it came to that, I see it as part of my duty as a GP to support a patient to do what is best for him- or herself. There would be help. I would help."

"Really?"

"Really."

I have had this conversation before, or one like it, with a Macmillan cancer nurse. Should doctors assist in euthanasia in cases of terminal illness involving great suffering where the patient has decided to end it? The nurse thinks not; I think they should. "Why do you think so?" she asks. "Because I think someone with cancer already suffers from immense social isolation. I don't think that anyone facing such a terrible and degrading illness should have to endure the additional isolation of having to execute themselves alone. Like a heroin addict jacking up in a back alley. I believe dying should be a social act, a time of acceptance and togetherness."

So Jocetta Bailey's avowal makes all the difference to me. "I'll finish the course," I say.

She nods, reaches for her briefcase. "I had hoped you would say that. Now we need to look at medication. We may need to boost your dose of antidepressants. There's no point being unrealistic. No one gets through this without help. Lots of it. And if the school gate is getting you down, maybe you should get away from it all for a while."

Chapter Eleven

Getting Across

A WEEK LATER, we are standing on the pier in Oban, on the west coast of Scotland, waiting for the ferry to Tiree to pull in. It has been a long drive. We are all tired, the car a litter of crayons, half-completed sudoku puzzles, biscuit wrappers, and banana skins, like the floor of a monkey's cage. But the sight of the harbor in the late-afternoon light lifts us — sun bouncing off the granite blocks of the quay, the little squall of painted fishing boats, the wide dazzle of sea and islands.

There is something magical, too, about watching the ferry come in to berth. Entering the harbor wall, it begins its long curve to port, sending out an oblique wash across the bay. The great diesel engines that have driven it across the Sound of Mull are cut, power transferred to the more delicate electric motors in the bow. The whole five-thousand-ton weight seems to hover on a point, before sliding smoothly into place alongside the pier.

"When can we get on? When?" Michaela and Kitty chant, swinging over a quayside rope holding Rabbit and Dolly Jayne.

"Come away from that side!" I say sharply, with a vision of Kitty chasing the doll down the narrow fissure that separates the boat from the pier.

"There's no need to shout, Mummy," says Kitty solemnly, with delicate four-year-old umbrage.

And I think of my own mother, who got vertigo on cliff tops, in the towers of ruined castles across Scotland, in the upper gallery of a church.

A ferryman in blue overalls and a weathered West Highland complexion gestures the children wordlessly back. He unfastens the quayside rope and pulls up an iron stairway. The foot passengers begin to descend with that tottering gait and slightly dazed look of people whose retinas are drunk on sunshine and 360-degree views.

"How long will it take, Mummy?" asks Michaela when we have bumped the car into the hold and made our way up the narrow staircases, through the smells of frying fat and stale beer, out onto the open rear deck.

"About four hours."

"Four hours! That's so long!" she says, her patience exhausted now that we are a single journey from our goal. "Will Grandpa be there to meet us?"

"Yes."

"How long are we staying?"

"Ten days. Nine nights."

"Will we swim every day?"

"It depends on the weather. But as often as possible."

"Will Grandpa buy us an ice cream every day?"

I smile. "Who knows? Maybe."

"Grandpa likes buying us ice creams," comments Michaela.

"Yes, he does, doesn't he?"

As always, contemplating this benign, rosy-cheeked vision of my father, I am startled. It seems impossible that the sometimes oppressive figure of my childhood has metamorphosed into this jolly Father Christmas. But for the children, it seems, their grandfather is an unambivalent source of pleasure. For them, he holds no fear. "*Why* does he?" asks Michaela.

"Well, when you're older, you enjoy giving children pleasure. Especially your own grandchildren. It's nice."

"When Grandpa buys us an ice cream, he has one, too," says Michaela with a child's observational powers.

"Yes, that's true, isn't it?" A thought comes to mind. "You know, maybe Grandpa likes buying you ice creams because he didn't get enough of them when he was a kid."

Michaela's eyes widen. "Why?"

"Well, it was wartime, you see. And during the Second World War, Grandpa's father was a prisoner with the Japanese. For several years, no one knew whether he was alive or dead, not even my grandma. So Grandpa didn't see enough of his father when he was little. And when he *did* come back, Grandpa got a shock—he hardly knew him. Maybe that's partly why he likes buying you ice creams. It's like doing the things for you that there wasn't always someone around to do for him. Who knows?"

MIRIAM HAS LAID the table with a hand-embroidered white tablecloth. There are cut glasses, napkins, and wildflowers from the shore in front of the house. We take our places on the long pine benches, while the children head for the swing, which my father has made from a piece of old sacking and rope and which is hung from the steep wooden staircase that leads to the attic rooms. They kick it out in wide loops that fall just short of the table. At seventy-two, my father has built his own house and can arrange it as he likes. The main room has several picture windows looking out over the sea and is filled with a large red and gold rug. At one end is the long table where meals take place; at the other, a stove bracketed by two armchairs. The space in between is scattered with beanbags. A free-standing telescope is positioned at one of the windows. Upstairs, there is a pair of rooms, one of which serves as Miriam's studio, the other as my father's study. This is furnished with a plain trestle table, like an architect's drawing board, and two extra beds for grandchildren. He has made the mattresses himself, from lengths of PVC material lashed together with blue and white cord. At the end of each of these beds he has inserted a porthole window, with a spectacular view of sea and cliffs, which the sleeper can look out at while lying down.

We chat about the journey and the weather, while the children run about the house laying claim to things: the study upstairs, the Georgian doll's house from my own childhood—now a drafty hutch without its original furniture—the beanbags, and the telescope, which they peer down intently but have to duck their heads round to have a chance of seeing anything.

We don't talk about cancer for the moment. We don't need to. During this time on chemotherapy, my father has phoned each day at 4:00 p.m. It is a window of opportunity between his day's work—checking the cottages, fetching the boats on and off the water, fixing problems with loos or showers, managing his workers, fielding tricky customers—and his evening shift, spent processing sales calls and bookings. These phone calls have been a space out of time and out of any previous relationship we have had. In them I have been free to express my fears, my shock and fury at my altered body, the helpless anguish at any thought of leaving the children early. And my father has listened.

In the long years under my father's roof, this is not something that I remember. Expression of feelings was discouraged. In our narrow beds after my mother died, each of us wept alone, slept alone, eventually left home alone. We were the White Russians, lucky to escape with our lives, carrying our exile with us. The closest we would ever get to a homeland again was the flare of a lit match before a chipped icon, in lonely bedsits across London. Mother Russia gone, we fell apart in disputes. But the isolation had begun long before that. My parents seemed too busy, too stretched by the pressing physical needs of all their children, the blows that life had dealt them, to take on much in the way of answering to the emotional needs of their brood. My sense is of a great roar—the din of this large, striving, talented, damaged, vital, visceral family, framed by my father's disturbed drive, his furious discontent, which no action or outcome could assuage, my mother's fateful reticence. Behind it were pieces of silence, the haunting spaces between objects, offcuts, which later in life, you find yourself drawn to.

Grief is not polite. It is not dainty. It does not announce itself in respectful requests and orderly tears. It is more likely to tear the world apart, to open its rib cage and send everyone running. It may be articulate in atrocities and silent in a drawing room. I believe that if I had spoken to my father at any point, as a dependent under his roof, I would have been given short shrift. He had not space. Mistrustful of himself, overwhelmed by the solitary responsibility for these children, he surrendered himself to the elemental fury of "keeping the show on the road." Life was a brute business, full of random cruelty and injustice, where everything that was most dear could be extinguished in a second. The best that could be done was to shrink it to a set of duties that could safely be discharged. This tribe of children—now seven, with the addition of Miriam's two—had to be fed, clothed, shod, and educated. They had to have a few life skills hammered into them. And they had to be gotten safely out into the world.

Struggling to maintain the coordinates of a middle-class family life, with no space for suffering, my father ran his home like a military operation. His labor to underpin it was unremitting. There was the long drive into Aberdeen each day to get to work and take two of his children to the schools they had attended before my mother died, on roads that were treacherous and often snowed up. Once home again, there was a hill of tasks: chopping logs; managing the generator (the house had no electricity); feeding children; feeding animals; cleaning the house; cleaning the stables; directing homework. There was the evening ritual of the accounts, as he struggled to make ends meet. Tax returns, bookings and inventories for the letting cottages he still maintained twenty miles away. There were children's illnesses, some serious, some not so serious, all terrifying given my mother's death. There were eruptions from the sex lives of this brood of adolescents, which had to be controlled. Other signs of disorder—petty stealing, sleeplessness, bed-wetting, rageful outbursts—also had to be controlled, or crushed; none could be allowed to derail the central mission. Children had to make the correct choices of subjects at school, university, career. They must also learn to see the Truth correctly, about the world and themselves, or they might go astray in life and make wrong choices, as he felt that he himself had done.

Love was not on the menu. Or not anything that could easily be recognized as such. You might know love in the fury that greeted you if you were back later than you had promised; in the excoriating contempt if you were caught smoking yourself half to death in your wretchedness. ("Reaching for your crutch again, eh?" came the heavy sneer. "You think that's going to help?") You might know it in the obsessive nightly rounds he made to check for gas leaks in the Superser heaters. Alarming, those sudden appearances in the darkness of your bedroom, his tall form clad in the tartan dressing gown my grandmother had sewn, a large torch in his hand. Is he sleepwalking? Is he conscious? He doesn't trust the evidence of his senses: the minute he has checked that gas supply is shut off, he bends to check again.

You would know it in the forbidding stare that greeted you if you asked to borrow some money, a piece of paper, a stamp. What is going to become of a child who at nineteen is still not capable of buying herself a stamp?

You would know it particularly if, for whatever reason—a night spent in tears, the feeling that you simply could not face another grim industrialized meal—you failed to greet Miriam in the morning as she stood nervously at the head of the table in place of my mother. "Good morning, Miriam!" My father would proffer us our lines. "Good morning, Miriam!" If we said nothing, or failed to address her in the correct tone, his tolerance was breached. He might rear up at the end of the table, knocking his chair to the floor. He might shove a few children against a doorjamb. There were punishments. There were exercises in obedience, drawn from his time spent in military service. "Think you're clever, eh? Think that's good enough! Well, let me tell you, life is a bit harder than *that*!" he might say, lifting a fist beneath a child's chin until the teeth rattled. "You're going to have to stiffen *up* a bit! You're going to have to stiffen *up*!"

Then, because none of this is simple, and none of it final, and because people are endlessly, ineluctably mixed, not one thing, nor another, but many things in outright contradiction to one another, and because, once you have lost a parent, it is not given to you in this life — unless you have some belief in ameliorative reincarnation — to be offered another one, he stole the show again. In his grief, indivisible from rage, he took himself off to sit on the stone step outside the door, self-banished. Rain or snow. Shame was his final trump card. During my mother's illness, his hair—like the dog's—had gone white at the edges. We all knew he couldn't cope. We all knew he couldn't manage. *Help. Please, someone. Help.* Once, one of my sisters lifted the phone to dial 911. When a voice at the other end politely asked what she wanted, she put the receiver down without a word. *Click.* Then the isolation reverberated: the graveyard, next door, made a tunnel for the wind. There was the *wheep wheep* of the oystercatcher and, half a mile distant, at the nearest farm, the roar of Farmer Michie yelling at his wife and his beasts.

But now, in these nicely framed conversations, by phone, between a father of seventy-two and a daughter of forty-five, taking place at precisely four o'clock each afternoon, lasting for perhaps half an hour, there is a space of humanity, for listening, for decency. I am R's responsibility now, not his. My situation doesn't have to torment him with things he has failed to fix. Nor can my cancer be laid at his door: it has been clearly traced to a mutated gene, and on my mother's side of the family, moreover. So he can listen. And as he listens, I have a sense of having found my voice, a voice that was lost in childhood, around the age of seven, a little younger perhaps, a little older, but a voice that I failed to recover across my adult life, though I sought it in drink, depression, the odd scrap of lyric poetry. At the end of the day, it is something to be able to talk to your father, in your own voice, in middle age. What would life have been like, I can't help wondering, if I had been given this earlier? What could I not have done with it?

We talk of medical appointments and the effects of chemotherapy. We talk of cancer and the possibility of dying. We talk of the children, their feats of derring-do, their progress at school. We talk of his business: glitches in the IT systems, wayward employees, fluctuations in exchange rates that have an impact on visitors from abroad. We talk of the vagaries of EU-driven health and safety regulations that stop him getting his boats on the water in the old way. We talk a little of history, of literature, of walks we would like to do. We have never talked so much, or so freely together, in our lives. But one thing we don't talk about is my mother, although she is a presence behind each conversation. She is waiting to step out from within the living rock, hefts of masonry falling around her, a tender smile on her lips. *My mother,* I want to say. *Who was she? Please, talk to me about my mother.*

So my feet have made this journey, through sickness and difficulty, because if I am to face this possibility of dying, I want to know who she was, this woman whom I seem condemned to follow, though it was the mission of my life to do almost anything else.

For a week, we don't come near it. We wander along the shore, exploring rock pools, the motley treasures of the tide line. We make trips to the western beaches, all white sand and big Atlantic rollers, and to the holy island of Iona. The children go in and out of the fiercely cold sea ten times a day. Sometimes my father and Miriam, or R, go with them. From a hollow in the dunes, I watch them, the taller figures of the adults moving slowly, while the children track in endless accelerated circles about them, breaking orbit now and again to run after a particularly lovely shell, a glossy frill of wave. Or they squat for long minutes by their fortress, excavating the sandy trenches in preparation for the tide. We stop for ice creams at some of my father's favorite spots: an old military bridge built by General Wade, when "the English redcoats were trying to get a grip on an unruly Highlands"; a meadow close to a ruined broch, with countless varieties of vetch and a view of distant hay fields dropping into the sea; a rocky outcrop on Iona, known as St. Columba's Pillow, where the saint is said to have gone to pray.

Then I realize that our stay is almost over, and if I don't do it now, I never will. I am going to have to make an active effort to tear this silence apart. "I want to talk about Mummy," I say one evening after supper, when the children are playing outside. "I want to talk about what it was like for her. When she was dying."

Miriam gets up quickly and excuses herself. "I think you need time together on your own. I have always felt that." It is the first time we have been left alone in this way, with my mother's name headlined. "So much of my own experience seems to be repeating hers," I say to my father, by way of justification. "I feel I need to know."

We sit in the armchairs on either side of the stove, while the back door to the sea is left open. Through it the blue shapes of mountains stretch out on every hand: the looming silhouette of Ben More, Mull's largest peak; beyond it, on the mainland, the twin peaks of Ben Cruachan, one a step lower than the other; the shaggy ridges of Glencoe; the long sleeping lion's back of Ben Nevis. The air is very still. There is a chittering of meadow pipits in the grass outside, the periodic whirr of swallows skimming about after gnats.

I don't know why my father moved to an island after my mother died. The obvious answer is that he had always loved the west coast of Scotland, and that this was as good a place as any to start his holiday business. Land was cheap on Tiree and there were decent transport links in the form of the daily ferry to and from Oban during the summer months and an old RAF landing strip that served as a base for light aircraft from Glasgow.

But my imagination always supplied other answers. An island is a place apart, a place you have to leave the mainland for. It is a place you have to make an effort to get to, a place you have to make an effort to leave. It is a place where day is divided not by the humble peal of the church bell, which might have suited my mother, but by the great tonnage of the Caledonian MacBrayne ferry—its hooter blasting across the bay, its outsize red funnel—bringing engine parts, petrol, rope, nails, bread, people, and post. A place of big horizons. Full of wind and weather. Where history lapses quickly into myth.

My father would tell the story of St. Columba, the sixth-century Irish saint. Born to a noble family, he is said to have fallen out with his father and his brothers before setting sail in a rush coracle from the northernmost tip of Ireland. He made his home on the island of Iona: a knob of pink granite, just breaking the surface of the Atlantic, scalloped round by white sandy beaches, where the water, in summer, is of a turquoise so brilliant it stops the heart. To remember, or to forget. History does not record.

"Your mother and I," my father says, clearing his throat, his hands clasped loosely in his lap. "We were always in the middle of things. *In medias res*. Five children, umpteen animals. There was not a lot of space to reflect."

I give internal assent. Five children, two dogs, horses, several cats, rabbits, ducks, and chickens. My father fighting elections for the Labour Party. Renovating houses in his "spare time" to try to boost the family income. Charging round the countryside with a political agent (a lackadaisical fellow—who could ever equal my father's demoniacal energy?), mugging up on the complexities of the Common Agricultural Policy and fishing rights in the North Sea, before practicing his oratory at the supper table. There were septic tank and drainage issues. There were rotten beams and recalcitrant voters. There was the rise of Scottish nationalism, which made an ugly dent in the Labour vote; he fought and lost elections in 1970 and 1974. All of this would have been fine if it had been done with a light heart. But it wasn't. The disappointment was devastating, the disorientation immense. My parents' rows, which would erupt in the night from time to time in the early days in Parsonage Farm House, became more frequent. My father had left the civil service to enter politics. There was no Plan B.

"Your mother had had a sore back for some time. She would talk about it occasionally. She was carrying a heavy load—washing, cooking, caring for you all. We didn't think much of it." My father clears his throat again, shifts his feet. "It may be . . . it may be I was at fault in not attending sufficiently. But there was always a lot happening. All those children, all those animals. I don't know whether you remember the meetings we used to have?" he says with delicate interrogation.

Ah yes, those meetings. I nod wordlessly. They were long a source of gloomy humor between my siblings and me. On Sunday, we would meet to discuss the family timetable. Sometimes the question of animals would come up, which ones we might do without. My father was overwhelmed by the financial and logistical responsibility he carried for all this life teeming about him. As we worked our way down the list—no creature was ever dispensed with—his mood darkened. We were confused. We all knew the story of Jude the Obscure, his brave love with Sue Bridehead sunk under the weight of poverty and parenting. The scene where Little Father Time, the eldest son, hangs himself and his siblings from the back of the door. *Done because we are too menny,* says the note pinned across his chest.

"Looking back on it, I think I can see that your mother may have been severely depressed for months before she was diagnosed. She may have had low mood for years before that. On my side, there had been three electoral defeats. There was going back to work for the civil service in Aberdeen, which was . . . frankly, frustrating. And there were the normal stresses and strains as you all entered adolescence. Our life at that time . . ." My father pauses, hesitating over his words. "It wasn't exactly a bundle of laughs."

I remember my father's return home from the office each evening. A kind of habitual gloom, once so foreign to his nature, seemed to have settled over him. There was our anxious appraisal of his mood. My mother's pitiful attempts to appease him with cups of tea and food he didn't want. Her gifts to him he rejected. It may be that his to her she also rejected. There was a feeling that everything was wrong: the house, the job, the children.

The dream had come unstuck. My mother made efforts at happiness in spite of it. She cooked beautiful meals. She did the washing and the cleaning. She tried to manage the household expenses and would come to him with pathetic pride to boast of how she had bought this chicken or that tin of baked beans for a few pennies less because it was on sale. Was she like a child, expecting praise? Did she make my father feel his lonely responsibility more acutely? At any rate, he was not impressed. He refused to smile at her, refused to warm to her.

He would withdraw to his study to do his accounts. His discontent filled the house. It made us all feel guilty, unworthy, and afraid.

"It was summer 1978 when your mother first went to the doctor. The back pain that she had had for years had got worse. Now she had pain in her tummy, too. Your mother had a tendency to procrastinate, to hope for the best. And it may be the doctor was at fault, too." My father pauses. "He colluded with doing nothing, with sweeping the whole thing into the long grass instead of referring her on for urgent specialist examination. We lost time. When it became clear, after surgery, that she had in fact been severely ill, the GP came back to visit her. Your mummy refused to see him."

My mother must have been frightened. She must have been in pain. The symptoms would have persisted for some time before she took the step of making an appointment with the GP. So much easier to do this for one of the children—that happy bunting of appointments over the years for vaccinations, whooping coughs, measles, dislocated shoulders, earaches, verrucas—than for herself.

And then, after building herself up to it—why *did* she have no energy? What *was* that pain in her stomach?—she encountered a GP who didn't take her seriously enough. He would be patronizing, perhaps, with just that flavor of contempt, short of outright rudeness, that is the worse for being kept within the bounds of ruddy joviality. My mother was a middle-aged woman in a foreign country. She would have had the diffidence of her gender and her nation in this context.

Lower-back pain, the doctor might have quipped, scarcely troubling to examine her. What does she expect? With five children, she must be bending and fetching a hundred times a day! Good Lord! If he had a penny for every patient who came to him with lower-back pain, he could spend the rest of his life on the golf course!

"There was not a very long delay," says my father quietly. "We lost a month or two perhaps. Then she went under the care of a very humane and able surgeon called Professor McGillivray. He was in his late fifties, based at Aberdeen Royal Infirmary. Your mummy got outstanding treatment from there on. There is no question about that—from the surgeons and also from the nursing staff. She couldn't have had better. Professor McGillivray operated immediately: he did a hysterectomy with removal of her ovaries. That was mid-October, 1978."

My mother's hysterectomy. October 1978. I remember the atmosphere in the house. Tears, darkness. I seem to remember corridors and the angles of doorways, half-shut, people behind them whispering. My mother, who was not given to expressing her feelings, was in a state of grief about the forthcoming surgery and the loss of her womb, as my parents referred to it. I couldn't understand it. Why should she regret this organ? It had done its job, hadn't it? It had produced five children. Far too many anyway, I thought nastily. Why should she feel such intensity of grief about its removal?

I must have expressed something of this confusion, because I remember someone—it would have been my father—explaining that a womb is a large part of a woman's identity. That for my mother, the power to create children, her fertility, was very much bound up with her sense of purpose in life. I wasn't entirely convinced by this. But I took it on trust, grateful to have an explanation at all. Clearly, there were things I didn't understand, despite being a woman myself.

I still find it hard to think about this period with equanimity. My mother was facing the possibility of a diagnosis of cancer. She was facing the possibility of dying. For one of the first times in our life together, she was allowing herself to express her feelings. Or those feelings were so powerful that they overrode her normal restraint. But at no point did anyone mention the word *cancer* to me. At no point did I realize that there was more at stake in the forthcoming surgery than the removal of a superfluous organ. And because I understood nothing, I stood apart from her. I looked at her coldly, with misgiving. I judged her.

When we went to see my mother in Aberdeen Royal Infirmary,

I was profoundly shocked by her appearance. She was thin, her hair grey. She looked at me from a gaunt face. What had happened? It was as if the hospital had taken her in a well person and turned her overnight into a sick one.

"What is happening?" I asked my father at home. It seemed a treachery, as a seventeen-year-old daughter, just entering my domain as a woman, to inquire about my mother's looks when she was in hospital having such surgery. But I was frightened. "Why does Mummy look like that?"

"Your mother has been through a very hard time. She has had a difficult operation," said my father. "It's taken it out of her. But when she comes out of hospital, we're all going to look after her. We're going to build up her strength and make sure she gets better again."

We decided to cook a meal to celebrate her homecoming, and fixed on rump steak as the most special and exotic thing we could think of to give her, though none of us had any idea how to cook it. I remember standing with my father in the butcher's shop while the butcher, a large man with shattered veins across his cheeks, moved his fingers gently among the pieces of meat.

"Div ye want it tenderized?" he asked finally, draping a piece carefully over his hand, like a bleeding cloth. The accent was on the last syllable, with a harsh inflection, though his voice was gentle enough. "Div ye want the meat tenderized?" None of us had any idea what that was. Eventually, my father explained that it meant doing something to the meat to make it softer and easier to eat. Under the circumstances, it sounded like a good idea.

So we stood in silence as the butcher passed it slowly through a machine, a kind of guillotine with steel rakes that scored the flesh deeply, so that it came out looking like a plowed field. Later, when we set the cooked meat in front of my mother, it bothered me very much that it still bore those lines, which I found extremely unattractive. In any event, my mother seemed scarcely to have the strength to hold her knife and fork. After taking a few mouthfuls and telling us how delicious it was, she went upstairs to bed.

"Don't worry," said my father. "Mummy just needs time to get her strength back. But she's going to be fine."

I went back to Oxford, University College, where I was studying English literature and language. I was painfully shy and lacked confidence. I smoked too much. I did not sleep well. Frightened of the college dining hall, with its long tables and candelabra, its portraits of famous men staring down at us, I took to eating my meals alone in my room. They were minimal anyway, consisting of packets of crisps and biscuits bought at a newsstand on the High Street.

You could not say I was a happy young person. You could not say I was well-adjusted. I was clearly disturbed, with my monotonous black clothes, my cigarettes, and my solitary meals. But I made friends, got on with my work, and found myself a boyfriend, a handsome fellow whose confident public-school drawl went some way to compensating for my own silence. I was no different from thousands of other young people who turn up at the portals of Oxford, almost against the laws of probability—bearing the smell of their particular domestic misery, their particular social or economic pain—and pass through, leaving not a trace behind.

"After Mummy's surgery, I phoned Professor McGillivray to hear the results of the biopsy," says my father. "He was a humane man. I think he had some doubts about telling me in that way, over the phone. I was working in Glasgow that day. I phoned him just before I took the train home. I told him I wanted to understand clearly and fully what was going on. But I overestimated my own strength."

My father lifts his head and looks out toward the sea. With his white hair and erect posture, he reminds me of the Lismore lighthouse, its slim white column stuck out on a rock just beyond the bay, its wide beam striking out rhythmically through the night. People have different kinds of courage. It's taken me most of my life to understand that. And this is my father's: he does not abandon his post; he endures. "I think from that point, Mummy couldn't have been taken care of by anyone," he says with native eloquence. "Not by Professor McGillivray, nor by the nurses, nor by Scott Hutchison, the minister, nor even by me."

The train from Glasgow crosses from the west to the east coast before taking its long, leisurely, shore-hugging loop up toward Aberdeen. You pass the dark chimneys of Dundee. Then there is the cliff-top silhouette of Dunnottar Castle, near Stonehaven—in summer an emerald pasture stitched in daisies; in winter a wave-lashed spit you wouldn't dare to approach. Then the fishermen's houses at Fittie, the long, low huddle of them, their granite backs all turned to the sea, windows facing inward for warmth.

My father would have sat alone. He would have put his brief-case on the floor beside him or between his legs. Not up in the lug-gage rack; there would have been an instinct to keep things close, to hold tight. He would have been wearing his black coat, or something like it—a more demotic, less glamorous version, perhaps, bought from the men's section of Marks & Spencer. The carriage would have been full of other men returning home, snapping their newspapers, jostling for legroom, joking about football or work. He would have kept very still. He would not have moved at all as the chimneys and fields flashed past.

The homecoming would have been unspeakable. My mother's gaze fastened on him, looking instantly away, returning to check the truth of what she had seen. What did she think, what did she do? What does any of us think, or do, in such a situation? It is her hands I see. Those long slender fingers, the gracefully articulated knuckles, and her rings: the engagement ring, with its alternating sapphires and diamonds, and the slim platinum wedding band.

Did she lift a hand to brush away a wisp of hair at her temple, just beginning to grey? Did she smooth away imaginary creases in her apron? Did she go through quickly to pour a splash of boiling water into a teapot for my father? Or bend to open the door of the oven, her face filled with a rush of heat, the tart fragrance of an apple pie, before turning—her voice suddenly uncontrollably sharp—to tell a child to settle down please and get on with her homework?

Unspeakable, too, the pain of being surrounded by all those

children, their young lives about to be smashed by a force over which no one had the least control. "I thought I could take it," said my father quietly. "But I overestimated my own strength for that."

Silly child. The voice in my heart leaps up. Did you think because he had no words, married Miriam on the instant, scarcely mentioned your mother's name for a quarter of a century, sold many of their joint possessions, rarely volunteered a memory or a shared spring of joy, that he had no love for her? *These are not empty-hearted whose low sound reverbs no hollowness.* Sorrow is not the outward form and shape of grief. It is *that within which passeth show.* Silly child, the voice inside me jubilates. How wrong could you be, threading your way between external signs, and making no sense? So it takes me a moment to catch up with what my father is saying next. And I hear it from a distance, like a submarine explosion, where you feel the impact later in a sudden surge of choppy water. "Chemotherapy," he is saying. "Your mother started chemotherapy almost immediately."

When the doctors first told me I was to have chemotherapy, I was more horrified by the word than by the phenomenon itself, about which I knew little. The word resonated with sinister associations: chemical warfare, baldness and degradation, women in kerchiefs, limping along at the margins of life. As I made my way through treatment, the word lost its power to shock, while in its place I developed an unshakable horror of the phenomenon itself. Hearing for the first time that my mother had had to endure it, that original totemic dread returns, with a force magnified by experience. My mother! My beautiful mother! They pumped her full of poisons. They brought her low. They made her sick and wretched before she died. A mute howl sets up in me. *My mother. My beautiful mother. And I never knew.*

But any expression of emotion will frighten my father. If I burst out, reproach him in any way, or even seem too affected by what he has said, there will be another interregnum of silence—and I won't hear what I need to hear.

"Do you remember what kind of treatment she was given?" I say quietly, as if we were discussing the health of a stranger. "Could you tell me a bit about it?"

My father can't remember much about the details of the chemotherapy. The names of the drugs escape him, although he's sure that, if it is important to me, he could find the names written down somewhere. What he does remember is how quickly she responded. "It was almost instant," he says. "It had the force of a miracle. She seemed herself again. She had energy."

It is a story I am now familiar with. Up to 80 percent of women who take chemotherapy for advanced ovarian cancer have a positive response. They experience remission, with the cancer either stabilizing or regressing. With the most aggressive chemotherapy, the median duration of this remission is now twenty-two months. In my mother's day, it was ten months. At that time, the majority of women diagnosed with advanced ovarian cancer were dead within two years. My father would not have known this. He would have seen my mother suddenly feeling better and, without someone to tell him to the contrary, would have begun to hope.

What about nausea? I ask. Did the chemotherapy make her very ill? Did it make her tired, depressed? Did she lose her hair? Where did she go to have it, and did he go with her?

She did suffer sickness, says my father carefully, though he doesn't remember it being debilitating for more than a few days after each treatment. She was tired, certainly. But she functioned. She resumed many of her normal duties, looking after us all and so forth. She didn't lose her hair. She went for treatment every few weeks at the Aberdeen Royal Infirmary. He remembers all this business with blood counts that I have been having; if her immune system was too depressed, she couldn't be given the drugs. And no, he didn't go with her. She seemed to want to do it on her own. It was part of how she did things. "She had great dignity throughout her illness," he says. "Your mummy walked tall. She walked very tall."

I find this difficult. Did my mother *really* want to go alone, or did she just think it was her duty? Had she internalized the great shame that surrounds the illness, even to this day? Did it combine with her own natural diffidence to prevent her reaching for support? Or was this self-reliant pride her way of seizing back control over a situation that had deprived her of all choices in life, except how she endured the loss of it?

"Did it change her appearance?" I ask in a sudden afterthought, remembering how much I hated her as an adolescent—with a complex, self-divided, guilt-ridden hatred—for what I regarded as the loss of her looks.

My father sighs. "I would like to say it didn't change her, that she remained herself. But that wouldn't be true. The chemotherapy did change her. It diminished her physically. She looked less well on it."

Now the knife is under my breast; it takes a few ragged cuts. How well I know this part of the story, from a different vantage point. I saw my mother grey. I saw her thin. It was as if she were drained of her life force, ashen from within. Her gestures fell away, her words were without commitment. It wounded me, in the very core of myself, that imperious eighteen-year-old-girl self that needed my mother to be strong in order for my own life to prosper. Cruel girl. Cruel youth. I understood nothing. Seeing my mother like that, I took her weakness for voluntary withdrawal, and I could not forgive her.

"We passed most of a year with Mummy on chemotherapy. She seemed to be gathering strength, or so we hoped. And then at Christmas, we made a trip to Edinburgh, and Mummy climbed Arthur's Seat. She was slower, of course. But she did it, unaided. It was a great moment. It seemed as if everything might be OK. I allowed myself to hope. Looking back on it, I think I was living in a fool's paradise."

Hope. The gift without which no doctor can heal, no life can be lived. A fool's paradise. A fundamental human right.

My father gets up and opens the little door of the iron stove. He looks wistfully at the wicker basket of logs to the right of it, the logs all sawed neatly to the same length, sitting snug and tinder-dry together. Then he looks out at the open door. But no, there's really no justification for it. The evening is still warm.

He would like to be up and doing now. He would like a job, gathering sticks for kindling to make a fire on the beach, perhaps. Setting the heavy stones round in a ring, sinking them into the sand, to bulwark the early flames. He would like to be making a little dry nest in the middle, fetching twists of paper, inserting a firelighter or two if he is making things easy for himself. Cupping his hands about the flame and blowing gently: *Whoo whoo. Whoo whoo.* And then, when it's up and crackling, the little blue flame snapping numinously against the white sand, he would like to fetch the kettle, grimed with the soot of a thousand fires, and the plastic cups that date from forty years ago and camping trips with my mother. "Cup of tea, anyone?" he would ask pleasantly. "Cup of tea?"

For a moment, I think that he might be going to walk away. But no. He resumes his seat, feet loosely apart, hands clasped in his lap. He has taken it on this time. He has made his commitment and will see it through. For some reason, his feet, with the inexpensive brown leather shoes he buys from a supermarket in Oban, seem poignant to me. They are blunt and round toed, like a child's. They always were a shade small for his height.

"And then, a month later, at the end of January," he says simply, "the world just fell in. It was a very big shock. Nothing could be done."

DOUGLAS, THE HEAD PORTER at University College, is knocking at the door of my room. His knock is sharp and peremptory. It makes the old wooden door shake. Douglas served in the Royal Horse Artillery during the Second World War; he was at Dunkirk. You didn't mess with him. "Your father is on the phone," he says, his white head appearing round the corner of the door. "You need to come now!"

College rooms did not have telephones. If parents needed to

contact a child, they would leave a message with the porter, who would transcribe it and then deposit the note into one of the wooden pigeonholes opposite his reception area.

So this singling out was different. Douglas, too, was different. He was not his normal jovial self. He seemed rattled, unsettled. He was also infected with a sense of speed, as if his loyalty to my father meant he had to hustle me from my armchair by the electric fire, down the stone stairs, and along the wall of the main quad toward the Porter's Lodge.

I remember hurrying to keep up with him. I remember the bewildered pride at being seen alone with him in the quad. (We all sought his approval, this former soldier, with his tough, wisecracking humor and decorations for bravery.) And I remember the rain — a soft, fine rain — that made the dark wool of his uniform steam a little, so that it smelled of sacking and damp sheep.

"WAS MUMMY AFRAID of dying?"

My father looks past me through the open door. Outside, the light is just turning from that endless empyrean of a perfect Hebridean day to something darker and more intense. It seems to show up the glacial scoring in the rocks opposite, which I have never noticed before.

The light here is different. It doesn't so much reveal a landscape as invent it. A little shawl of sea mist is tossed over the bay, and everything disappears: mountains, shore, horizon. A few seconds later, shafts of sun conjure up whole valleys, long vistas of rivers, and secret upland meadows. Then the storm clouds come in. Gravity loses its hold: the land and the sea swap places.

But on certain summer evenings, when the light stands still, you might think you hold time in the palm of your hand. The waves keep up their flurried slapping, tying their threads together, loosing them, tying up, and loosing. It is never finished, this work of creating and destroying. It seems a freedom to me to be unclear whether we are sitting here, my father and I, at this moment. If not, we might as well be. If life is an illusion, so, too, is its opposite. And people are not the less present for being dead.

"Your mother had faith," says my father. "*In fide vade*. That was her motto." He adds, with emotion, "She walked tall, your mother. She came out of that ward like a queen. She must have been afraid, but that isn't my memory of that time."

When she was a young girl, my mother went to a convent school in Cobham, Surrey. The nuns would have taught her the Creed there, a little elementary Latin liturgy. She would have known the smell of candles in a stone interior, an altar strewn with flowers. She would have known ritual and order. Later, she went to Wycombe Abbey School, where they started each day with chapel and took communion on Sundays. During my childhood, the church played a part in our lives. Mostly, it was the humble social church, giver of the year's ritual, with its flint steeple and gold weather vane in the shape of a cockerel. The church of polished pews and tapestried hassocks; of freezing Nativity ceremonies, with tinfoil crowns and mumbling Josephs; of plaited loaves at Harvest; and of painted eggs at Easter. Later, it was the Scottish kirk, bleaker perhaps, but recognizable in format, with its oak-carved pews and extensive graveyard. But I think I always knew that for my mother it was more than this. It was also the church of the holy fathers, of St. Paul's miraculous conversion, of the loaves and the fishes, of wafer and wine, of last things, and of the tongues of flame descending.

In fide vade. What is religious faith in head-on collision with individual death and the forced abandonment of five children? My mother's faith, and what it meant to her, is a place I cannot go. I do know that around the time of her dying, she made friends with the Reverend Scott Hutchison. A former athlete who had competed in rugby and boxing, he had been crippled by polio at age twenty-one. He was a huge man—taller even than my father—and would appear at the house in his black cassock, struggling up the stairs on his calipers, cracking jokes. He had an affection for my mother, and she for him. My father stayed downstairs during these visits.

Was my mother afraid of dying?

But perhaps I don't need to repeat this question. My father is seventy-two. His hair is white, though still thick and vigorous on his head. Nowadays, he is a man who has an afternoon sleep. He sits with Miriam, one on each side of the stove in the outsize armchairs. He pulls a little lever in the base: the chair tips back at a sharp angle; a footrest shoots out at the front—it is a trick he delights in exhibiting to grandchildren. And when he gets up from his siesta, which lasts for half an hour, his spine juts forward in the way of people whose bones no longer bend themselves so easily back to the true.

"Did Mummy say anything about us . . . what she wanted for us?"

My father looks up. He has been lost in a reverie. From the open door, there comes the sound of an outboard motor, a friendly puttering that has probably been carried for miles. There is the *wheep wheep* of an oystercatcher, the little background slapping of the waves.

Was it the phrase *walked tall*? Did it bring my mother in front of him, her back always so straight, her limbs long and graceful? I once came down a mountain behind one of my sisters and saw how she traveled down through heather and bog in a kind of trance, without glancing at her feet. I remember thinking that this was how my mother would have come down a mountain, that something in this poise was hereditary.

My parents' relationship was stormy, but it was a love affair nonetheless. They met when my mother was twenty-one, in her last year of studying English literature at Oxford. My father was twenty-three, just back from two years of National Service. They were married two years later: in High Wycombe parish church, my mother in an ivory silk gown with a long train, my father in a top hat and morning dress. How hopeful it would all have seemed. What a blessed union of love and good fortune.

But this time I do need to repeat the question. "Did Mummy say anything about what she wanted for us?"

My father looks unsure. "How do you mean?"

"I mean, did she say anything about how she wanted us brought up, what she hoped for for us?"

"Well, she wanted you to be happy, of course. She wanted that more than anything in the world."

Pause. "Did she say anything about what she wanted for us in particular, given that she was dying?"

My father blinks in a slightly dazed way. "I think she trusted that I would . . . You see . . . it was all so very fast at the end . . . "

Ah, what a dangerous game of brinkmanship my parents played at the end. My sister and I both away at university, called back at the last minute. The cancer might well have killed her a few days earlier. It might have deprived her of consciousness before she had seen us.

What then? I would have received a call at college, presumably, to say that my mother was dead. That she had died of a cancer I never knew she had, and that I had better come home immediately for the funeral.

"We didn't know when to call you back," says my father. "We were unsure. Just at the point when I was beginning to wonder, some ladies who were being kind to us, cooking meals for us and so forth, began to talk to me and say that it was time."

So it was not my mother. At no point had she expressed the desire to have her eldest daughters with her as she died. She had thought it was for the best, probably, to leave us in our lonely idyll. Hear no evil, see no evil. Perhaps it had been a consoling fantasy to think of us as happy, in that faraway golden world, untouched by the things that were happening at home.

Perhaps, knowing the joy of having my father's attention focused on her again after so many years of difficulty and division, she wanted to relax in the pleasure of being cared for and did not want to share it with tumultuous teenage daughters. Or perhaps there were always too many. That when it came to it, death so fast and furious, she did not have the energy to negotiate another set of needs. She would have been extremely weak; she would have been overwhelmed. She must have often been in great pain.

"I wish I'd known," I permit myself to say in a small voice. "That Mummy had cancer. That she was on chemotherapy. That she was dying."

My father sighs. He shifts his round-ended shoes. He gives a sniff. "In plea of mitigation," he says finally. "It was all so very fast at the end. It was really so terrifyingly fast . . ."

Nowadays, if you're lucky, there are grief counselors. There are bereavement specialists and family therapists. They have organizations like SeeSaw to help children facing the loss of a parent. They have children's help lines and memory boxes. What did my parents have? They had the doctors. They had Scott Hutchison, the minister. They had some friendly neighbors, helping with meals. They did the best they could.

We go through to the cottage next door, where my father wants to show me some things he has stored in the loft. He disappears for a few minutes and reappears with a large manila envelope and a pile of my old drawings.

At the sight of the manila envelope, my heart leaps up. Secretly, I have always cherished a longing for my mother to have left me one particular jewel, a favorite ring or necklace. Secretly, too, I always believed that she must have left me a letter somewhere, that at some point in the whole process she would have wished to speak to me. When my father appears with the envelope, I think: This is it. Here is the letter I always knew she must have written, talking to me at length and lovingly in her own voice. Explaining everything, even the silence.

But no. An old penny slips out of the envelope and rolls across the table. There is a picture of Britannia on the back, her shield beside her, and a date: 1966. It was probably a gift from my maternal grandfather, who worked in a bank and liked to send us commemorative coins. There is also the letter my father wrote in response to messages of condolence, in which he talks of the time of "divine grace" he and my mother shared before she died.

He seems to want to focus on this. "The surgeon had some doubts, you see. He felt that perhaps Mummy had been made to suffer needlessly in her last year, with treatments that offered little chance of a cure. I said no. A thousand, thousand times no. The treatment gave us time. It was a time of grace. And that was priceless."

I know that during my mother's illness and her dying, my parents drew absolutely close again. Perhaps their love, always encumbered—their first child born a year after they were married, four more following in a few short years—was permitted a little free space in the face of death. Perhaps my father, so apt to lose himself in restless anxiety and self-doubt, is of a nature to find himself in a crisis.

I am profoundly grateful for it. I could never wish it otherwise. But is it churlish of me to carry a sadness because it is also a time in which I played no part, a time from which I was excluded? To hide my disappointment, I pick up the envelope and tip it upside down. Inside, there is one last thing: an old silver sugar caster he has kept for me. I haven't seen it for years. With its fat base and cylindrical top, it used to sit on the dresser in the kitchen in Parsonage Farm House. We used it to sprinkle sugar over a Victoria sponge, warm from the oven, or apple pancakes. It belongs to the early, hopeful days of my parents' marriage, when my father had his post in the civil service in London, and they looked fair to accumulate a silver collection, like my maternal grandparents. Now, with a big dent along one side, it refuses to stand upright.

I pick it up, relishing the feel of the old, soft metal, and shake it gently at my ear. There is a little wincing rattle. A few ancient grains. My inheritance, I think wryly, and put it down again. But in truth, I have lived without objects for so long, I no longer need them. I have had to find another way round.

I pull the drawings toward me. There is a thick pile, done in HB pencil and charcoal across my teenage years. My father rescued them from the dustbin where I put them after my mother's death: one of those acts of putting away, whether of things or people, that can happen in the face of trauma. After all these years, I am pleased to see them. Mostly, they are life drawings of my family.

There are sketches of my sisters, one crouched in front of a book, a long plait snaking down her back, the soles of her feet curved behind her. Another is leaning against a doorway, with a graceful smile and strong limbs, like a fifteen-year-old version of my mother. My grandmother appears, with her wide forehead and hooded eyes, then a picture of my father, in which those same eyes look straight out of the page. But the picture that stops me in my tracks is of my mother. She is sitting on the sofa, her elbow resting on the arm and her head propped in her hand. She looks tired. She is wearing the old brown dressing gown that I hated so much. With its skimpy cloth and faded embroidered yoke, it seemed to me to symbolize everything that had gone wrong with her life. Now I would like to press my face into it. To plunge myself into the smell. The sweet, forgotten smell of her.

"It's strange," I murmur. "No one said a word to me. But it's as if I knew all along. What else is this a picture of? Those hollow eyes. And her hands—she's hardly got the strength to hold her head up."

My father is visibly upset. He gets up, looks at the drawing again, frowns. At this point the children rattle round the corner of the house on their scooters, skidding to a smart halt on the gravel. "Mummy! Grandpa! Hot chocolate!" they cry. "Miriam has made hot chocolate. You've got to come now!"

"Your mother loved life," says my father before he goes. "She wasn't one to haul things into the light particularly . . . She would have been appalled to think of you unhappy. To think of you focusing on the dark, the negative. She loved life. She loved to look after things. She had a strong instinct for that . . ." He shrugs; the ghost of a smile crosses his face. "I remember once we took a journey on the train from Canterbury to Margate. Five children, two dogs. The pram. The picnic. It seemed to take all day. There wasn't room for anyone else in the carriage. That was our life, really . . . We were a whole world to ourselves . . . A whole world."

Chapter Twelve

Except It Weigh Less than a Feather

About a year ago, halfway through writing this book, I thought I would finish it with a scene in the Pitt Rivers Museum in Oxford. We're there during a half-term break for a lecture aimed at children. Standing in the main hall, under the Victorian arches, between the skeleton of a sperm whale and a large case of butterflies, we are listening to a young man with shiny black curls and a brilliant smile tell us something about ancient Egyptian beliefs in the afterlife.

"They believed that when you died, you didn't stop existing, you just took a journey to the afterlife. The afterlife wasn't that much different from this life, in fact. You needed food and drink, somewhere to sleep, games to play, spells to keep you safe, and people to help you do your work."

He indicates a series of clay models on the table in front of him: boats designed to transport wealthy Egyptians from the east to the west bank of the Nile, where the afterlife began, boats stuffed with tiny pots for food and drink, bales of mattresses, pillows, stools and chairs, miniature board games, and laborer servants with sickles and hoes. It's a little like a modern-day camping expedition.

"So you see, it was very comfortable, really. Eventually, all your family and friends would join you there. And it had the great advantage that it went on forever. But there was only *one thing* . . ."

He pauses, and looks intently round at the children. "Before you could take the trip, you had to pass a special test."

The children's eyes grow wide. They take on that slightly glazed look with which children treat the emphatic utterances of adults. I have the feeling that if they could, they would take a step backward. But hemmed in between the butterfly case and the table, their little bodies are stuck fast.

"When you died, they took the heart out of your body and put it on a great pair of scales," he says. "On the other side there was an ostrich feather. They thought that if your heart was weighed down with all the bad things you had done in your life, it would be heavier than the feather. Only if your heart was lighter than the feather could you take the trip to the afterlife. If it wasn't . . . well then, they took it off the scales and threw it into a lake below, where a horrible monster called Ammit—half-hippopotamus, half-crocodile— would eat it up."

He snaps his teeth shut in imitation. The children blink, swallow hard. "Oh, you'd all probably be OK. It's your parents I'm not so sure about!" he quips. Then he invites them to come forward and feel the ostrich feather on the table in front of him. As they do so, he gives them other things against which to measure its weight: a pebble, a peck of grain, a copper ring. I watch first Michaela, then Kitty, close their eyes like obedient dolls. Pure concentration: best achieved by shutting down other senses. What do they make of it, I wonder, standing there with the feather in one hand, in the other, the cool slab of pebble, the warm texture of the grain?

For me, this idea, which I have never heard before, is a revelation. It captures something about depression, its dark, bewildering shame. It's no accident that religious leaders the world over have taken a light heart as an index of spiritual enlightenment. The business of life is to live, the duty of the heart to be light. Buddha, St. Francis, St. Julian of Norwich. All shall be well and all manner of things shall be well.

"I probably shouldn't say this," said a woman at Kitty's fourth birthday party, "but I have a bad feeling about cancer patients.

When I worked near the Churchill, I used to see them at the back of the hospital having a fag, dragging their little drips from chemotherapy behind them . . . Can you believe it? I'm sorry, but I just couldn't cope with that."

Hatred of the victim. It's a familiar model. Such wretches do not deserve society's scarce medical resources, still less its pity. At the time, sitting on the edge of the bouncy castle, waves of nausea passing over me with each jolt of the broiling plastic, I have no words to answer her.

And though I still find it crass, this punitive model, I have to admit I have my own version. It goes like this: If society spends thousands of pounds paying its top technocrats to cut bits out of you; storing your tissue for analysis for the redemption of future generations, which may include your own children; pumping you full of poisons to try to prolong your individual life, together with expensive medication to ensure you suffer as little as possible in the process, do you then have a right to sadness? To live a life of anxiety, or indeterminacy? Surely not. Surely a life thus rescued— Lazarus from the dead—must be lived with every cell, every atom, dedicated to the praise of life itself—if not with the first, fine, careless rapture of youth, at least with the barked triumph of a midlife phoenix, a thing risen from the waste of its own ashes.

In practice, it is not so simple. The heart is an intractable organ. It has a tendency to go its own way. "Well done," Tariq Dhanjani said, offering me his hand in congratulation at the end of chemotherapy. "You've got through. Now you can go away and get on with it. If you take this slip to reception, you can make an appointment to see us again in six months' time."

Six months, Doctor? Six months! But what if I die in that time? What if it comes back to get me? Surely you need to be doing blood tests, scans, investigations . . .

There is no blood test that can tell you whether you are clear of cancer, he says. There are tests that can detect raised markers within the blood and tell you whether the "burden of tumor" has increased. But nothing that can tell you whether you are clear. The most reliable indicators of the return of cancer are patients' own reports on their health. "If it comes back, you will know," he says with an ominousness of which he seems unaware. And how will I know exactly? "Oh, headaches, joint pain, unexplained weight loss," he murmurs vaguely. And then, when pressed, he stands a little stiffer and talks as if dictating bullet points for a patient leaflet: a headache like a tight band about the head, which persists day and night and is unaffected by medication. Night fevers, drenching sweats. Unusual pains that do not go away, especially in the bones. Untoward lumps and bumps, a rash in the site of the scar, difficulties in breathing . . .

Convinced they are withholding scans for reasons of cost, I demand to see MacBryde. He comes out of his cubicle, in his beautiful wool suit, to back up his junior. "If we knew whether cancer was still present in your body, we would know a great deal. And we don't. The tests are largely pointless."

I have difficulty believing him: it's too counterintuitive. We have it drummed into us so thoroughly that finding cancer early prolongs survival. Surely finding recurred cancer early must also affect outcome. But no, the literature supports what MacBryde is saying. If you can find primary, local cancer early, you have a chance of cutting it out or poisoning it to extinction. But once cancer has metastasized, or spread, it has changed its nature. You can no longer eradicate it; only delay its progress. If it's coming to get you, it will. Repeat scanning may detect recurred cancer at an earlier stage, but it has no impact on prolonging survival. Mostly it throws up what MacBryde calls "artifacts," things that may be consistent with cancer, cause a great deal of anxiety, require further investigation, but usually don't turn out to be cancer at all.

"Are you basically saying to me that if you can't affect outcome, you might as well delay knowledge as long as possible?" I ask finally.

"You've got it, more or less," says MacBryde with a pained shrug. "I've had ladies passing out on the floor in front of me when they hear." He indicates a buffed spot on the linoleum in front of him, now hazed in sunshine. "Right there on the floor in front of me."

The task, it seems, is to go away and wait. No, no, that is entirely the wrong way of thinking about it. The task is to go away and "get on with your life," as Deborah Lovelace, Don MacBryde, Tariq Dhanjani, so many young, brainy, good-looking consultants all, in their different ways, put it. But what life exactly? And how?

Kate Carr, in her book *It's Not Like That, Actually,* describes the isolation of dealing with her own uncertain situation. Facing a high risk of recurrence, she lives alone with her fear for years. There is a moment of watching her husband and children running down a hill holding hands. This is how it will be if she isn't there, she thinks. Just that tight circle, without her. When her five-year checkup is passed, everyone celebrates. She is safe; she is through. They can all relax. She is left at the party with a clammy-handed presentiment, which she can communicate to no one. How can she ruin their party? In fact, it turns out that her presentiment is correct. One morning, seven years after its first appearance, the cancer has returned; a year later she is dead.

I know the graphs. The black line tracking the distribution of mortality in any cohort of breast-cancer sufferers. It takes a big hike about a year after treatment, then falls away. There is another hike again at four or five years; no one knows why. Then more falling away, until it reaches a point a little ways off the x axis, where it chugs along indefinitely, like a kite in a low wind, marking the incidence of deaths of women after five, eleven, even seventeen years.

"ALL OVER NOW? Looking good. Hair growing back!" says someone at the school gate. "Marvelous. Marvelous. You must feel so *relieved* it's all *finished.*"

People want closure. They want it badly. Once chemotherapy is over, you have "beaten" the disease. They stick a pair of Victory wings on you and tell you how nice your hair looks. This is kindly meant; people are genuinely happy to see you beginning to look healthy. But what it doesn't deal with is the fact that you feel as raw as a newborn baby. You have the Moro reflexes at the big wide world around you. You need to be swaddled tight, held close. For the hands that held you through the hell of treatment are drawing back now. The hospital, with which you have a love-hate relationship as intense as that with your ancestral family, is withdrawing from you. Just the smell of it can turn your stomach, but when a fire erupts in the roof, threatening to shut down operations, you are glued to the television with tears streaming down your face. There are no more visits from the Macmillan nurse. No visits to or from the doctor. You are on your own now. Waiting. No, no. You are on your own now, getting on with your life.

The dialogues I remember from those days have a disjointed quality. There is my interior voice, still pressing and urgent. Will I live? Will I die? Will my children be left motherless? How would motherlessness work itself out across the long sweep of their lives? Is there any way it could be made less catastrophic than it was in mine?

And then there are the lines that others are speaking over my head. Hair growing back? Wonderful! Looking good! You must be so *happy* it's all over! You must be so *relieved* to have it *behind* you!

If I try to enter this dialogue, express a little of my uncertainty, it becomes unstable. A fugitive look enters my interlocutor's face, dark and flickering, as if she has just glimpsed a rat escaped from a plague ship. I am well aware that the words *cancer* and *terminal* are about as welcome in a school playground as the figures of poverty, old age, and disease in a medieval garden of romance. But I force myself to speak of them, out of a kind of loyalty to my own existence, a feeling that all this experience can no longer remain unspoken.

"It's not quite like that," I murmur. "With cancer, there's always a chance of it coming back, at which point the outlook is not so good."

"Oh, you can't think like *that*!" says Molly or Mandy or Tilly or Tami, with that brittle voice that is kept in reserve, like the best bone china in the back of the cupboard. "Of *course* you're going to be fine. I *know* you are. You just have to be *positive*."

* * *

AT THE SUPPORT GROUP, I learn that Lil is dying. Her PhD on French female mystics of the early medieval period will never be finished. She brought up four children in a ramshackle house in Gloucestershire before discovering her cancer at the age of fifty. After treatment, she decided to do what she had always wanted to do: a degree in history. It turned out that gentle Lil—known for the lightness of her Victoria sponges and her tireless support of the Women's Institute—was good at it. Very. She got a First in her undergraduate degree and went on to study for a PhD.

Making endless trips to libraries and abbeys throughout France, in the footsteps of her women saints, she comes back with boxes full of papers, irrepressible. Her children return from busy lives in London to find their mother buried in her study, the house needing attention and no proper food on the table. Only the dogs, three Labradors, still get routinely fed, three identical bowls at the back door, a can of dog food in each. The children crack jokes about their mother, the "bus-pass boffin," and leave, vaguely disquieted.

Then Lil begins to get headaches. Normal medication doesn't seem to dent them. One evening, she finds she can't see the print on her computer screen. It does a delicate pas de deux—as they used to do at her dancing class in the village hall when she was seven, so that the pink slippers flashed in and out of each other, so pretty in the freezing air—and disappears.

It is another few weeks—no one is in a hurry to press this news—before a brain scan reveals the cause: a tumor the size of a walnut behind the right eye, pressing on the main optic nerve. Inoperable. A course of radiation may retard the growth but can't get rid of it. The house is in commotion. Her children scour the Internet, ordering quantities of specialist optical equipment, magnifying glasses and large-print computer screens, to help her work. But the cancer is moving fast now. The headaches are worse, and how could she have failed to notice that pain in her right hip? Soon she finds it easier to work from her bed.

Jim is dying, too. The last time I see Jim, who has cancer of the pancreas, his wife, Annette, has just gotten away from it all on a pottery course in Pembrokeshire. "I had a wonderful time, wonderful!" she says in a gush of excitement, like a girl gone on her first trip to the continent, bringing back stories for skeptical siblings. "But perhaps I shouldn't have gone away for so long."

We inhabit the silence for a while, as the statement reaches off. I take it she means that when she came home, Jim was in a bad way, had been left too much to his own devices, with his breathlessness and his pain and his not being able to leave the house without assistance. That this trial run of separation had been a little too much like the real thing.

"Perhaps we'll all do a little relaxation exercise, if that's all right," says the group facilitator in her best now-we'll-all-turn-to-page-ninety-three-of-our-hymn-books-and-find-our-biggest-voices voice. "We'll work on relaxing our muscle groups one by one, starting with the feet, moving on to the legs, then to the arms and the hands. And when we're in a nice relaxed state, we'll think of a place that's very special to us, a place we love from holidays perhaps, or just a place we love to go to, particularly warm and peaceful and relaxing, and we'll just stay there for a while and take time to imagine it in all its special, special detail."

In the support group, we talk of losses. The physical losses are relatively easy to chronicle. Multiple surgeries, general anesthetics, radiotherapy, chemotherapy. We are not what we were. We haven't got much stamina. Our bones ache. And our minds. We cry a lot.

Someone goes back to work too soon and can't manage. She finds herself in the ladies' toilets weeping uncontrollably. She has always been a coper, known for her level temperament and her ability to handle many projects simultaneously. With a shade too much alacrity, her boss offers to sign her off on sick leave. But at home, the walls close in. And at night, she can't sleep.

There is a nod of recognition from Ted, a retired boilerman from Bicester. We don't know what kind of cancer he has because he rarely speaks. He simply sits, week after week, his long bony hands resting loosely on his knees, smiling sometimes, and nodding, as if the women's voices express things he can't get to himself.

A woman of about sixty years old, slim, with an alert manner and clear blue eyes, laughs as she tells us how she used to run big commercial projects for a major builder. "Oh, you'd never believe it now, would you!" she says. "But yep, that was me—with my hard hat on, marching up and down, barking orders at teams of workmen. I had the whole lot in my head, every light fitting and washer in every unit on the whole site. Everyone came to me. I couldn't possibly do that job now. I can't even remember where the damn socket is for the hair dryer!"

Judith had a heavyweight career running the legal department of a building society, but had to take early retirement after chemotherapy. "I found I couldn't retain the detail of a contract," she says quietly. "Nor follow an argument so well. I had to face it—I wasn't really up to that job anymore." So now she is doing a degree in Spanish with the Open University and spending more time with her grandchildren.

Other losses are more subtle, harder to articulate. We touch on them glancingly. There are losses of relationship, of identity. A woman who had an income, breasts, hair, a sex life, a future, and now does not, can be disorientated. A man who had a career, colleagues, status, strength, and virility, and now has only some or none of these things, may feel worthless.

Like an ocean liner, oblivious in its trajectory, cancer bears down on smaller craft, leaving smashed flotsam in its wake. Friendships, marriages, family relations, all come under pressure. They may be strengthened. Or they may fracture. "I don't know where we are now," says one woman of her relationship with her supposed best friend. The friend sent an expensive bouquet at diagnosis, but otherwise did not contact her throughout her illness. "I know it's because she was frightened. But where does that leave me?"

"It's difficult to talk to him," says Megan quietly of her husband. "He's very supportive in practical terms, taking me to checkups and scans and so on. But he doesn't want to talk about the cancer. If I try, he gets up and leaves the room. My daughters get upset if I mention it—they just tell me that I have to put it behind me and be positive. As for my friends, well, I think that at the end of the day, after all the excitement, people just want the good news, really."

We are silent. We know Megan's circumstances. Her cancer has spread to her bones. Cure is no longer an option. The only possible good news is that the disease is stable. We hope and pray for this with every scan. But how lonely to face a shortened life within a home that does not allow you the expression of vulnerability. Should a dying person be condemned to a kind of solitary confinement?

"I think, if you are all agreeable, we will do a little breathing exercise now," says the facilitator. "We will practice breathing in to a count of three . . . and out to a count of four. As we breathe in, we are going to focus all our attention on the present. On the cool sensation of the breath going through our nostrils, the warm feeling as it flows out of our mouths. We will focus only on this present moment, allowing the little anxious thoughts to drift into our awareness, and then out again, to float off like a cloud."

Like Chekhov's three sisters, who never got to Moscow, we are in mourning for our lives. Something has gone wrong; something has been taken from us. A promise of vitality, the open horizon of the future. How deeply shared assumptions of longevity seem to imprint normal social discourse. They are the currency of communication. There has been a death. It's hard to put words to it. There may be a rebirth, too. We are not sure yet. Sitting in the colored armchairs with our stubbled fuzz, learning how to breathe, we are like ugly grubs, waiting to be born.

ONE DAY, MICHAELA is watching a news item about a celebrity television actor dying of cancer. "Mummy has the kind of cancer you get better from," it prompts her to assert. I sit in the room saying nothing, careful neither to affirm nor deny her statement.

"Mummy has the kind of cancer you get better from," repeats Kitty, with a sweet and absolute trust in her elder sister.

After a couple of minutes, I slip quietly from the room, go upstairs, and ask R to lie down beside me. "Hold me, please. Please hold me."

The sun is shining, but I feel cold. To the crime of treacherous health, have I added deceit? From my most painful experience, and from any number of books I have read, I know that you cannot shield children from life, that worse things may result if you think you can. But I know no other way to do it. I refuse to have them spend their childhood in fear. I refuse to allow cancer to take their childhood away from them.

Some of the books for children have a section entitled: "When Cancer Comes Back." We avoid this section ruthlessly. We do aberrant cells; surgeons removing unwanted lumps; toxic medicines that make your hair fall out and your body too weak to get out of bed. We do repeated hospitalizations, disorientating changes to routine, disrupted family dynamics. We do the unfairness at having a sick mother who can't do the things with you that other mums are doing. We even do a bit of Mummy and Daddy getting in rages because they're frightened and can't always cope. But what we don't do is recurrence. We don't do cancer coming back. We just don't go there.

"You can ask me any questions you like," I trill endlessly to the children during chemotherapy and for months afterward. "You must feel free to ask me anything, anything that comes to mind."

"Yes, Mummy, you've already told me that a zillion, squillion times," says Michaela wearily in front of the TV. "Now, can you be quiet and let me watch King Stupid?"

But when she comes at me, am I ready for her? Am I, hell. Because the need for taboos didn't drop out of history with the great white heat of the Enlightenment. It didn't vanish in a puff of smoke with the rise of science, historical determinism, industrialized medicine. Why would it? Has science made the world a less frightening place? Does knowledge decrease by one jot the quantity of anxiety or pain in the world? Perhaps it does, and even the act of writing this is a monstrous historical ingratitude for all that hard-won progress. Or perhaps prohibition simply seeks another level, like dammed water. And pain expands, in a version of ideal gases under Boyle's law, to fill the volume of space available.

It is a beautiful spring day, and Michaela and I are walking down the hill to school. The pink frills of the currant blossom tumble down their stalks. There are hyacinths and clumps of primroses in the little front gardens of our suburban street. I have lived to see another spring, and this is progress. I will also soon go into hospital for reconstruction. More surgery. More absence, each separation from the children enacting the larger threatened one.

"What is a godparent, Mummy?" asks Michaela, who is doing a project at school on the significance of objects given to a child at birth. We spent an hour last night looking for the antique silver coin that my friend Jeremy Atiyah had given her when she was born. Something about Jeremy's premature death at age forty-two, the forthcoming surgery, and the fact that we fail to find the coin combine to produce a feeling of extreme fragility in me, as if everything and everyone I touch must perish.

"A godparent sends you a card on your birthday," I murmur. "Hopefully, they take an interest in your life. Perhaps we should think of finding you another one . . . ?"

Michaela ignores this and focuses on her original question. "Yes, Mummy, but what are they *for*?"

"Well, as I say, they will usually send you a birthday card. Perhaps even a present. They might come and visit from time to time. And hopefully they would take an interest in . . ."

She looks disappointed. "Yes, but what are they . . . you know . . . *for*?"

I have a sudden sense of my own mental rigidity, of having missed the point, iterating all this faff about birthday cards. I stop dead in the middle of the street. "Do you mean . . . the bit about looking after children if the parents die? Is that what you mean, Michaela?"

There is a sudden burst as her dark eyes meet mine.

"Michaela, are you sort of asking what would happen to you if Daddy and I died?"

She looks away again. Doesn't nod. It would be an admission of having done the unthinkable, of having tried to imagine a world without her parents in it. But something in her posture—her solid body at a slight angle to mine, eyes fixed on the pavement—and the intentness with which she waits for my response tells me I am on the right track.

"Michaela, if I die, Daddy and Aunt Jane will look after you. Primarily, it would be Daddy. But also, I would hope that Aunt Jane would be very much involved in bringing you up. Because she loves you very much, and I would be happier if there was a woman involved, too. And if Daddy and I both died—and that's not going to happen, you understand, that's about as likely as seeing an elephant flying—it would be Aunt Jane and Auntie Beatrice together. They would do it. You would go to live with your cousins, and they would bring you up. Even though you would always be sad because you didn't have us, and you would never stop missing us in some way, and that would be very hard, there would always be people who loved you. You would go forward in life. Do you understand?"

Afterward, I think there is a lightening between us. She gives a skip. Sweet skip. The syncopated beat of childhood. I pick a currant blossom, crush it in my palm, and hold it up to her. We inhale the sweet, tart smell. We chat a bit about what objects other children have brought into class. Jake has brought a silver christening mug. Naomi brought the christening dress her own mother had worn as a baby. Amaani brought a child's burka, for the time when her father will take her to the mosque. When she is finished with the subject, Michaela streams away from me down the street. "C'mon, Mummy, catch me! You never run! C'mon, catch me!"

Kitty, too, has her preoccupations. "Mummy, how old will Grandpa be when he dies? How old was your mummy when she died? How old was your dog when he died? How old is Grandma?

How old will I be when I die? How old is the oldest woman in the world?"

Between drawing, painting, playing with friends, scootering, bouncing on the trampoline, jokes and laughter, swinging on the monkey bars, endless tea parties with her dolls and soft toys, these questions persist across the ages of four and five. I offer simple factual answers and reassure her that by the time she dies she will be so old it is hardly worth thinking about. At one point, I take to reading snippets out of the newspaper to her: a woman in Scotland who survived to the age of 108, a Buddhist nun in Tibet who lived well past the age of 110, no one is clear how long. She wants to know details. The Scottish woman attributes her longevity to eating porridge for breakfast every morning and to never touching a drop of alcohol. The Buddhist nun lives a life of austerity and ritual up in the mountains. There is a picture of her in a Sunday magazine. She has all her teeth. And her face is as smooth and unlined as that of a young frog.

"This is Dolly Jayne. She likes strawberries and chocolates," says Kitty. "She likes jelly and ice cream. Her favorite meal is macaroni and cheese. She likes peas. But she doesn't like Brussels sprouts. I'm her mummy. So you're her grandma, Mummy. Because I'm her mummy."

Ah, Grandma. The heft of the knife. What are the chances of that? Inheritance of a *BRCA1* mutation brings with it so much uncertainty. There is the one-in-five chance of dying of this cancer in the next few years. I have had my ovaries removed so I can't die of ovarian cancer. But there is still the 2 to 3 percent residual risk of developing cancer of the peritoneum, the fine membrane that covers the inner organs, which kills 95 percent of people who get it. With both breasts removed, I carry roughly a 10 percent risk of developing another primary breast cancer in any residual breast tissue. There is also a slightly raised risk of other cancers: of uterus, bowel, and pancreas. By now I know the family histories of several women bearing *BRCA* mutations. The stories vary. Some are riven with a kind of cross-generational holocaust of female members: aunts, sisters, daughters, mothers who have died young. Others are

less unfortunate: they lose only the odd member, from one generation to the next. And individual carriers, who have had prophylactic surgery, may even survive to a decent age and see something of
their grandchildren.

"We never discharge you," says Deborah Lovelace at the cancer
genetics clinic one day. "We never leave you on your own."

She stands as if expecting gratitude, or a medal to be pinned to
her chest, while I look at her in utter dismay. It takes me fully two
years to assimilate her meaning. Once you test positive for a mutation, there will never be a point at which you are discharged into
the general population to take your biological risks with the rest of
your gender and age. Your odds have shifted. The best you can do is
to be watchful. So a harmless game of dolls turns lethal.

Sometimes Kitty, riding along in the car to Tesco, taking a
trip to the park or the swimming pool, will announce to people
apropos of nothing: "Mummy's mummy's dead. Mummy's mummy
died."

It is a statement that has no obvious sequitur. If the person
whom she addresses is not close to us, they might say: "Really?" in
a startled voice and turn to look at me queryingly. If I'm feeling on
top of things, I say to Kitty evenly: "Yes, it's very sad, isn't it? And
how she would have loved to have known you!"

If I'm feeling low—too many other women's mothers at the
school gate, coming to make flapjacks with their grandchildren or
help out their daughters with a bit of cooking or child care—I grip
the steering wheel grimly. "Yes, it's a bugger, isn't it?" and fall silent.

I don't know whether Kitty adds the next bit in her mind: if
Mummy's mummy can die, might my mummy die, too?

And the truth is, *I can't afford to ask*. If she asks me directly, I
won't be able to lie to her. I will have to say that there are great
hopes but no promises. And that would seem cruel. So I say nothing. I leave her on her own in her world, her five-year-old interior,
already infinitely complex world, full of questions and unknowing.
And she continues to assert, from time to time, apropos of nothing:
"Mummy's mummy's dead . . . Mummy's mummy died . . ."

*   *   *

THROUGH A SUMMER, I make fortnightly visits to the hospital to have inflated the silicone implants that have been inserted behind my chest muscle at the time of the second mastectomy. I lie stripped to the waist, while a surgeon bends over me with a syringe filled with saline silicone solution: 35 cc's each time. The chest skin must be stretched gradually before it reaches the required flexibility and these expander implants can be replaced with the final ones.

The surgeon is gentle and courteous. He tells me about a recent skiing trip he took with his family in the French Alps. About the football he plays on Saturday mornings to clear his head. When he has finished, he cleans the area with an antiseptic wipe and tells me I may feel a little "tight" for a few days.

I go away with the feeling that an iron box has been inserted beneath my chest. But I am pleased with them, these new breasts. I study them shyly in front of the mirror. The scars are ugly. But the shape is good. In time, perhaps, the scars will fade, and these implants will not feel like an alien body that my own body is fighting to reject. In time, perhaps, I will come to see them as my own—or at least, most of the time, come to forget that they are not.

But this process of adjustment is different for each one of us. "Too hard!" says Michaela one day when we are lying in the big bed, reading a story. "Your new breasts are too hard!"

I laugh at her. "You just haven't found the right position yet."

We shuffle about each other, like a pair of moles in a burrow, wedging in pillows and pushing them away again, in an effort to get comfortable. But everywhere she places her head, my chest seems to bounce it back again. "They're no good," says Michaela. "I don't like your new breasts. They're like rocks!"

Truly, the *feel* of them was not something I considered. As we trailed from one cramped NHS consultation room to another, from one harassed surgeon to another, studying the gory photo albums, the technicalities of flesh transfer, the life cycle of scars, the *feel* of my new breasts was not something we talked about. When I asked a breast-care nurse whether it might be possible to talk to women who had had different types of reconstruction, she referred me to one of the charities that might be able to help. But we had no time for this. We could barely get the children fed, dressed, to school on time; make our medical appointments; process basic administration. We were making decisions against the clock; there was no time for extras. At no point did I consider that it might one day matter to me, or my husband or my children, what these new breasts *felt* like. Now it seems absurd to me, shameful even. But there it is. We all did the best we could. And it didn't run to this.

"Well, I like them, Michaela," I say ruefully. "I really do. They've got a nice shape. And they make me feel better about myself."

"Well, I don't," she says bluntly, warming to her theme. "I like your *old* breasts. These ones are no good! You shouldn't have got them!"

I sigh. "You know what, Michaela, we all did the best we could. The doctors, me, Daddy, you, and Kitty. We all did the very best we could. It's natural you should miss my old breasts. They were lovely. We were all very fond of them . . . But now we have to get used to these new ones."

Grief is a dangerous element, like the sea. You step in, the ground shelves, suddenly you are up in over your shoulders. Already, the people left behind on the shore look tiny and they haven't even noticed you've gone.

"You know, I wish . . ." says Michaela with sudden energy, and breaks off.

"Yes?"

"I wish it hadn't . . ." She looks away.

Open-ended states of mind, like wishing, longing, regretting, hoping, are not characteristic of her. Mostly, her statements are of the wanting, intending, or planning nature: "At six o'clock, *Raven*'s on the TV; they're on to gold challenges now. On Saturday, me and Francesca are going to wear our character skirts to do the Hungarian dance at ballet. When I grow up, I'm going to be a doctor." She is focused, goal directed, determined. So the helplessness of a wishing statement is unusual. It feels important to me. "Yes—what were you going to say?" I prompt.

She shakes her head, looks away again.

"No, say it. Please. What is it you wish?"

"I wish . . . I wish we could go back to . . . before it happened . . . and that it never . . . that we . . . without it."

"Do you mean you wish we could go back to the time before the cancer happened and that it didn't happen? That maybe you wish we could have that time again without it having happened?"

She nods. "Yes," she says quietly.

Your children are not your children, says the poet Khalil Gibran. *They are the sons and daughters of Life's longing for itself . . . You may give them your love but not your thoughts, For they have their own thoughts. You may house their bodies but not their souls, For their souls dwell in the house of tomorrow, which you cannot visit, not even in your dreams.*

I stroke the bedcover carefully, thinking for a few moments. It is the first time Michaela has expressed such a thought to me, and it moves me very much. I understand her longing; it is something I have felt myself—that the cancer has robbed me of time, the time of the children being little. And I understand the vehemence, too, with which she responds to my next question.

"We have all been through a great deal," I say. "The truth is that we wouldn't be the same people if we went back and didn't have that experience. Do you feel that maybe you have learned quite a bit from it?"

She shakes her head vigorously. "No!"

"Nothing at all?"

"No!"

This vehemence, her loyalty to her own truth, tells me more clearly than direct speech how much she has suffered. It also reminds me of my own refusal to greet the Reverend Hutchison when he arrived after my mother's death. I could not bow my head in prayer. Any god who had designed a world in which my mother was cut down in this way was a monster. I could not yield to his representative.

"And if you could go back to . . . to before it happened," I say carefully, "and have the time again without it having happened, what is it that you would most want from it?"

"To be normal," she says without hesitation.

"Normal?"

She nods.

"So have you felt abnormal? That you were different from everyone else?"

She looks down at her book, falls silent.

There is a flash of realization. Of course. Difference. Always difference. Every day at school, she has been the child of the mother who has cancer. She has gone home at the end of the day to the house with the sick mother. To the father who is always struggling to cope with one medical emergency after another. Distracted, loving, but worn out. To a mother often weakened by treatment, terrified for her life. And what are the other mothers doing in the meantime? They are taking their children to the pick-your-own farm, cycling along the towpath to the open-air pool, making two-tone jelly, having a party with witch's-hair spaghetti for Halloween. They are planning their summer holidays, a visit from Grandma, which secondary schools their children will attend. Farmed out to friends at crisis points during chemotherapy and surgery, Michaela has been a shy visitor to all this stability, this matrilineal heritage. She will have made her comparisons. Why ever *wouldn't* she want to be normal?

The ash branch taps gently on the window. "You know, Michaela, I think perhaps there are several children in your class who will feel something of what you have expressed. They may look at other children like you and think that you have something they don't. There is Jake, for example, whose parents are separated. He has to cope with the fact that his daddy is not living in his house anymore, and every night it is just him and his mum. There is Beatrice, who can't see her daddy very much because he lives in America and has another family there. They probably look at you and feel that it's not fair, and feel sad for themselves. In fact, throughout childhood, a great many children feel different. It is a very hard thing. Even when you are grown-up it is a hard thing."

Michaela makes a grimace of distaste. I can see that the last thing she needs to hear is that this miserable feeling carries on into the unimaginable dreary wastes of adulthood. "Read the story, Mummy."

"Don't you want to talk a bit more?"

She puts her thumb in her mouth, twirls Rabbit's ears round her hand. "Read!"

A few weeks later, browsing the tatty bookshelves at Maggie's, trying to postpone the moment at which I must leave the scuffed green unit and venture out into civvy street again, I come across a title I haven't seen before: *Your Family and Cancer*. It's written by an American doctor, Wendy Schlessel Harpham, who had three young children when she was diagnosed with malignant myeloma. In the back is a booklet, *Becky and the Worry Cup*, written in conjunction with her eldest daughter and aimed at children.

It tells the story of Becky, who is seven when her mother is diagnosed. Becky watches as her mother is stripped of her hair, her physical strength, and, eventually, her medical practice. It shows Becky's lonely rages when her mother is unable to attend a special ballet performance, a school tea or play, when she can't play with Becky as other mothers do, or take her to the park, a friend's house, or the swimming pool. We watch Becky struggling with her fear and frustration, lashing out at her mother, being ashamed of her for her baldness, and lavishing affection on her dog. We watch her terror when, one morning, after her mother has been taken into hospital with a sudden medical emergency, Becky finds her mum's bed empty and thinks she has gone forever.

I read the book to Michaela and Kitty individually across several weeks, a chapter at a time. Afterward, I ask them questions, as instructed. "Did you feel anything like this? Does this remind you of anything you felt?"

"I can't remember," says Kitty a little wistfully, and picks up her doll. "Dolly Jayne might. She was older than me when it happened."

"I think I may have felt that," says Michaela, connecting with Becky's sense of injustice about having a mother who couldn't do anything active with her. "I can't remember. Why don't you just *read*."

But they are rapt. It is the first story we've read whose heroine is a little girl like them, going through the experience of a mother with cancer. A believable little girl, with an open, loving nature that is confused by fury and shame, balked affection, the underlying fear of the loss of her mother. "You've read more to Michaela than me!" complains Kitty. "It's not fair!" "Kitty's got ahead of me. It's my turn now!" says Michaela. They refuse point-blank to talk about their feelings, and insist that almost nothing in the book remotely resembles anything they have felt. But they follow Becky's story as avidly as they would study their own faces in the mirror.

Children's grief is not direct. It comes to you in ways you couldn't have expected, in ways you couldn't have predicted. It leaves you winded, with a catch in your throat, and no compass.

"I hate you," Michaela has said, over and over, at various stages of treatment. "I hate you, I hate you, I hate you!" This anger is a mercy, so much more bearable than watching the white exhaustion of the little girl carrying the burden by herself. "Yes, that's natural." I brace myself. "I felt the same way about my own mother often, and particularly when she was ill."

For the alternative, however, I am less well prepared. She comes to me from behind, throws her arms around my waist, leans her cheek into my back. "I love you, Mama," she says in her sweet, high voice. It is her voice that reminds me how little she is, despite her physical robustness, her exuberant embrace of life, her monkey bars and maths problems, her footballing, scootering, running, wrestling, cartwheeling, ice-skating, tree climbing, sudoku puzzling, and trampolining. How vulnerable, how breakable. "I love you too much."

I don't ask her what she means by this. We both know that "too much" is how you love when the object of that love is unreliable — or capable of disappearing.

Kitty, too, clings to me from time to time. "Don't go, Mummy! Don't go!" she says at bedtime. "I love you. For ever and ever." If my back is sore and I try to abbreviate our nighttime ritual, she seizes my hand and smothers it with kisses, causing me to stop dead and burst into startled laughter. Where does that come from, that gesture of prostrate adoration, half-mocking, half-earnest? Ah yes, it was me, all those years ago, spilling off the train from Edinburgh, dropping to my knees by my mother's bed, my wet face pressed into her dying hand. Is this genetic predisposition? Do certain bodily gestures repeat themselves as precisely as hair or eye color? Or is it the work of premourning, as the psychologists might call it, an attempt to defuse the terror of an event by enacting it in advance? Is Kitty (God forbid) getting her good-byes in early? Or—wild, expressive child that she is—is she simply reaching for the brightest colors in the paint box, the most theatrical outfits on the peg, just because they are there?

"R, IF I DIE, will you put the children first?"

"Yes." The reply is prompt, effortless. There is no division, no doubt. R is a good man, a loving father. He will do what is needed. But I want him to consider it: division and doubt. I am trying to teach him about a world of complexity, where an adult's desires are not the same as a child's, where impulses run crosswise and people in proximity run on parallel lines and may do great hurt to one another—the world that I emerged from.

"I mean, before your own needs. If you meet someone else, will you remember that your needs are not necessarily the same as theirs? That your desires are different? That what may be good for you immediately is not necessarily good for them, in any simple way? Because children are so very vulnerable. They have no say."

"I will," he says. "I will."

As for my own mother, I am in close communication with her. She is a dialogue inside me, healthy or otherwise. Rage, grief, yearning, love, bitterness, defeat, aspiration, the voices knock back and forth inside my breast. Hell, my mother and I, we don't need any-thing as banal as existence.

When I had my second miscarriage, I was overcome by grief, not just for the baby that might have been, but also for the preg-nancy itself: the sensation of nausea, the blue line in the window of the pregnancy test, the tenderness of my nipples. The fetus had been dead two weeks, the doctors told me, indicating an empty hollow on the screen. But I couldn't take it in. I mourned that dead dream just the same. And the mourning was fierce. If you had drawn a piece of fine paper across my nipples at any point for weeks afterward, they would have bled, so primed were they for that vanished life, so deeply did they mourn that particular dream of motherhood.

Are my feelings for my mother like this, a grappling after some-thing that should have been expulsed long ago, like the "products of conception," as the doctor referred to them, which, if retained, risk causing infection, scarring, a loss of fertility? How biology mocked me then, poor woman, carrying that dead dream inside me! Is this what it is? Or not.

Lovely Persephone went down into the underworld and thought of nothing but her mother. Demeter never gave up the search for her beloved daughter. Hades presented and re-presented those pomegranate seeds, desire smelting into helpless self-disgust at her refusal.

Finally, the goddess of spring ate just six. She must have been starving, down there in the empty places, the echo chambers of the heart. What did Hades think when he saw the seeds split on her lips, that melancholy devil? Did tears well over the reddened rims of his eyes? Did he feel triumph, shame, fury, calculation, adora-tion, despair?

Each day, as I reach out to switch on a kettle, wipe the children's faces, pick up a broom or a pen, it is my mother's hands I see before me. Mine are not quite so long as hers, not quite so graceful. But they are of the same genus. Fine wrists; slim palms; the knuckles gracefully articulated. And it is her voice I hear telling the children to mind the cracks in the pavement, to walk round and not under a ladder, to eat up their carrots so that they can see in the dark.

This book has given me my voice. It is only the beginning. It is so very much too little, too late. But it is a voice. Beyond the shame, beyond the garment of silence that others wove for me, I have gone up into my mountain. I have also sat at the kitchen table each day, with pen and paper, and—despite the crumbs on the surfaces, the chipped tiles in the garden, the unplanted flower beds, the dereliction of the fences, this foregrounded mortality—have allowed hot coals to sink into my tongue. I have done well. Really, I wouldn't have thought I had it in me.

At night, I turn to R. "Please hold me?"

"Mmmmn," he says sleepily.

"Please hold me, R. I'm frightened."

Turning toward me, he begins the long journey up from sleep. I feel him exiting its laborious wynds. What place does he go to each night, this place apart, which will persist whether I do or not? Sometimes, from within it, he murmurs something to me, or lifts a hand and gently strokes his collarbone with index and middle fingers, delicately, almost meditatively. The self-reflexive tenderness of this gesture always affects me with a tug of sadness, as if I had failed to love him well enough, or as if, despite our long marriage, he had always been promised to someone else.

How will it be for him if he is left alone? I wonder. For better or for worse, our marriage vows said all those years ago—and which we would have been embarrassed to take seriously. Joint Life First Death, as the life insurance policy puts it, guaranteeing to pay the balance of the mortgage in the event of either of us dying before the end of the twenty-five-year term, which we took very seriously indeed.

We come into the world alone. There is the long journey of childhood, too often too much alone, and then, if we are fortunate, we go on to create a simulacrum of intimacy with lovers, friends, spouses, children. This little nest, stitched into a cliff side, is so very fragile. It must be reinforced each day in a hundred different ways or its mortal frailty will be exposed. And yet it is the strongest thing we have. And can never be broken. And can never be denied. Anna Akmatova lived on to bear witness against the Gulag that murdered her son. Judas executed himself for his betrayal. Love is where we live. It is all we have. Denying it, we deny the happiest, most hopeful part of ourselves.

"Not sleeping?" asks R, picking up the clock to check the eerie green phosphorescence of the dials: 4:00 a.m. He curses softly. Then places a warm hand at the base of my spine. It is the same hand that helped me up from a chair in the late stages of pregnancy, gave me an extra push in our walks during chemotherapy, when even the shallowest incline caused shortage of breath. "Too bad."

It is his great kindness to me, a promise made me in the first forty-eight hours after diagnosis—that he would not leave me alone in my terror. "No. You don't have to do the nights on your own," he said, knowing my history of insomnia. "I'll be there with you. Whatever it takes."

In the first weeks, I wake several times a night in slaking baths of terror. Terror beats its heart between us like a newborn babe. We nurse it together, taking turns. It does not allow R to leave the room, so primal is the fear of being abandoned. *Don't go. Don't leave me.* If you go out of that door, down those stairs, off in that car, I might never see you again. *Never.*

Gradually, this all-consuming form of it recedes. Terror begins to crawl across the floorboards, to lift itself up on the household furniture. It starts playing games of peekaboo round the sofas and the doorways, foraging in the cupboards for wooden spoons and saucepans. But if Mum is absent just a little too long, terror collapses. It has heart palpitations, breathing difficulties. "You are going to be *fine*. Absolutely *fine*," says an aunt who survived cancer. "You lie on your back on the floor, take a paper bag, and breathe into it. In two three four, out two three four. That's what you do. You're going to be fine. I know you are. Just fine!"

We go for longer and longer stretches of "normal" life, taking the children to school, picking them up, going to a park, a swimming pool, a friend's house. Sometimes terror recedes for a period of hours. Then something happens. Someone says: "How *are* you? But how *are* you?" in too pointed a way; I imagine tumors growing everywhere. A mother talks of secondary schools; I go into a spin. Kitty falls off her scooter. I see her far down the street, tumbling over the handlebars. And I can't get there. A stranger picks her up, a Middle Eastern man who takes a beautifully laundered white handkerchief out of his pocket and wipes her bloody nose so tenderly I want to kiss his hands. Afterward, I am inconsolable. What will happen if I'm not here? What? Will other mothers comfort her? But other mothers are merciless. I know this. They have to be. In the wild, a mother elephant will reject an orphaned baby that tries to attach itself. If it persists, the mother will turn violent. A famished child is frightening. A teacher, nurse, social worker . . . they will give only the precise amount that they are paid to give. So my little girl, her heart as bright as an apple blossom, would reach without being given. How many times must a child reach before, finding nothing, she closes up in herself and dies a death, the death of the heart?

There are the support-group notices. Minty is in a hospice now. Minty with her wild sense of humor, her endless knitting when the fear was on her, her parachute jumps to raise funds for Breast Cancer Research. And it's been a long time since we've seen Ted.

Every few months, I report to the hospital for a checkup. The doctor, a different one each time, places slim, cool hands along the clavicle bone, under the armpits, behind the neck, feeling for swollen lymph nodes. Then she asks me to lie down on the bed. Standing over me, she keels her weight into the flats of her palms, feeling the soft inner tissue of spleen and liver. Finding no obvious cause for concern, she goes over to the basin and begins to wash her hands. "You can get dressed now." I fumble my buttons back together with trembling hands. *Not me today. Not me.* I am free to go. But driving through the dust of the Fulham traffic, past the Shepherd's Bush water tower, its transparent plastic cylinder eerily still now (what has happened to all that water? Such a volume can't just disappear), we don't say much. We don't need to. We both heard the man at the table opposite in the waiting room, fifty or so, breathing on a pocket handkerchief of lung tissue. We both saw the woman with the distorted belly—ascites—and her distraught husband.

We begin to make plans. At first, they seem dangerous, too great a claim on life. The bigger ones have been put on hold: career, bringing up children, living to see grandchildren, saving for a pension. But gradually, little ones start to grow. We plan a holiday. Just a small one, a night away perhaps, or even a weekend. We think of how we will spend Christmas, though it is several months away. I make an apple pie. Stitch the elastic on Michaela's new ballet pumps. We take it a step at a time. We are learning how to walk again.

Sometimes, I go whole nights without waking R. I get up and look out the window. I am learning to trust the darkness a little. I know that Judith or Megan or Ted is awake, too, or likely to be in the course of the night. Mentally, I blow them a kiss, my compatriots in this strange country, the treacherous land after cancer. Along the tatty suburban street, past the plane trees and the box hedge, comes a fox with a hacking cough. She stops in the middle of the road and turns her face to give me a look, straight up into my eyes, as I stand at the window. She seems to look at me more intently than any living creature, human or otherwise, has ever done. Her eyes are a green quill slicing into me. But her cough is alarming. Has she swallowed poison? Is she going to give birth? I can't tell. After several moments, she turns and, with a dip of her haunches, crosses the street and slips under a fence. One of the many burrows that track across these gardens. Then there is the noise of the milk truck. The strange electronic wheeze of its engine as it makes its way up the street, the stacked crates of bottles bumping tremblingly against one another. Back in bed, R mumbles something in his sleep. I keel closer to him for warmth, settling into the lee of his breathing. "Love you," he murmurs, half in and half out of sleep, lifting a hand to stroke his clavicle bone. "Love you, too," I murmur, with my eyes wide open. This is how we live. This is how we love.

Acknowledgments

IN TELLING William Marsden's story, I made use of Frieda Sandwith's biography, *Surgeon Compassionate* (London: P. Davies, 1960). The account of Fanny Burney's mastectomy is a historical reconstruction based largely on a letter she wrote to her sister, Esther, in 1812. I also drew on Claire Harman's *Fanny Burney: A Biography* (London: HarperCollins, 2000); Kate Chisholm's *Fanny Burney: Her Life* (London: Chatto and Windus, 1998); D. J. Larrey's *Memoirs of Military Surgery* (tr. John Waller; London: Cox, 1815); and Robert Richardson's *Larrey: Surgeon to Napoleon's Imperial Guard* (London: John Murray, 1974). Mike Greenall, consultant breast cancer surgeon at Oxford's John Radcliffe Hospital, kindly helped me try to imagine what it might have been like to perform such surgery in 1811. I should not that some of the incidental characters in this chapter have been invented.

I am very grateful to Rose Davidson, my editor in the UK, and Nan Graham, of Scribner in New York, for their support and invaluable editorial insight, and also to Kara Watson, who gave this manuscript close and thoughtful attention throughout. But perhaps the biggest thanks of all goes to my friend Laura and my husband, there with me every step of the way.